John's Use of Matthew

# John's Use of Matthew

James W. Barker

WIPF & STOCK · Eugene, Oregon

Wipf and Stock Publishers
199 W 8th Ave, Suite 3
Eugene, OR 97401

John's Use of Matthew
By Barker, James W.
Copyright © 2015 by Barker, James W. All rights reserved.
Softcover ISBN-13: 978-1-6667-1426-5
Hardcover ISBN-13: 978-1-6667-1427-2
eBook ISBN-13: 978-1-6667-1428-9
Publication date 3/23/2021
Previously published by Fortress Press, 2015

This edition is a scanned facsimile of the original edition published in 2015.

*In loving memory of my dear friend and mentor*
*David Laird Dungan*
οὐκ ἔστιν μαθητὴς ὑπὲρ τὸν διδάσκαλον

# Contents

| | | |
|---|---|---|
| | Acknowledgements | ix |
| | Abbreviations | xi |
| | Introduction | xv |
| 1. | John and the Synoptics | 1 |
| 2. | Methodology and Hermeneutic | 15 |
| 3. | Ecclesial Authority | 37 |
| 4. | Proof from Prophecy | 63 |
| 5. | Samaritan Inclusion or Exclusion? | 93 |
| 6. | Conclusion | 107 |
| | Bibliography | 115 |
| | Index of Ancient Sources | 139 |
| | Index of Subjects and Modern Authors | 149 |

# Acknowledgements

This book is a revised version of my 2011 dissertation at Vanderbilt University in Nashville, Tennessee. I would like to thank the members of my committee, most especially my advisor Amy-Jill Levine for her unwavering support throughout my graduate studies, dissertation writing, and beyond. Also, I always felt supported by the other members of the committee, Susan Hylen (New Testament), J. Patout Burns (Early Christian Studies), Annalisa Azzoni (Hebrew Bible/Semitic philology), and David Petrain (Classical Studies/Greek philology).

I have had the pleasure of corresponding with a number of scholars who graciously offered their feedback, insights, and support for my work: my thanks to Paul Anderson of George Fox University; Guy Bar-Oz and Ram Bouchnik of the University of Haifa; Charles Hill of Reformed Theological Seminary, Orlando; Chris Keith of St. Mary's University, Twickenham; and Bronwen Wickkiser of Wabash College. I also express gratitude to my second-cousin B. F. Barker for sharing his vast knowledge of animal husbandry, which informed chapter four.

I presented an abbreviated version of chapter three in a joint session of the John, Jesus, and History and Synoptic Gospels groups at the 2014 Society of Biblical Literature annual meeting in San Diego, California; my thanks to Paul Anderson for extending the invitation and to Elaine Pagels for responding. I also presented an abbreviated version of chapter four to the task force on John's Gospel and the Old Testament at the 2015 Catholic Biblical Association annual meeting in New Orleans, Louisiana; my thanks to Gregory Glazov at Seton Hall

University for extending that invitation and to Rev. Lawrence Frizzell for responding.

I am deeply appreciative of the unending love and support my family has shown. My sincerest thanks to my wife, Katy, above all (Sir. 26:1); also to our children, Jacob and Hannah; my parents, James and Dianne; my sister and brother-in-law, Leanne and Rex; my father-, mother- and sisters-in-law, Emil, Diana, Jennifer, and Marie, as well as her husband Justin.

I am very grateful to Neil Elliott at Fortress Press for supporting the publication of my work. Finally, I lovingly dedicate this book to my undergraduate mentor in the Department of Religious Studies at the University of Tennessee, Knoxville, David Dungan (1936–2008); I wish that he could have seen this project come to completion, but—especially through friendship with Mrs. Anne Dungan—I know how proud he would be.

# Abbreviations

AB — Anchor Bible
ACW — Ancient Christian Writers
AGJU — Arbeiten zur Geschichte des antiken Judentums und des Urchristentums
AnBib — Analecta Biblica
ANTC — Abingdon New Testament Commentaries
ArBib — The Aramaic Bible
ATANT — Abhandlungen zur Theologie des Alten und Neuen Testaments
A[Y]BRL — Anchor [Yale] Bible Reference Library
BBB — Bonner biblische Beiträge
BDAG — Danker, Frederick W., Walter Bauer, William F. Arndt, and F. Wilbur Gingrich. Greek-English Lexicon of the New Testament and Other Early Christian Literature. 3d ed. Chicago: University of Chicago Press, 2000
BECNT — Baker Exegetical Commentary on the New Testament
BETL — Bibliotheca Ephemeridum Theologicarum Lovaniensium
*Bib* — *Biblica*
*BibInt* — *Biblical Interpretation*
BNTC — Black's New Testament Commentaries
BWANT — Beiträge zur Wissenschaft vom Alten und Neuen Testament
BZNW — Beihefte zur Zeitschrift für die neutestamentliche Wissenschaft
CBET — Contributions to Biblical Exegesis and Theology
*CBQ* — *Catholic Biblical Quarterly*
DJD — Discoveries in the Judaean Desert

| | |
|---|---|
| EBib | Etudes biblique |
| ETL | Ephemerides Theologicae Lovanienses |
| ETS | Erfurter theologische Studien |
| FB | Forschung zur Bibel |
| GBS | Guides to Biblical Scholarship |
| GCS | Die griechischen christlichen Schriftsteller der ersten drei Jahrhunderte |
| GELS | *A Greek-English Lexicon of the Septuagint.* Takamitsu Muraoka. Leuven: Peeters, 2009 |
| GKC | *Genesius' Hebrew Grammar.* Edited by E. Kautzsch. Translated by A. E. Cowley. 2d. ed. Oxford, 1910 |
| HNT | Handbuch zum Neuen Testament |
| HTB | Histoire du texte biblique. Lausanne, 1996– |
| HTKNT | Herders Theologischer Kommentar zum Neuen Testament |
| ICC | International Critical Commentary |
| JAOS | *Journal of the American Oriental Society* |
| Jastrow | Jastrow, M. *A Dictionary of the Targumim, the Talmud Babli and Yerushalmi, and the Mishnaic Literature.* 2d ed. New York, 1903 |
| JBL | *Journal of Biblical Literature* |
| JETS | *Journal of the Evangelical Theological Society* |
| JSHJ | *Journal for the Study of the Historical Jesus* |
| JSNT | *Journal for the Study of the New Testament* |
| JSNTSup | Journal for the Study of the New Testament Supplement Series |
| JTS | *Journal of Theological Studies* |
| KJV | King James Version |
| LD | Lectio Divina |
| LEH | Lust, Johan, Erik Eynikel, and Katrin Hauspie, eds. *Greek-English Lexicon of the Septuagint.* Rev. ed. Stuttgart: Deutsche Bibelgesellschaft, 2003 |
| LNTS | Library of New Testament Studies |
| LSJ | Liddell, Henry George, Robert Scott, Henry Stuart Jones. *A Greek-English Lexicon.* 9th ed. with revised supplement. Oxford: Clarendon, 1996 |
| LXX | Septuagint |
| MM | Moulton, James H., and George Milligan. *The Vocabulary of the Greek New Testament.* London, 1930. Repr., Peabody: Hendrickson, 1997 |

# ABBREVIATIONS

| | |
|---|---|
| MT | Masoretic Text |
| NA²⁷ | *Novum Testamentum Graece*, Nestle-Aland, 27th ed. |
| NASB | New American Standard Bible |
| NCBC | New Cambridge Bible Commentary |
| NICNT | New International Commentary on the New Testament |
| NIGTC | New International Greek Testament Commentary |
| NIV | New International Version |
| NJB | New Jerusalem Bible |
| *NovT* | *Novum Testamentum* |
| NovTSup | Supplements to Novum Testamentum |
| NRSV | New Revised Standard Version |
| NTD | Das Neue Testament Deutsch |
| NTL | New Testament Library |
| *NTS* | *New Testament Studies* |
| NTTS | New Testament Tools and Studies |
| *OrSyr* | *L'orient syrien* |
| PO | Patrologia Orientalis |
| PTMS | Pittsburgh Theological Monograph Series |
| QD | Quaestiones Disputatae |
| *RB* | *Revue biblique* |
| RBS | Resources for Biblical Study |
| *RevExp* | *Review and Expositor* |
| RSV | Revised Standard Version |
| SANT | Studien zum Alten und Neuen Testaments |
| SBL | Society of Biblical Literature |
| SBLDS | Society of Biblical Literature Dissertation Series |
| SBLECL | Society of Biblical Literature Early Christianity and Its Literature |
| SBLSP | Society of Biblical Literature Seminar Papers |
| SCS | Septuagint and Cognate Studies |
| SNTSMS | Society for New Testament Studies Monograph Series |
| SP | Sacra Pagina |

| | |
|---|---|
| StBibLit | Studies in Biblical Literature (Lang) |
| Str-B | Strack, H. L., and P. Billerbeck. *Kommentar zum Neuen Testament aus Talmud und Midrasch*. 6 vols. Munich, 1922–61 |
| *TDNT* | *Theological Dictionary of the New Testament*. Edited by Gerhard Kittel and Gerhard Friedrich. Translated by Geoffrey W. Bromiley. 10 vols. Grand Rapids: Eerdmans, 1964–76 |
| THKNT | Theologischer Handkommentar zum Neuen Testament |
| *TLG* | *Thesaurus Linguae Graecae: Canon of Greek Authors and Works*. Edited by Luci Berkowitz and Karl A. Squitier. 3d ed. New York: Oxford University Press, 1990 |
| TSAJ | Texte und Studien zum antiken Judentum |
| TU | Texte und Untersuchungen |
| UNT | Untersuchungen zum Neuen Testament |
| *VC* | *Vigiliae Christianae* |
| WBC | Word Biblical Commentary |
| WUNT | Wissenschaftliche Untersuchungen zum Neuen Testament |
| *ZAW* | *Zeitschrift für die alttestamentliche Wissenschaft* |
| *ZNW* | *Zeitschrift für die neutestamentliche Wissenschaft* |

# Introduction

This book is a revised version of my 2011 dissertation, which was directed by Amy-Jill Levine at Vanderbilt. In Spring 2007, I was searching for a dissertation topic while I was serving as a teaching assistant for Professor Levine's introductory New Testament course in the divinity school. We spent one week on the Gospel of John, and so I read Moody Smith's *John among the Gospels*.[1] I had done quite a bit of work on the Synoptic problem, but I had never worked on John and the Synoptics, so I did not realize how contested the field was. The next week we happened to read the extracanonical *Protevangelium of James*, and I noticed several places where it had to be dependent on the canonical Gospels of Matthew and Luke—even though the *Protevangelium* appears to be a self-standing narrative. I began wondering whether John might relate to the Synoptics in similarly subtle ways.[2]

Strictly for the sake of argument, I asked how someone might make a case for John's use of the Synoptics. I picked the Gospel of Matthew because, on the one hand, I had recently taken a course on it with Professor Levine and, on the other hand, Matthew is generally considered the least likely of John's sources. I began reading Matthew

---

1. D. Moody Smith, *John among the Gospels* (2d ed.; Columbia: University of South Carolina Press, 2001).
2. I later discovered that Smith had asked similarly whether John ought to be considered the first apocryphal gospel: D. Moody Smith, "The Problem of John and the Synoptics in Light of the Relation between Apocryphal and Canonical Gospels," in *John and the Synoptics*, ed. Adelbert Denaux (BETL 101; Leuven: Leuven University Press, 1992), 147–62.

in Greek on one day and then reading John in Greek on the next day. I did this for several weeks until I had gotten through both gospels approximately ten times. I was compiling a long list of parallels, and I was becoming convinced that Matthew's gospel had to be one of John's sources. When I engaged earlier scholars, I found that we had isolated many of the same parallels; there were also a few that I had missed as well as a few places where I had something new to say. I took my preliminary conclusions to my *Doktormutter* A.-J., and right away she noted how ironic it would be for me to write about John's dependence on one of the Synoptics, given that she had written her dissertation at Duke University under Moody Smith, who maintained Johannine independence. At the same time, she gladly supported my inquiry and patiently guided the project to completion.

That project has culminated in the publication of this book, which consists of five chapters and a conclusion. Chapter 1 sketches the history of research on John's relation to the Synoptics from the second century to the present day. In the patristic era, key figures include Tatian, who constructed one gospel harmony out of the four eventually canonical gospels; Origen, who emphasized that John simply cannot be harmonized with the Synoptics and that the attempt to do so is dizzying; and Augustine, who insisted that the four separate gospels can be interpreted harmoniously, free of any contradiction. In the twentieth century, Hans Windisch upheld the older belief that John was dependent on all three Synoptics, but Windisch offered a newer interpretation that John intended his gospel to replace them.[3] Before Windisch's hypothesis could take hold, Percival Gardner-Smith shifted the consensus to the view that John's synoptic parallels arise via independent oral tradition;[4] in effect, John could not have wanted to replace the Synoptics, because he had never read them. Debates between literary dependence and oral tradition have continued, and currently there is no firm consensus. Even though scholars

---

3. Hans Windisch, *Johannes und die Synoptiker: wollte der vierte Evangelist die Älteren Evangelien ergänzen oder ersetzen?* (UNT 12; Leipzig: J.C. Hinrichs, 1926).
4. Percival Gardner-Smith, *Saint John and the Synoptic Gospels* (Cambridge: Cambridge University Press, 1938; repr. 2011).

increasingly consider John dependent on one or more of the Synoptics, Matthew remains the Fourth Gospel's least likely written source. I intend to show that John's use of Matthew is far likelier than previous scholarship has realized.

Chapter 2 explains my methodology and hermeneutic. John did not use Matthew in the same way, or to the same extent, that Matthew used Mark. In other words, there are far fewer parallels, and John's parallels show very little verbatim agreement. Therefore, many scholars still follow Gardner-Smith in attributing John's synoptic material to oral tradition. To claim literary dependence rather than oral tradition, I employ Helmut Koester's minimalist criterion that a subsequent text must reveal knowledge of redactional work found in the source text.[5] If the Gospel of John reflects knowledge of the redacted Gospel of Matthew, then Windisch's question resurfaces and deserves an answer: Did John want to supplement or to supplant Matthew? On the analogy of extracanonical gospels, I argue that John intended his gospel to be read alongside Matthew's, not instead of it.

I then take up three case studies in successive chapters. Chapter 3 pertains to ecclesial authority. According to Matthew, Jesus gives the disciples the rabbinic authority to "bind and loose," that is, to discriminate between prohibited and permitted practices. According to John, Jesus gives the disciples the authority to forgive sins and to refuse forgiveness. The sayings evince striking grammatical and syntactic similarities, and at least since the third century these logia have been interpreted in light of one another. Since a single word in Aramaic (שרי) and in Greek (λύω) can signify both *loosen* and *forgive*, many scholars consider these sayings independent, orally transmitted variants that mean the same thing. I reassess the semantic arguments for oral tradition, and I conclude instead that the sayings mean very different things and yet John's logion must depend on Matthew's. Matthew wanted the disciples to determine what counts as sin, to convict sin, and then to forgive penitent sinners. To guard against

---

5. Helmut Koester, "Written Gospel or Oral Tradition?," *JBL* 113, no. 2 (1994): 293–97.

laxity in the church, John re-inscribed the disciples' right to withhold forgiveness.

Chapter 4 concerns proofs from prophecy, specifically that Jesus' riding a donkey into Jerusalem at the beginning of passion week fulfills Zechariah's oracle about Israel's king coming on a donkey. The species of an ass and the enactment of Zechariah's prophecy are widely claimed as traditional elements, and so scholars predominantly assume that Matthew and John merely made explicit what was already implicit in Mark and Luke. I show that this argument tacitly and unfairly harmonizes the four gospels. John's Matthean material turn out to be more idiosyncratic than is typically acknowledged. Many scholars also assert that Matthew and John, as well as Justin Martyr and Irenaeus, could have independently adopted the Zechariah quotation from a *testimonium,* an early Christian collection of messianic Old Testament prophecies. However, upon closer examination, there is no evidence for a first- or second-century *testimonium* containing Zechariah's prophecy. Neither does John's quotation derive from any extant text of Zechariah. Instead, as Edwin Freed argued fifty years ago, John's wording can be explained entirely by Matthew's narrative of Jesus' entry into Jerusalem.[6] John intentionally corrects and supplements Matthew by depicting Jesus atop only one donkey (Matthew has Jesus simultaneously riding two donkeys) and by explaining why no one could understand the prophetic significance of Jesus' actions at the time.

Chapter 5 concerns the inclusion or exclusion of Samaritans from the church. According to Matthew, Jesus commands the disciples not to evangelize in any Samarian city. According to John, Jesus spends two days in a Samarian city, where the Samaritans confess him to be the Savior of the world. In this case, I argue somewhat counterintuitively that the Fourth Gospel differs so much that John must be intentionally reversing Matthew's prohibition. The key link between John and Matthew is a metaphorical evangelistic saying about fields being ready for harvest, which allows John's Samarian narrative to harmonize with,

---

6. Edwin D. Freed, "The Entry into Jerusalem in the Gospel of John," *JBL* 80, no. 4 (1961): 329–38.

and to reinterpret, Matthew's mission discourse. When read together, Jesus was not trying to exclude the Samaritans when he forbade the disciples from preaching to them. On the contrary, Jesus himself was already in Samaria revealing himself to the Samaritans. Chapter 6 concludes the book by summarizing my findings regarding John's use of Matthew in the light of the perennial question of John's relation to the Synoptics.

# 1

# John and the Synoptics

A cursory reading of the Gospels reveals that very few episodes in John occur in Matthew, Mark, and Luke. Characters and events common to all four include John the Baptist, Jesus feeding the five thousand, a woman anointing Jesus with oil, and the passion narrative. Even when John narrates parallel stories, however, many of the details differ. For example, the Fourth Gospel never says that Jesus was baptized, and Jesus does not institute the Eucharist at the Last Supper. Moreover, in John's gospel, Jesus never teaches in parables or performs exorcisms; such words and deeds are commonplace in the Synoptics. Finally, in terms of time and space, John narrates multiple trips back and forth between Galilee and Jerusalem over a two-year period (there are three Passovers in the Fourth Gospel), whereas the Synoptics mention only one trip to Jerusalem for a single celebration of Passover, coinciding with the passion. Readers have observed all of these differences since the second century, and scholars have imagined wide-ranging possibilities concerning John's knowledge, use, and opinion of the Synoptics. This chapter sketches the history of these investigations.[1]

---

1. This *Forschungsbericht* is intended to be representative rather than exhaustive; for a much more

## The First Seventeen Hundred Years

In the mid-second century, Tatian constructed a harmony of the four gospels called the *Diatessaron*. Thanks to Louis Leloir's painstaking numbering, we can observe Tatian's process of incorporating Johannine narratives.[2] The *Diatessaron* opened with a quotation from John's prologue (§1) before turning to Matthew's and Luke's nativity stories. After relating Jesus' baptism and temptation, Tatian included the wedding at Cana in John 2 (§12). Tatian later harmonized the feeding of the 5000 in John 6 with synoptic accounts (§34), Matthew's in particular. Thereafter, Tatian worked back to Jesus' conversation with the Samaritan woman in John 4 (§37). Tatian also included the Sabbath controversy in John 5 (§39) as well as Jesus' celebration of the Feast of Tabernacles in John 7 (§47). Tatian later presented Jesus' dialogue with Nicodemus in John 3 (§56), which—along with the remainder of the Fourth Gospel—Tatian relocated to passion week. Throughout the passion narrative, Tatian harmonized John and the Synoptics; for example, at the crucifixion (§73) Jesus said not only "Father forgive them" (Luke 23:34) but also "Woman, behold your son" (John 19:26). The *Diatessaron* included only one Passover, and so Jesus' ministry would have comprised less than one calendar year. Overall, Tatian recognized extensive disagreements among the Gospels, and he resolved them of contradiction by rewriting one harmonious narrative. The *Diatessaron* gained wide popularity and was most likely the earliest form of the gospels in the Syrian church, given the name *Mepharreshe* for the "separate" old Syriac translations of Matthew, Mark, Luke, and John.

Irenaeus of Lyons (c. 130–c. 200) is the earliest extant author to list the names of the evangelists as Matthew, Mark, Luke, and John, and Irenaeus considered John one of Jesus' disciples (*Haer.* 3.11.1). Irenaeus

---

extensive review of modern scholarship, I heartily recommend D. Moody Smith, *John among the Gospels* (2d ed.; Columbia: University of South Carolina Press, 2001).

2. Louis Leloir, "Le Diatessaron de Tatien," *OrSyr* 1 (1956): 208–31, 313–34. For a *Forschungsbericht* on *Diatessaron* studies, see William L. Petersen, *Tatian's Diatessaron: Its Creation Dissemination, Significance, and History in Scholarship* (Supplements to Vigiliae Christianae 25; Leiden: Brill, 1994); see pp. 314–18 for Petersen's description of Leloir's "unrivaled" contribution.

was also the first Christian to insist that the Church use all four of these gospels—no more, no less. Irenaeus argued that just as there are four zones and four winds in the earth, so there are four gospels as pillars of the church (*Haer.* 3.11.8). He did not explicitly acknowledge the differences between John and the Synoptics, yet his argument would disallow Tatian's harmony, which would destroy the fourfold form of the gospel (*Haer.* 3.11.9). Roughly contemporaneous with Irenaeus, Clement of Alexandria c. 150–c. 215)—in a famous one-liner recorded by Eusebius (*Hist. eccl.* 6.14.7)—described John's gospel as spiritual (πνευματικόν) and the Synoptics as corporeal (τὰ σωματικά).

Origen (c. 185–c. 254), Clement's successor at the Catechetical School in Alexandria, most significantly advanced the early study of John's relation to the Synoptics. Origen's *Commentary on John* honestly assessed the disagreements among the gospels: "If someone carefully examined the Gospels with regard to the historical disharmony that each one shows . . . , then the person would surely become dizzy from trying to confirm the Gospels as true" (*Comm. Jo.* 10.3). Accordingly, Origen argued that the four canonical gospels cannot always be true in a historical sense; instead they must be true in a spiritual sense. Origen concluded:

> I do not condemn . . . (the four evangelists) for how they alter in different ways what happened historically—these differences being useful for some mystical objective. So they refer to what happened in one place as happening in another, or something at this time as happening at another, and something announced in such-and-such a way has been reproduced with some alteration. For the Gospels set out to tell the truth spiritually and corporeally [that is, literally] at the same time, where it was possible; but where it was not possible to do both, they prefer the spiritual to the corporeal—often preserving the spiritual truth in a lie, so to speak. (*Comm. Jo.* 10.5)

Origen did not deny the gospels' literal discrepancies, which he knew could cause some readers to deem the gospels false or unreliable or uninspired (*Comm. Jo.* 10.3). Origen attempted to defend the inspiration, reliability, and veracity of the gospels by privileging spiritual truth over historical truth.

The Neoplatonist philosopher Porphyry (c. 232–c. 303) read the four gospels, noticed their differences, and reached the opposite of Origen's conclusion.³ Porphyry did not distinguish between two kinds of truth, and if the gospels contradicted each other anywhere, then they were unreliable everywhere. For example, during the crucifixion Jesus uttered the cry of dereliction according to Matthew (27:46) and Mark (15:34); Jesus commended his spirit to the Father according to Luke (23:46); and Jesus said "it is finished" according to John (19:30). Porphyry suggested that these discordant (ἀσύμφωνος) accounts reflected either the deaths of several men or the death of one man that was inaccurately recorded by several people (*apocr.* 2.12). According to Porphyry, inconsistencies about Jesus' death cast doubt on everything else written in the Gospels. Porphyry wrote during a century of empire-wide persecution of Christians, and he was a towering intellectual in his epoch. Subsequent Christians could not ignore such thoroughgoing polemic.

Eusebius of Caesarea (c. 260–340) was not only the first to respond to Porphyry but also the first to assert that John wrote his gospel after having read the Synoptics:⁴

> So then, first let it be agreed: the Gospel according to (John) has been read in all the churches under heaven. For indeed, let it be clear in this way that it was truly reasonable to the ancients that it be counted in fourth position relative to the other three. The previously written three had already been distributed unto everyone, even to (John). He accepted the three, they say, and testified to the truth in them. The only thing lacking in the previous writing was the narrative about what had been done in the earliest times and at the beginning of the preaching by Christ. And indeed the word is true. (*Hist. eccl.* 3.24.2)

Eusebius also said that the Synoptics mainly recorded "what had been done by the Savior after the confinement of John the Baptist in prison"

---

3. I consider Porphyry the most likely polemicist in Macarius Magnes's *Apocriticus*; for discussion, see Pieter W. van der Horst, "Macarius Magnes and the Unnamed Anti-Christian Polemicist: A Review Article," in *Jews and Christians in Their Graeco-Roman Context: Selected Essays on Early Judaism, Samaritanism, Hellenism, and Christianity* (WUNT 196; Tübingen: Mohr Siebeck, 2006), 181–89.
4. T. Scott Manor ("Papias, Origen, and Eusebius: The Criticisms and Defense of the Gospel of John," *VC* 67, no. 1 [2013]: 1–21) has argued persuasively that Eusebius, in opposition to Origen, most likely inserted the testimony about John receiving and approving the Synoptics.

(*Hist. eccl.* 3.24.8), whereas John wrote "what also had been done by the Savior throughout the time passed over in silence by the earlier evangelists" (*Hist. eccl.* 3.24.11); Eusebius added that "to those who understand this, the Gospels no longer seem to disagree with one another" (*Hist. eccl.* 3.24.13). However, Origen had already shown the inadequacy of this argument (*Comm. Jo.* 10.3). John's gospel clearly states that John the Baptist identified Jesus as the lamb of God on two consecutive days in Bethany (1:29, 35–36), that the next day Jesus returned to Galilee (1:43), and that three days later Jesus attended the wedding at Cana (2:1). These six days in no way allow for the forty-day temptation, which Mark (1:12) says immediately followed Jesus' baptism. Eusebius's conclusion was far too simplistic to refute Porphyry's criticisms.

A century after Porphyry had died, his polemic still necessitated the extensive treatise by Augustine (354–430), *On the Harmony of the Gospels*. Augustine attempted to prove that the gospels do not contradict each other, because his unnamed adversaries had denied the accuracy of the four gospels. Consequently, some people decided not to become believers, and some believers doubted their faith (*Cons.* 1.10). Augustine assumed that John knew all three written Synoptics (*Cons.* 1.4), yet Augustine recognized how little material the Fourth Gospel had in common with the Synoptics; he listed the testimony of John the Baptist, the feeding of the 5000 and walking on the Sea of Tiberias, the anointing at Bethany, and the passion (*Cons.* 4.19). On these occasions, Augustine referred to John as coming back down to earth to join Matthew, Mark, and Luke (*Cons.* 4.15), for John had left the synoptists on the earth and peered into heaven to depict Jesus' divinity (*Cons.* 1.7).

Augustine readily acknowledged John's differences. For example, in the Synoptics, Simon of Cyrene carried Jesus' cross, and in John's gospel Jesus carries the cross himself. Augustine nonetheless believed both accounts to be historically accurate: Jesus carried the cross initially, but along the way Simon of Cyrene was compelled to carry it (*Cons.* 3.10). Similarly, since John places the temple incident at the beginning of Jesus' ministry and the Synoptics narrate it in the course of passion week, Augustine concluded that Jesus must have disrupted the temple on two separate occasions (*Cons.* 2.129).[5] In contrast with Origen, then, Augustine insisted on the historical and literal truth of all four gospels despite their discrepancies. According to Augustine, the gospels did not contain any real contradictions, and so—*contra* Porphyry—all four provided reliable histories.

For the most part, one or another patristic testimony would be employed down to the eighteenth century. Augustine's philosophical characterization was that the Synoptics appeal to the mind's active virtue, whereas John appeals to the contemplative (*Cons.* 1.8; 4.20); Thomas Aquinas (1225-1274) quoted Augustine's active/contemplative distinction in the prologue to his commentary on John. Augustine also described the Gospel of John as loftier than the Synoptics (*Cons.* 4.19), and Martin Luther (1483-1546) once wrote that "John's Gospel is the one, fine, true, and chief gospel, and is far, far to be preferred over the other three and placed high above them."[6] In the preface to his commentary on the Gospel of John, John Calvin (1509-1564) echoed Clement of Alexandria in saying that the Synoptics show Christ's body while John shows his soul. In the mid-eighteenth century, Henry Owen accepted Eusebius's testimony that John, son of Zebedee, had read all three Synoptics and intended to supplement them.[7] Although these writers were aware of John's many differences from the Synoptics, these scholars rested on centuries of tradition asserting the non-contradiction of the gospels.

Deism challenged traditional assumptions. Peter Annet (1693-1769) paid especially close attention to the gospels' discrepancies.[8] For example, according to Mark (15:47; 16:1) and Luke (23:55; 24:1), Mary Magdalene and at least one other woman saw where Jesus was buried

---

5. In less significant chronological discrepancies (e.g., when precisely Jesus healed Peter's mother-in-law), Augustine suggested that the evangelists narrated events in the order they recollected them (*Cons.* 2.51).
6. E. Theodore Bachmann, ed., *Luther's Works, Vol. 35: Word and Sacrament I* (Philadelphia: Muhlenberg, 1960), 362.
7. Henry Owen, *Observations on the Four Gospels: Tending Chiefly to Ascertain the Times of Their Publication and to Illustrate the Form and Manner of Their Composition* (London: T. Payne, 1764), 107.
8. For discussion of Annet, see William Baird, *History of New Testament Research, Vol. 1: From Deism to Tübingen* (Minneapolis: Augsburg Fortress, 1992), 49-52.

on Friday, and on Sunday the women returned to anoint Jesus' corpse with spices. However, John (19:39) says that Jesus had already been buried with a hundred pounds of spices—something the women would have known if they had actually seen him buried. According to Annet, John contradicts the Synoptics here, and their respective accounts cannot be reconciled.[9] Annet further concluded that the Gospels defy harmonization:

> For the witnesses, as they are called, do not all agree, in any one circumstance which they relate concerning it; but palpably contradict one another in every particular they give us of it. I wonder what harmony all the evangelists would make . . . compared with one another, seeing the four we have are so harmonious![10]

Like Origin, Annet honestly assessed the gospels' contradictions. Unlike Origin, Annet assumed no spiritual truth to contemplate in historical falsehood.

## The Last Two Hundred Years

Deism stimulated the development of the historical-critical method, and source-critical study of the gospels became much more rigorous as scholars proposed new models of literary dependence and raised new questions concerning oral tradition. In the nineteenth and twentieth centuries, a new consensus began to emerge: John knew Mark and Luke, but not Matthew. Ferdinand Christian Baur (1847) concluded that John had a literary connection to Mark and Luke, whereas John's Matthean parallels derived from oral tradition.[11] Similarly, Theodor Zahn (1909) determined that John was acquainted "especially with Mark, apparently also with Luke."[12] Benjamin Bacon (1910) held that

---

9. Peter Annet, *The Resurrection of Jesus Considered: In Answer to the Trial of the Witnesses* (London: 1744), 35; moreover, according to Annet, the repeated attempts to anoint Jesus' corpse shows that no one expected Jesus to rise from the dead, thereby implying that Jesus never predicted his resurrection.
10. Ibid., 69.
11. Ferdinand Christian Baur, *Kritische Untersuchungen über die kanonischen Evangelien:ihr Verhaltniß zu einander, ihren Charakter und Ursprung* (Tübingen, 1847), 280; see 239–80, Das Verhältniß zu den synoptischen Evangelien.
12. Theodor Zahn, *Introduction to the New Testament*, trans. M. W. Jacobus, et al. (3 vols.; Edinburgh: T&T Clark, 1909) 3:254–98, ch. 67: "The Relation of the Fourth Gospel to the Earlier Gospels"; the German edition was published 1897–99.

John based his gospel on Mark while also using Luke a great deal; in John, "Matthew is practically ignored."[13] B. H. Streeter (1925) demonstrated John's use of Mark and Luke, but Streeter found no conclusive evidence that John used Matthew.[14]

Against this backdrop, Hans Windisch (1926) reasserted John's use of all three Synoptic Gospels.[15] However, Windisch was more concerned with authorial intent than literary dependence. In other words, he questioned what John really thought of the Synoptics. Windisch offered a taxonomy of four answers to this question, and he concluded that John had wanted to supplant the Synoptics altogether. (1) According to the supplemental theory (*Ergänzungstheorie*), John wrote to fill in the gaps of the Synoptics, and John sometimes overlapped with, and corrected, synoptic narratives; since the patristic era, this had been the predominant explanation of John's motivation. (2) According to the independence theory (*Unabhängigkeitstheorie*), John's gospel preserved accurate, eyewitness testimony without having read the Synoptics; this hypothesis placed more emphasis on John's differences, yet it maintained a theologically conservative position regarding the gospels' historical reliability. (3) According to the interpretation theory (*Interpretationstheorie*), also known as the surpassing theory (*Überbietungstheorie*), John offered a deeper theological meaning than is found in the Synoptics; this hypothesis is associated with the Tübingen School, which regarded John as a "higher synthesis."[16] (4) Windisch argued for the replacement hypothesis (*Verdrängungshypothese*), which he also referred to as substitution (*Ersatzhypothese*) and elimination (*Beseitigungshypothese*); he concluded

---

13. Benjamin W. Bacon, *The Fourth Gospel in Research and Debate: A Series of Essays on Problems concerning the Origin and Value of the Anonymous Writings attributed to the Apostle John* (New York: Moffat, Yard and Company, 1910), 368; see 356–84, ch. 14: Johannine Treatment of Synoptic Material. See also idem, *An Introduction to the New Testament* (New York: Macmillan, 1900), 264, regarding John and the Synoptics on the feeding of the five thousand: "The relation of our Gospel to (Matthew?), Mark, and Luke could hardly receive more convincing illustration."
14. Burnett Hillman Streeter, *The Four Gospels: A Study of Origins: Treating of the Manuscript Tradition, Sources, Authorship, & Dates* (London: Macmillan, 1925), 393–426, ch. 14: "The Fourth Gospel and the Synoptics."
15. Hans Windisch, *Johannes und die Synoptiker: wollte der vierte Evangelist die Älteren Evangelien ergänzen oder ersetzen?* (UNT 12; Leipzig: J.C. Hinrichs, 1926), 42–54; for a highly commendable discussion of Windisch's work, see Smith, *John among the Gospels*, 19–43.
16. Windisch, *Johannes und die Synoptiker*, 24.

that "John adhered to the one gospel principle, and *his* gospel should have been *the* gospel."[17] Windisch agreed with centuries of scholars who thought that John had read all three Synoptics, but Windisch strongly disagreed with the longstanding assumption of the Fourth Gospel's compatibility with its predecessors.

Windisch's solution did not gain wide acceptance, because New Testament scholarship took a sharp turn: oral tradition soon took precedence over literary dependence. If John had heard general Synoptic tradition rather than having read particular Synoptic Gospels, then John could not have attempted to eliminate Matthew, Mark, and Luke. Percival Gardner-Smith's 100-page *Saint John and the Synoptic Gospels* (1938) marks this "turn of the tide."[18] Gardner-Smith returned to the "more cautious" and practically unanimous opinion that John had used Mark and Luke.[19] Yet Gardner-Smith found this view unconvincing, resting on two main problems: previous studies had not given nearly enough attention to the role of oral tradition in the first century; neither had they adequately explained John's differences from the Synoptics.[20]

Gardner-Smith succeeded in raising doubts about literary dependence, thereby shifting the burden of proof—even in cases of very close parallels. For example, when a woman anoints Jesus according to Matthew, Mark, and Luke, she uses an alabaster container of ointment; in Mark and John, it is "expensive, genuine nard ointment" costing "three hundred denarii," and to the woman's detractors Jesus says that "the poor, you (always) have with you, but me you do not always have" (Matt. 26:11; Mark 14:7; John 12:8).[21]

---

17. Ibid., 132.
18. Percival Gardner-Smith, *Saint John and the Synoptic Gospels* (Cambridge: Cambridge University Press, 1938; repr. 2011). The "turn of the tide" statement vis-à-vis Gardner-Smith comes from C. H. Dodd, *Historical Tradition in the Fourth Gospel* (Cambridge: Cambridge University Press, 1963), 8 n. 2; for a careful reception history of Gardner-Smith's book, see Jos Verheyden, "P. Gardner-Smith and 'The Turn of the Tide,'" in *John and the Synoptics*, ed. Adelbert Denaux (BETL 101; Leuven: Leuven University Press, 1992), 423–52.
19. Gardner-Smith, *Saint John and the Synoptic Gospels*, vii.
20. Ibid., x–xi.
21. ἀλάβαστρον μύρου (Matt. 26:7; Mark 14:3; Luke 7:37); μύρου νάρδου πιστικῆς πολυτελοῦς/πολυτίμου (Mark 14:3; John 12:3); δηναρίων τριακοσίων/τριακοσίων δηναρίων (Mark 14:5; John 12:5); γὰρ τοὺς πτωχοὺς . . . ἔχετε μεθ' ἑαυτῶν . . . ἐμὲ δὲ οὐ πάντοτε ἔχετε (Matt. 26:11; Mark 14:7; John 12:8); John

Despite verbatim agreement of seventeen Greek words between Mark and John, Gardner-Smith asserted, "All these . . . are of a kind very easily remembered, striking in character, and therefore likely to become stereotyped in oral tradition."[22] Ironically, then, some of the strongest evidence for John's literary dependence on the Synoptics could be claimed just as easily in support of oral tradition.

Several of the most influential Johannine studies of the twentieth century followed Gardner-Smith. Rudolf Bultmann held that John drew upon oral tradition rather than written gospels, although an ecclesiastical redactor occasionally aligned the final edition of the Fourth Gospel with the Synoptics.[23] C. H. Dodd painstakingly argued that John's sayings and narratives lack strong enough connections for establishing literary dependence on the Synoptics; Dodd argued instead for John's use of Synoptic tradition.[24] Citing Dodd approvingly, Raymond Brown and Rudolf Schnackenburg likewise concluded that John did not use any of the Synoptic Gospels.[25] At the same time, C. K. Barrett maintained that John knew the texts of Mark and Luke.[26] Also, albeit in different ways, M.-É. Boismard and Frans Neirynck reasserted John's use of all three Synoptics.[27] Despite these notable exceptions, the consensus had shifted to Johannine independence.

Current scholarship explains John's relation to the Synoptics in a

---

includes "always" in both clauses, and Mark also says with regard to the poor, "and when you want, you can do good to them."

22. Gardner-Smith, *Saint John and the Synoptic Gospels*, 49.
23. Rudolf Bultmann, *The Gospel of John: A Commentary*, trans. G. R. Beasley-Murray (Philadelphia: Westminster, 1971); the first German edition was published in 1941. See also D. Moody Smith, *The Composition and Order of the Fourth Gospel: Bultmann's Literary Theory* (New Haven: Yale University Press, 1965).
24. Dodd, *Historical Tradition in the Fourth Gospel*, 9.
25. Raymond Brown, *The Gospel according to John* (2 vols.; AB 29–29A; Garden City: Doubleday, 1966–70), 1:xliv–xlvii; Rudolf Schnackenburg, *The Gospel according to St. John*, trans. Kevin Smyth, et al. (3 vols.; HTKNT 4; New York: Herder & Herder; Seabury; Crossroad, 1968–82; repr. New York: Crossroad, 1990), 1:26–43, ch. 2: Relationship to the Synoptics; the German edition was published from 1965–75.
26. C. K. Barrett, *The Gospel according to St. John: An Introduction with Commentary and Notes on the Greek Text* (2d ed.; Philadelphia: Westminster, 1978), 15–17; 1st ed. published in 1955.
27. M.-É. Boismard et al., *Synopse des quatre Évangiles en français: avec parallèles des apocryphes et des pères* (3 vols.; Paris: Cerf, 1965–77); see also Frans Neirynck et al., *Jean et les Synoptiques: Examen critique de l'exégèse de M.-É. Boismard* (BETL 49; Leuven: Leuven University Press, 1979); Maurits Sabbe, "John and the Synoptists: Neirynck vs. Boismard," *ETL* 56, no. 1 (1980): 125–31. I will discuss Boismard and Neirynck further in the following chapter, because they are exceptional in defending John's use of Matthew and their arguments are methodologically significant.

variety of ways. To be sure, scholars such as Craig Keener maintain Johannine independence.[28] Yet other explanations abound. Frank Schleritt renews the attempt to reconstruct a pre-Johannine Passion Narrative as a hypothetical source mediating John's synoptic parallels.[29] Contesting the long-held assumption that John was written last, Mark Matson and others argue for Luke's literary dependence on John.[30] Paul Anderson posits even earlier and ongoing reciprocal influences between Johannine and Synoptic traditions.[31] Other recent studies situate John in the context of oral culture, oral performance, and memory studies.[32] Different questions often yield different answers—sometimes reaching an impasse. The same Johannine details (for example, Jesus' washing his disciples' feet and having his side pierced) can be claimed as either very early tradition or very late redaction.[33] In the end, it remains far easier to identify synoptic parallels in John than to explain convincingly how they got there.

As consensus has evaporated, scholars have increasingly reclaimed John's indebtedness to one or more of the Synoptics. Richard Bauckham holds that John intended his gospel to complement Mark's;[34] Bauckham also considers the Fourth Gospel a record of eyewitness testimony.[35] Udo Schnelle has argued for John's use of Mark and Luke.[36]

---

28. Craig Keener, *The Gospel of John: A Commentary* (2 vols.; Peabody, Mass.: Hendrickson, 2003), 1:40–42.
29. Frank Schleritt, *Der vorjohanneische Passionsbericht: Eine historisch-kritische und theologische Untersuchung zu Joh 2,13-22; 11,47-14,31 und 18,1-20,29* (BZNW 154; Berlin: de Gruyter, 2007).
30. Mark A. Matson, *In Dialogue with Another Gospel? The Influence of the Fourth Gospel on the Passion Narrative of the Gospel of Luke* (SBLDS 178; Atlanta: Society of Biblical Literature, 2001); see also F. Lamar Cribbs, "A Study of the Contacts that Exist between St. Luke and St. John," *SBL Seminar Papers, 1973* (2 vols.; Cambridge, Mass.: Society of Biblical Literature, 1973), 1:1–93; idem, "The Agreements that Exist between Luke and John," *SBL Seminar Papers, 1979* (2 vols.; Missoula, Mont.: Society of Biblical Literature, 1979), 1:215–61; J. Ramsey Michaels, *The Gospel of John* (NICNT; Grand Rapids: Eerdmans, 2010); Barbara Shellard, "The Relationship of Luke and John: A Fresh Look at an Old Problem," *JTS* 46, no. 1 (1995): 71–98.
31. Paul N. Anderson, *The Fourth Gospel and the Quest for Jesus: Modern Foundations Reconsidered* (London: T&T Clark, 2006).
32. E.g., Anthony Le Donne and Tom Thatcher, eds., *The Fourth Gospel in First-Century Media Culture* (LNTS 426; London: T&T Clark, 2011); see especially James D. G. Dunn, "John's Gospel and the Oral Gospel Tradition," in *Fourth Gospel in First-Century Media Culture*, 157–85; see also Mark Jennings, "The Fourth Gospel's Reversal of Mark in John 13,31–14,3," *Bib* 94, no. 2 (2013): 210–36.
33. For a brief comparison of von Wahlde and Schleritt, see my review of Frank Schleritt, *Der vorjohanneische Passionsbericht*, *CBQ* 74, no. 2 (2012): 397–98, here 398.
34. Richard Bauckham, "John for Readers of Mark," in *The Gospels for All Christians: Rethinking the Gospel Audiences* (ed. Richard Bauckham; Grand Rapids: Eerdmans, 1998), 147–71, here 170.
35. Richard Bauckham, *Jesus and the Eyewitnesses: The Gospels as Eyewitness Testimony* (Grand Rapids: Eerdmans, 2006), 358–468.

In separate studies, Thomas Brodie and Steven Hunt have attempted to demonstrate John's use of all three Synoptics.[37] Similarly, commentaries by Ulrich Wilckens, Hartwig Thyen, and Andrew Lincoln presume that—in addition to oral tradition—John made use of all three Synoptics and that John expected his readers to make comparisons with the synoptic parallels.[38] Also, according to Urban C. von Wahlde's reconstruction, the Gospel of John's third and final compositional stage reflects knowledge of all three Synoptics.[39] In my estimation, these studies collectively signify a demurral to Windisch's and Gardner-Smith's conclusions. *Pace* Windisch, John's limited use of, and differences from, the Synoptics need not entail John's attempt to eliminate them. *Pace* Gardner-Smith, while it may not be possible to explain satisfactorily all of John's differences from the Synoptics, literary dependence seems just as likely as oral tradition.

### John's Relation to Matthew

Michael Bird recently considered John "literarily independent" of the Synoptics, yet Bird qualified, "At some point (John) has come across Mark, perhaps Luke, and, who knows, maybe even Matthew."[40]

---

36. Udo Schnelle, *Das Evangelium nach Johannes* (2d ed.; THKNT 4; Leipzig: Evangelische Verlagsanstalt, 2000), 13–17. See also idem, *The History and Theology of the New Testament Writings*, trans. M. Eugene Boring (Minneapolis: Fortress Press, 1998), 496–502; there he concluded that John knew Mark and perhaps Luke as well, but Shnelle also included a few instances of John's use of Matthew, for example, Matthew's binding and loosing saying (18:18) and John's forgiving and retaining sins logion (20:23).
37. Thomas L. Brodie, *The Quest for the Origin of John's Gospel: A Source-Oriented Approach* (New York: Oxford University Press, 1993); Steven A. Hunt, *Rewriting the Feeding of the Five Thousand: John 6.1–15 as a Test Case for Johannine Dependence on the Synoptic Gospels* (StBibLit 125; New York: Peter Lang, 2011).
38. Ulrich Wilckens, *Das Evangelium nach Johannes* (NTD 4; Göttingen: Vandenhoeck & Ruprecht, 2000), 4; Hartwig Thyen, *Das Johannesevangelium* (HNT 6; Tübingen: Mohr Siebeck, 2005), 4; Andrew T. Lincoln, *The Gospel according to Saint John* (BNTC; London: Continuum, 2005; repr. Peabody, Mass.: Hendrickson, 2006), 32–33.
39. Urban C. von Wahlde, *The Gospel and Letters of John* (3 vols.; ECC; Grand Rapids: Eerdmans, 2010), 1:370; by my count, von Wahlde only claims one example of John's use of Matthew, which I examine in the following chapter.
40. Michael F. Bird, *The Gospel of the Lord: How the Early Church Wrote the Story of Jesus* (Grand Rapids: Eerdmans, 2014), 213. Jörg Frey ("Das Vierte Evangelium auf dem Hintergrund der älteren Evangelientradition: Zum Problem: Johannes und die Synoptiker," in *Johannesevangelium—Mitte oder Rand des Kanons? Neue Standortbestimmungen*, ed. Thomas Söding et al. [QD 203; Freiburg: Herder, 2003], 60–118, here 113) similarly concluded that John's use of Matthew cannot be ruled out, although it is less probable than John's use of Mark or Luke.

Commentators have similarly pointed out that a connection between John and Matthew is improbable or at least very difficult to demonstrate;[41] for example, Schnackenburg simply concluded, "Special contacts between Matthew and John are rare and unimportant."[42] Nevertheless, there is a long history of identifying these agreements. In the fourth century, Eusebius of Caesarea compiled the earliest extant list of John–Matthew parallels.[43] John's contacts with Matthew in the passion narrative also figure prominently in separate studies by Nils Dahl, Peder Borgen, Anton Dauer, and Josef Pichler.[44] These four scholars argue for oral tradition rather than literary dependence, although they allow for the possibility that Matthew's written gospel influenced ongoing oral tradition. Taking into account this long history of research, Table 1.1 lists the sixteen most prevalent John–Matthew parallels.[45]

---

41. E.g., D. A. Carson, *The Gospel according to John* (Pillar New Testament Commentary; Grand Rapids: Eerdmans, 1991), 51; Leon Morris, *The Gospel according to John* (rev. ed.; NICNT; Grand Rapids: Eerdmans, 1995), 43; Ben Witherington III, *John's Wisdom: A Commentary on the Fourth Gospel* (Louisville: Westminster John Knox, 1995), 7.
42. Schnackenburg, *Gospel according to St. John*, 1:30.
43. Eusebius's Canon VII consist of John–Matthew parallels. NA[27] includes the Eusebian canons and sections on pp. 84*–89*, with introduction on p. 78*; for discussion, see David Laird Dungan, *A History of the Synoptic Problem: The Canon, the Text, the Composition, and the Interpretation of the Gospels* (ABRL; New York: Doubleday, 1999), 108–11.
44. Nils A. Dahl, "Die Passionsgeschichte bei Matthäus," *NTS* 2, no. 1 (1955–56): 17–32; Peder Borgen, "John and the Synoptics in the Passion Narrative," *NTS* 5, no. 4 (1958–59): 246–59; Anton Dauer, *Die Passionsgeschichte im Johannesevangelium: Eine traditionsgeschichtliche und theologische Untersuchung zu Joh 18,1–19,30* (SANT 30; Munich: Kösel-Verlag, 1972); Josef Pichler, "Setzt die Johannespassion Matthäus voraus?" in *The Death of Jesus in the Fourth Gospel*, ed. G. van Belle (BETL 200; Leuven: Leuven University Press, 2007), 495–505.
45. In addition to previously cited works by Borgen, Brodie, Dahl, Dauer, Lincoln, Schnelle, Streeter, Wilckens, and Windisch, the following studies have contributed to this list: Rosel Baum-Bodenbender, *Hoheit in Niedrigkeit: Johanneische Christologie im Prozeß Jesu vor Pilatus (Joh 18,28–19,16a)* (FB 49; Würzburg: Echter Verlag, 1984), 176–218; Gilbert Van Belle and David R. M. Godecharle, "C. H. Dodd on John 13:16 (and 15:20): St John's Knowledge of Matthew Revisited," in *Engaging with C. H. Dodd on the Gospel of John: Sixty Years of Tradition and Interpretation*, ed. Tom Thatcher and Catrin H. Williams (Cambridge: Cambridge University Press, 2013), 86–106; Bruno de Solages, *Jean et les Synoptiques* (Leiden: E. J. Brill, 1979), 99–113.

| | Table 1.1 John–Matthew Parallels | John | Matthew |
|---|---|---|---|
| 1 | Jesus calls Simon Peter the son of John/Jonah. | 1:42 | 16:17 |
| 2 | Jesus says either I am or you are the light of the world. | 8:12 | 5:14 |
| 3 | Zechariah 9:9 is quoted when Jesus enters Jerusalem. | 12:15 | 21:5 |
| 4 | Jesus says that slaves are not greater than their masters. | 13:16 | 10:24 |
| 5 | Jesus commands a disciple to put away his sword. | 18:11 | 26:52 |
| 6 | Caiaphas is specified as the high priest. | 18:13, 24 | 26:3, 57 |
| 7 | Releasing a prisoner at Passover is customary. | 18:39 | 27:15 |
| 8 | Soldiers put a crown of thorns on Jesus' head. | 19:2 | 27:29 |
| 9 | Pilate sits on the judgment seat (βῆμα). | 19:13 | 27:19 |
| 10 | Jesus' name is inscribed on the *titulus*. | 19:19 | 27:37 |
| 11 | Joseph of Arimathea is called a disciple. | 19:38 | 27:57 |
| 12 | Jesus is buried in a new tomb. | 19:41 | 27:60 |
| 13 | Mary Magdalene is *not* going to anoint Jesus' corpse. | 20:1 | 28:1 |
| 14 | An angel or two appear(s) to Mary Magdalene. | 20:12 | 28:2–3, 5 |
| 15 | The risen Jesus sends Mary Magdalene to his "brothers." | 20:17 | 28:10 |
| 16 | John's forgiving and retaining sins logion parallels Matthew's binding and loosing saying. | 20:23 | 18:18; cf. 16:19 |

As this chapter has shown, currently there is no firm consensus for explaining John's relation to the Synoptics. As has been the case for the last two hundred years, however, scholars still consider Matthew the least likely gospel that John would have read. At the same time, previous scholarship has generated a fairly long and impressive list of agreements between the two gospels, and these require a detailed explanation. The time has come to reinvestigate the relationship between John and Matthew.

2

## Methodology and Hermeneutic

When I say that John used Matthew, I do not mean that John's use of Matthew was systematic and thoroughgoing, as in the way Matthew and Luke used Mark.[1] John's relationship to the Synoptics is much more complicated, and so in this chapter I discuss my methodology and hermeneutic. Given scholars' relative inattention to John's relation to Matthew, I am—for the most part—content to demonstrate that a relationship exists. I use redaction criticism not only to determine whether John depends on Matthew but also to explain how John altered Matthew. John made both major and minor alterations, and I by no means imply that John accepted Matthew uncritically.[2] Instead, I propose interpreting John in light of "apocryphal" gospels, particularly infancy gospels that clearly depend on, and recast, the canonical nativity stories. By a rewriting process known as *oppositio in imitando*,

---

1. See D. Moody Smith, *John among the Gospels* (2d ed.; Columbia: University of South Carolina Press, 2001), 6: "In principle, the problem of John and the Synoptics may not be different from the synoptic problem, but in fact the problem is exacerbated by the extent of the divergences of John from the Synoptics."
2. E.g., regarding Luke's use of Matthew, see Francis Watson, "A Response to Richard Bauckham and Heike Omerzu," *JSNT* 37, no. 2 (2014): 210–18, here 215: "it would be better to say that he *responds* to Matthew, sometimes critically" (emphasis Watson's).

John indeed offers correctives to Matthew, but John's corrections do not imply that he wanted his gospel to replace Matthew's.

## Methodology: Redaction Criticism

In this section, I explain my method for showing John's use of Matthew. John lacks extended verbatim agreements with the Synoptics, and so synoptic parallels are not always obvious in the Fourth Gospel. To discern Matthean parallels, I draw on Richard Hays's criteria for detecting echoes of Old Testament Scriptures in Paul's epistles.[3] Once a parallel is identified, I adhere to Helmut Koester's redaction-critical criterion for claiming literary dependence rather than oral tradition. Although I do not deny the importance of oral tradition, my case studies in the following chapters will make a stronger claim for John's use of Matthew's redacted gospel. So in this section, I show how Koester's methodology applies to previous scholarship on John's relation to Matthew. I also explain how my redaction-critical findings are compatible with recent studies involving social memory theory.

First and foremost, Matthew's gospel must have been accessible to John.[4] In this regard, I accept the conclusions of Graham Stanton and Daniel Ulrich, who have argued for a wide audience for the Gospel of Matthew.[5] Stanton wrote about the evangelist's plural communities and questioned whether Matthew would have written such an elaborate book for only one small group.[6] In a careful study of Matthew's references to missionary activity, Ulrich determined that the author "very likely . . . expected a large and expanding audience for the Gospel."[7] For example, Jesus twice predicts the preaching of this gospel to the entire world (24:14; 26:13),[8] and the gospel ends with Jesus' Great Commission (28:19-20).[9] In light of Stanton's and Ulrich's

---

3. Richard B. Hays, *Echoes of Scripture in the Letters of Paul* (New Haven: Yale University Press, 1989).
4. Regarding "availability," see Hays, *Echoes of Scripture in the Letters of Paul*, 29-30.
5. Graham N. Stanton, *A Gospel for a New People: Studies in Matthew* (Edinburgh: T&T Clark, 1992), 51; see also idem, "Revisiting Matthew's Communities," *SBL Seminar Papers, 1994* (SBLSP 33; Atlanta: Scholars Press, 1994), 9-23; Daniel W. Ulrich, "The Missional Audience of the Gospel of Matthew," *CBQ* 69, no. 1 (2007): 64-83.
6. Stanton, *Gospel for a New People*, 45-53.
7. Ulrich, "The Missional Audience of the Gospel of Matthew," 66.
8. Ibid., 66-67.

conclusions, I accept that Matthew's gospel would have been available to John.

Given Matthew's plausible accessibility, the next step is to identify parallel material based on verbal or structural similarities.[10] It is important to avoid "parallelomania,"[11] but an accumulation or concentration of verbal agreements may enhance the likelihood of a literary relationship.[12] *Sondergut* is the term for "special material" found in only one of the Synoptics, and the appearance of Matthean *Sondergut* in John may raise the probability of literary dependence.[13] It would nonetheless remain indeterminate whether John drew upon Matthew's written gospel, generally circulating tradition, or even a hypothetical source such as the pre-Johannine passion narrative.[14] While is essential to isolate Matthew-John parallels, the parallels do not *ipso facto* prove literary dependence.

In discussions of literary dependence, New Testament scholarship increasingly recognizes the role of memory and orality in the early transmission of Jesus material.[15] So it is important to acknowledge from the outset that literary, mnemonic, and oral transmission were not mutually exclusive processes.[16] Koester pays considerable attention to the role of oral tradition as well as the literary interrelations of the gospels. When facing a parallel saying or narrative, Koester prefers

---

9. Ibid., 70–71.
10. Regarding "volume," see Hays, *Echoes of Scripture in the Letters of Paul*, 30.
11. Samuel Sandmel, "Parallelomania," *JBL* 81, no. 1 (1962): 1–13; in this 1961 SBL presidential address, Sandmel defines parallelomania as "that extravagance among scholars which first overdoes the supposed similarity in passages and then proceeds to describe source and derivation as if implying literary connection flowing in an inevitable or predetermined direction" (p. 1).
12. Regarding "recurrence," see Hays, *Echoes of Scripture in the Letters of Paul*, 30; see also A.J. Bellinzoni, "The Gospel of Luke in the Apostolic Fathers: An Overview," in *Trajectories through the New Testament and the Apostolic Fathers*, ed. Andrew Gregory and Christopher Tuckett (Oxford: Oxford University Press, 2005), 45–68, here 51. Similarly, regarding the "existence of additional parallels," see Wolf-Dietrich Köhler, *Die Rezeption des Matthäusevangeliums in der Zeit vor Irenäus* (WUNT 24; Tübingen: Mohr Siebeck, 1987), 13.
13. Köhler, *Rezeption des Matthäusevangeliums in der Zeit vor Irenäus*, 14.
14. E.g., Frank Schleritt, *Der vorjohanneische Passionsbericht: Eine historisch-kritische und theologische Untersuchung zu Joh 2,13–22; 11,47–14,31 und 18,1–20,29* (BZNW 154; New York: Walter de Gruyter, 2007).
15. E.g., Samuel Byrskog, "The Transmission of the Jesus Tradition: Old and New Insights," *Early Christianity* 1, no. 3 (2010): 441–68.
16. See Andrew Gregory, "What Is Literary Dependence?," in *New Studies in the Synoptic Problem: Oxford Conference, April 2008: Essays in Honour of Christopher M. Tuckett*, ed. Paul Foster et al. (BETL 239; Leuven: Peeters, 2011), 87–114, here 104–7.

to err on the side of caution by presuming oral tradition unless a subsequent text shows clear signs of the *Redaktionsarbeit* of a source text: "How can we know when written documents are the source for... quotations and allusions? Redaction criticism is the answer. Whenever one observes words or phrases that derive from the author or redactor of a gospel writing, the existence of a written source must be assumed."[17] Koester's own dissertation (under the direction of Rudolf Bultmann at Marburg) utilized this methodological principle,[18] which became axiomatic in several dissertations Koester directed at Harvard.[19] After fifty years, Koester's redaction criterion remains the strictest method for demonstrating literary dependence.[20] For example, Andrew Gregory and Christopher Tuckett claim that Koester's criterion "actually offers assured results," yet they qualify that the strictness of the test can limits its usefulness.[21] That is, clear instances of recurring *Redaktionsarbeit* are rare,[22] and so a text could easily conceal the evidence of literary dependence.

John's knowledge of Matthean redaction entails three considerations: what counts as Matthean redaction; which direction dependence runs; and whether John's cognition of Matthew was visual or aural. Signs of Matthean redaction include Matthew's modifications

---

17. Helmut Koester, "Written Gospel or Oral Tradition?," *JBL* 113, no. 2 (1994): 293–97, here 297.
18. Helmut Köster, *Synoptische Überlieferung bei den Apostolischen Vätern* (TU 65; Berlin 1957), 3.
19. Arthur J. Bellinzoni, *The Sayings of Jesus in the Writings of Justin Martyr* (NovTSup 17; Leiden: Brill, 1967), 4; Melvyn R. Hillmer, "The Gospel of John in the Second Century" (Th.D. diss., Harvard Divinity School, 1966), 6; Leslie L. Kline, *The Sayings of Jesus in the Pseudo-Clementine Homilies* (SBLDS 14; Missoula, Mont.: Society of Biblical Literature, 1975), 10.
20. See, e.g., Bellinzoni, "Gospel of Luke in the Apostolic Fathers," 51; Mark Goodacre, *Thomas and the Gospels: The Case for Thomas's Familiarity with the Synoptics* (Grand Rapids: Eerdmans, 2012); Andrew F. Gregory and Christopher M. Tuckett, "Reflections on Method: What Constitutes Use of the Writings that later formed the New Testament in the Apostolic Fathers?," in *The Reception of the New Testament in the Apostolic Fathers,* ed. Andrew F. Gregory and Christopher M. Tuckett (New York: Oxford University Press, 2005), 61–82, here 71, 75–76.
21. Gregory and Tuckett, "Reflections on Method," 75–76.
22. E.g., Ignatius of Antioch says that Jesus was baptized by John "in order to fulfill all righteousness" (*Smyrn.* 1.1), and "to fulfill all righteousness" appears in Matt. 3:15 as a redactional addition to Mark. I agree with Paul Foster ("The Epistles of Ignatius of Antioch and the Writings that Later Formed the New Testament" in Gregory and Tuckett, *Reception of the New Testament,* 160–86, here 174–76, 185) that this meets Koester's criterion, even though his own study appealed instead to a hypothetical source; see Köster, *Synoptische Überlieferung,* 57–59. Elsewhere I have critiqued Koester and his students for inconsistently applying the redaction criterion by presupposing an orally transmitted "born again" baptismal saying: James W. Barker, "Written Gospel or Oral Tradition? Patristic Parallels to John 3:3, 5," *Early Christianity,* forthcoming.

to Mark, Matthew's characteristic vocabulary, and Matthew's distinctive sequence of pericopes.[23] Analogous to the text-critical principle of *lectio difficilior*, the direction of dependence can be discerned if John appears to correct Matthew. Finally, John could have encountered Matthew's text more or less directly: (1) John himself could have maintained visual contact with the Gospel of Matthew and copied the text; (2) John could have had someone else dictate the text to him; (3) John could have recalled Matthew's text from memory;[24] or (4) John could have heard something that originated from the Gospel of Matthew without necessarily knowing about the written gospel itself.

The notion that a written text influenced ongoing oral tradition is known as secondary orality.[25] I make no appeal to secondary orality, and my arguments do not specify whether John's use of Matthew was visual, aural, or mnemonic in any given parallel. In other words, as long as I can show Matthean redaction in John, I do not speculate whether John was remembering something he had heard from Matthew or paraphrasing Matthew based on having read the text or having heard it read aloud. According to my reconstruction, John's parallels are not unmediated by Matthew's redacted gospel, and so I claim John's literary dependence on Matthew.

I do not aspire to invent a new methodology or even to innovate an existing one. My goal is simply to demonstrate John's use of Matthew by employing Koester's redaction criterion, which remains the

---

23. For general introductions to redaction criticism, see Adela Yarbro Collins, "Redaction Criticism in Theory and Practice," in *Method and Meaning: Essays on New Testament Interpretation in Honor of Harold W. Attridge*, ed. Andrew B. McGowan and Kent Harold Richards (RBS 67; Atlanta: Society of Biblical Literature, 2011), 59–77; Norman Perrin, *What Is Redaction Criticism?* (GBS; Philadelphia: Fortress Press, 1969).
24. For the suggestion that John used Mark from memory, see Mark Jennings, "The Fourth Gospel's Reversal of Mark in John 13,31–14,3," *Bib* 94, no. 2 (2013): 210–36.
25. For an early appeal to secondary orality, see Risto Uro, "'Secondary Orality' in the Gospel of Thomas? Logion 14 as a Test Case," *Forum* 9, no. 3/4 (1993): 305–29; for secondary orality applied to John and the Synoptics, see, e.g., Michael Labahn, *Jesus als Lebensspender: Untersuchungen zu einer Geschichte der johanneischen Tradition anhand ihrer Wundergeschichten* (BZNW 98; Berlin: Walter de Gruyter, 1999). Gregory's ("What is Literary Dependence?," 91) description of secondary orality sounds more like simple recollection from memory. Outside of biblical studies, the term secondary orality refers to twentieth-century shifts from print media back to oral storytelling via media such as radio and television; see H. Porter Abbott, "Secondary Orality," in *Routledge Encyclopedia of Narrative Theory*, ed. David Herman, Manfred Jahn, and Marie-Laure Ryan (New York: Routledge, 2005), 521–22.

strictest test for source-critical claims. I do not deny continuing influence of oral tradition in the first and second centuries. My own case studies will show, though, that John knows Matthew's material in its redacted context rather than as isolated, orally transmitted sayings or stories. This methodology is perhaps easier to show than to tell, and so below I list three previous examples of John's purported use of Matthew, one that does not meet Koester's criterion and two that do.

The first example comes from Urban C. von Wahlde, who has completed a monumental commentary on the Fourth Gospel.[26] He reconstructs three stages of the gospel's composition, and he argues for John's use of all three Synoptics. By my count, there is only one instance where von Wahlde claims that John intentionally used Matthew's gospel. John 12:25 reads, "The one who loves his life loses it, and the one hating his life in this world guards it into life eternal." There are five synoptic parallels to this saying, and von Wahlde concludes: "it seems clear that the Johannine version is an attempt to incorporate a saying that the author was familiar with from the Synoptics and that he chose to echo Matt. 10:39 in his own version."[27] Matthew 10:39 reads, "The one who finds his life will lose it, and the one who lost his life on account of me will find it." A related saying occurs in all three Synoptics: "For whoever wants to save his life will lose it, but whoever will lose his life on account of me and the gospel will save it" (Mark 8:35; cf. Matt. 16:25; Luke 9:24).[28] Table 2.1 displays the Greek sayings as von Wahlde orders them.[29]

---

26. Urban C. von Wahlde, *The Gospel and Letters of John* (3 vols.; ECC; Grand Rapids: Eerdmans, 2010).
27. Ibid., 2:550.
28. Matthew and Luke omit "and the gospel;" Luke inserts the subject "this one" who will save his life.
29. Von Wahlde, *Gospel and Letters of John*, 2:549.

Table 2.1 Synopsis of Gospel Sayings about Losing One's Life

| | |
|---|---|
| John 12:25 | ὁ φιλῶν τὴν ψυχὴν αὐτοῦ ἀπολλύει αὐτήν |
| Matt. 10:39 | ὁ εὑρὼν τὴν ψυχὴν αὐτοῦ ἀπολέσει αὐτήν |
| Luke 17:33 | ὅς ἐὰν ζητήσῃ τὴν ψυχὴν αὐτοῦ περιποιήσασθαι ἀπολέσει αὐτήν |
| Matt. 16:25 | ὃς γὰρ ἐὰν θέλῃ τὴν ψυχὴν αὐτοῦ σῶσαι ἀπολέσει αὐτήν |
| Mark 8:35 | ὃς γὰρ ἐὰν θέλῃ τὴν ψυχὴν αὐτοῦ σῶσαι ἀπολέσει αὐτήν |
| Luke 9:24 | ὃς γὰρ ἂν θέλῃ τὴν ψυχὴν αὐτοῦ σῶσαι ἀπολέσει αὐτήν |
| John 12:25 | καὶ ὁ μισῶν τὴν ψυχὴν αὐτοῦ ἐν τῷ κόσμῳ τούτῳ εἰς ζωὴν αἰώνιον φυλάξει αὐτήν |
| Matt. 10:39 | καὶ ὁ ἀπολέσας τὴν ψυχὴν αὐτοῦ ἕνεκεν ἐμοῦ εὑρήσει αὐτήν |
| Luke 17:33 | ὃς δ' ἂν ἀπολέσῃ ζῳογονήσει αὐτήν |
| Matt. 16:25 | ὃς δ' ἂν ἀπολέσῃ τὴν ψυχὴν αὐτοῦ ἕνεκεν ἐμοῦ εὑρήσει αὐτήν |
| Mark 8:35 | ὃς δ' ἂν ἀπολέσει τὴν ψυχὴν αὐτοῦ ἕνεκεν ἐμοῦ καὶ τοῦ εὐαγγελίου σώσει αὐτήν |
| Luke 9:24 | ὃς δ' ἂν ἀπολέσῃ τὴν ψυχὴν αὐτοῦ ἕνεκεν ἐμοῦ οὗτος σώσει αὐτήν |

John's key differences with Matt. 10:39 are the words "this world" and "eternal life," which von Wahlde rightly identifies as characteristic Johannine vocabulary.[30] As compared with the triple-tradition saying, Matt. 10:39 and John 12:25 similarly use a simpler grammatical structure—namely a nominative articular participle—for the subjects "the one who finds/lost" and "the one who loves/hates"; the phrase "whoever wants to save" (Matt. 16:25//Mark 8:35//Luke 9:24) consists of a relative pronoun, conditional particle, subjunctive verb, plus infinitive verb. Such a complicated construction occurs nowhere in John's gospel,[31] whereas simpler nominative articular participles occur more than seventy times in the Fourth Gospel. For the sake of argument, then, I would suggest that if John had encountered the triple-tradition saying apart from Matthew (via Mark, Luke, or oral tradition), then John still might have conformed the aphorism to his own customary style.

---

30. Ibid., 2:549.
31. The closest example is "whoever drinks" (ὃς ἂν . . . πίῃ) in John 4:14.

In my estimation, von Wahlde understates the structural differences between the sayings. The Matthean logion presents a paradox, and the same antonymous verb pair occurs within each strophe: the one who "finds" will "lose," and the one who "loses" will "find." This forms a simple chiasm (a b b' a'), and the same structure holds throughout all five synoptic versions of the saying. By contrast, the Johannine logion evinces antithetic parallelism (a b a' b'), and no verbs are repeated: "loving" in the first strophe is the opposite of "hating" in the second strophe, and "losing" something in the first strophe contrasts with "protecting" in the second strophe. John's structure is unique within this cluster of sayings, and John's uniqueness weakens the case for literary dependence on Matt. 10:39.

Von Wahlde assigns John 12:25 to the final edition of the gospel, which inserted synoptic parallels in other instances. He notes, "It is possible that the author knew it independently of the Synoptics, but given the number of times he inserts material with Synoptic affinities, it is very unlikely that the similarity to the Synoptics here (and elsewhere) was accidental."[32] In other words, here von Wahlde appeals to purported, cumulative evidence. The problem is that John 12:25 would constitute the gospel's only direct use of Matthew. Thus it is less convincing—if not inadmissible—to enlist John's occasional use of Mark and Luke elsewhere as supporting evidence in the sole argument for John's use of Matthew. I am very complimentary of von Wahlde's overall project, though I think that this argument for John's dependence on Matthew does not prove more compelling than an argument for oral tradition.

A second example comes from M.-É. Boismard, who led one of the largest-scale inquiries into the composition of John's Gospel.[33] His *Synopse des quatre Évangiles en français* consists of three volumes: the synopsis proper, a commentary on the synopsis that reconstructs each

---

32. Von Wahlde, *Gospel and Letters of John*, 2:550 n. 4.
33. For an overview of Boismard's project, see Smith, *John among the Gospels*, 141–47; for a book-length refutation, see Frans Neirynck et al., *Jean et les synoptiques: Examen critique de l'exégèse de M.-É. Boismard* (BETL 49; Leuven: Leuven University Press, 1979); see also Maurits Sabbe, "John and the Synoptists: Neirynck vs. Boismard," *ETL* 56, no. 1 (1980): 125–31.

gospel's sources and redactional layers, and a commentary on the Gospel of John that is keyed to the pericopes delineated in the synopsis.[34] Boismard posits numerous literary sources for John, but the basic formulation is that the gospel was composed in three stages over several decades. Boismard's project has been criticized for being overly complicated and for not considering the role of oral tradition.[35]

Despite the criticisms of the overall endeavor, one of Boismard's findings meets Koester's redaction criterion for John's use of Matthew. Regarding John's imperial official (βασιλικός; 4:46b-54), scholars have long noted the story's commonalities with Matthew and Luke's centurion (ἑκατόνταρχος; Matt. 8:5–13; Q/Luke 7:1–10). Since John's differences outweigh his similarities with Matthew and Luke, scholars often appeal to oral tradition. All three versions follow the generic structure of a healing narrative: a statement of sickness, request for healing, performance of healing, and response of the crowd; an additional element of this story is that Jesus performs the healing remotely. The three gospels nonetheless describe the illness differently: Luke says only that the slave was about to die (7:2), while Matthew names paralysis (Matt. 8:6), and John says fever (4:52); John says specifically that "the fever left him" (ἀφῆκεν αὐτὸν ὁ πυρετός; John 4:52).[36] Boismard astutely read across Matthew's pericopes and observed that two sentences later, when Jesus heals Peter's mother-in-law, "the fever left her" (ἀφῆκεν αὐτὴν ὁ πυρετός; Matt. 8:15; cf. Mark 1:31b). Except for differently gendered pronouns, the sayings are verbatim. Matthew (8:13) and John (4:53) also call attention to the precise hour in which the boy was healed. Here Boismard makes a plausible case for John's knowledge of Matthean redaction, specifically Matthew's distinctive ordering of pericopes.[37]

---

34. M.-É. Boismard et al., *Synopse des quatre Évangiles en français: avec parallèles des apocryphes et des pères* (3 vols.; Paris: Cerf, 1965–77).
35. For Boismard's inattention to oral tradition, see Robert Kysar, review of M.-É. Boismard and A. Lamouille, with the collaboration of G. Rochais, *Synopse des quatre Évangiles en français*, Tome III, *JBL* 98, no. 4 (1979): 605–7, here 607; for being overly complicated, see Raymond Brown, review of M.-É. Boismard and A. Lamouille, *L'Évangile de Jean* (Synopse des quatre Évangiles en français 3), *CBQ* 40, n. 4 (1978): 624–28, here 625: "When it is charted, it looks like a twelve-man football team with a lot of motion in the backfield."
36. Boismard et al., *Synopse des quatre Évangiles*, 3:149.

My third and final example is Frans Neirynck's consideration of Matt. 28:9–10 as "sufficiently different from Mark to be taken as special material in Matthew, and sufficiently close to Mark to be accepted as Matthew's editorial composition."[38] In other words, Matt. 28:9–10 evinces both Matthean *Sondergut* and Matthean redaction, so Neirynck repeatedly argued that these two verses served as a written source for John 20:11–18.[39] Having no Markan parallel, Matt. 28:9 tells that the two Marys "grabbed (Jesus') feet" (ἐκράτησαν αὐτοῦ τοὺς πόδας), which interlocks with Jesus' command for Mary Magdalene to stop clinging to him (μή μου ἅπτου; John 20:17).[40] That is, Matthew tells that Mary took hold of Jesus but Jesus does not tell her to let go, whereas John has Jesus tell Mary to let go of him but does not mention that she had taken hold. In this instance, John reflects knowledge of Matthean *Sondergut*.

John also shows knowledge of Matthean redaction, specifically the way Matt. 28:10 changes Mark 16:6–7. The main difference is that Matthew turned Mark's angelophany into a Christophany.[41] At the same time, the instructions of the angel and Jesus are strikingly similar. The statements are not verbatim, but all the differences are synonymous. Table 2.2 displays these verses.[42] In Mark, the angel commands the women to go to Jesus' "disciples"; in Matthew, Jesus commands the women to go to his "brothers." In John 20:17, Jesus commands Mary Magdalene to go to his "brothers," and in 20:18 she tells the disciples that she has seen the Lord. Neirynck concludes that John's use of ἀδελφούς reflects knowledge of Matthean redaction.

---

37. Luke's story of Peter's mother-in-law (4:38–39) occurs long before Jesus encounters the centurion.
38. Frans Neirynck, "John and the Synoptics: 1975–1990," in *John and the Synoptics*, ed. Adelbert Denaux (BETL 101; Leuven: Leuven University Press, 1992), 3–62, here 34.
39. Frans Neirynck, "Les Femmes au Tombeau: Étude de la rédaction Matthéenne," NTS 15, no. 2 (1968–69): 168–90, esp. 176–84; idem, "John and the Synoptics," in *L'Évangile de Jean: Sources, Rédaction, Théologie*, ed. M. de Jonge, et al. (BETL 44; Leuven: Leuven University Press, 1977), 73–106, here 96–98; idem, "John and the Synoptics: The Empty Tomb Stories," NTS 30, no. 2 (1984): 161–87, here 166–71; idem, "John and the Synoptics: 1975–1990," 33–35; idem, "Note on Mt 28, 9–10," ETL 71, no. 1 (1995): 161–65.
40. This observation dates back at least as far as Augustine (*Tract. Ev. Jo.* 121.3).
41. Strictly speaking, Mark refers to a young man (νεανίσκος) rather than an angel (ἄγγελος).
42. For Neirynck's synopsis, see "Les Femmes au Tombeau," 183.

Table 2.2 Synopsis of Mark's Angelophany and Matthew's Christophany

| Mark 16:6ab, 7 | Matt. 28:10 |
|---|---|
| ὁ δὲ λέγει αὐταῖς | τότε λέγει αὐταῖς ὁ Ἰησοῦς |
| μὴ ἐκθαμβεῖσθε . . . | μὴ φοβεῖσθε· |
| ἀλλ' ὑπάγετε εἴπατε | ὑπάγετε ἀπαγγείλατε |
| τοῖς μαθηταῖς αὐτοῦ καὶ τῷ Πέτρῳ ὅτι | τοῖς ἀδελφοῖς μου ἵνα |
| προάγει ὑμᾶς εἰς τὴν Γαλιλαίαν | ἀπέλθωσιν εἰς τὴν Γαλιλαίαν |
| ἐκεῖ αὐτὸν ὄψεσθε, καθὼς εἶπεν ὑμῖν | κἀκεῖ με ὄψονται |

In summary, in von Wahlde's example (John 12:25//Matt. 10:39), "lose" (ἀπόλλυμι) and "soul" (ψυχή) are the main words in common, but the same words occur in a nearly identical variant, which is common to all three Synoptics (Matt. 16:25//Mark 8:35//Luke 9:24; cf. Luke 17:33). In contrast to this variant, Matthew (10:39) and John (12:25) do use the same kind of participle, and yet the structure of John's saying is entirely different than its synoptic counterparts. Since John 12:25 does not show any signs of Matthean redaction, oral tradition would be as likely, or more likely, than literary dependence. In Boismard's example, Jesus heals the imperial official's son, and "the fever left him" (John 4:52). Although Matthew does not say that the centurion's slave suffered from a fever, Matthew does narrate Jesus' healing of Peter's mother-in-law in the immediately ensuing pericope, and in that story "the fever left her" (Matt. 8:15). Here, then, John likely knows Matthew's redactional placement of a story. In Neirynck's example, John (20:17) knows that Jesus sent Mary Magdalene to the disciples, whom Jesus calls "brothers"; "brothers" constitutes a Matthean (28:10) redaction of Mark (16:7). Despite the strictness of Koester's redaction criterion, Neirynck and Boismard have used it to demonstrate John's use of Matthew. To my knowledge, these are the only previously adduced John–Matthew parallels that pass Koester's test, and so Boismard's and Neirynck's influence on my research cannot be overstated.

In concluding this section on redaction criticism, I would be remiss not to mention the significance of social memory theory in recent research on the gospels.[43] Some studies of orality and memory advance

---

43. For a broad study of social memory and the Fourth Gospel, see Tom Thatcher, *Why John Wrote a*

strong claims regarding eyewitness testimony and the historical reliability of the gospel tradition.[44] These particular claims have been met with strong criticism,[45] and I agree that New Testament scholars should not overstate the accuracy of largely unrecoverable past events and extended transmission processes. It is important to point out, though, that other social memory theorists offer strikingly similar words of caution.[46] Chris Keith explains clearly, "Collective memory refers to the representation of the past in light of the needs of the present with no automatic assumption at the outset concerning the degree to which that representation may reflect reality."[47] According to social memory theory, then, what is being remembered is not necessarily the same as what actually happened.

Social memory theory critiques many aspects of form criticism, but the two approaches show a great deal of continuity, given their interests in oral tradition.[48] This does not imply that social memory theory lacks attention to the processes of writing the gospels, although source and redaction criticism have perhaps been devalued in some studies of memory and the Gospels.[49] I hope that my conclusions will show redaction criticism and social memory theory to be quite

*Gospel: Jesus—Memory—History* (Louisville: Westminster John Knox, 2006). For overviews of social memory theory vis-à-vis the Gospels, see Stephen J. Davis, *Christ Child: Cultural Memories of a Young Jesus* (Synkrisis; New Haven: Yale University Press, 2014), 14–18; Eric Eve, *Behind the Gospels; Understanding the Oral Tradition* (Minneapolis: Fortress Press, 2014), 91–98; Chris Keith, *Jesus' Literacy: Scribal Culture and the Teacher from Galilee* (LNTS 413; New York: Bloomsbury T&T Clark, 2011), 50–70; Anthony Le Donne, *The Historiographical Jesus: Memory, Typology, and the Son of David* (Waco: Baylor University Press, 2009), 41–64; Rafael Rodriguez, *Structuring Early Christian Memory: Jesus in Tradition, Performance, and Text* (LNTS 407; New York: T&T Clark, 2010), 39–80.

44. E.g., Richard Bauckham, *Jesus and the Eyewitnesses: The Gospels as Eyewitness Testimony* (Grand Rapids: Eerdmans, 2006); Samuel Byrskog, *Story as History—History as Story: The Gospel Tradition in the Context of Ancient Oral History* (WUNT 123; Tübingen: Mohr Siebeck, 2000).

45. E.g., Zeba Crook, "Collective Memory Distortion and the Quest for the Historical Jesus," *JSHJ* 11, no. 1 (2013): 53–76; Paul Foster, "Memory, Orality, and the Fourth Gospel: Three Dead-Ends in Historical Jesus Research," *JSHJ* 10, no. 3 (2012): 191–227.

46. E.g., Jens Schröter, "The Gospels as Eyewitness Testimony? A Critical Examination of Richard Bauckham's *Jesus and the Eyewitnesses*," *JSNT* 31, no. 2 (2008): 195–209.

47. Chris Keith, "Social Memory Theory and the Gospels: The First Decade," *Early Christianity* 6 (2015), forthcoming (my thanks to Chris for sharing with me his pre-production manuscript); see also Chris Keith, "Memory and Authenticity: Jesus Tradition and What Really Happened," *ZNW* 102, no. 2 (2011): 155–77, here 172: "Indeed, the Gospels often contain competing, contradictory memories of Jesus that cannot all be historically accurate."

48. E.g., Byrskog is indebted to traditional form criticism, but he is not uncritical of its inconsistencies; see Samuel Byrskog, review of Rudolf Bultmann, *The History of the Synoptic Tradition*, *JBL* 122, no. 3 (2003): 549–55. See also Part Two of Keith, "Social Memory Theory and the Gospels," for critiques and affirmations of form criticism.

complementary methodologically.[50] I am especially interested in redactional activity that invents traditions and manufactures memories.[51] For example, in a recent study of King David, Jacob Wright describes the ancient Israelites as not simply remembering the past but "constructing and transmitting alternative memories" as well as writing "counterhistory" (*Gegengeschichte*).[52] The notions of counterhistory and countermemory aptly apply to the ways John recast certain narratives and sayings from Matthew's text.[53]

### Hermeneutic: Reading John as an Apocryphal Gospel

By demonstrating John's use of Matthew, I thereby raise the question of whether John wanted his gospel to be read alongside, or instead of, Matthew's. Hans Windisch concluded that John wrote a new gospel to replace the Synoptics, not to supplement them.[54] Despite how long ago Windisch wrote, this question retains currency and relevance.[55] In this section, I argue against Windisch's replacement hypothesis. I explain how extracanonical gospels construct self-standing narratives that nonetheless presuppose and supplement the canonical gospels. Even though John corrects Matthew in several instances, John's relationship to Matthew should be considered "opposition in imitation" (*oppositio in imitando*). John might have wanted to surpass Matthew, but John could not reasonably expect to supplant Matthew.

Windisch based his replacement hypothesis on the Fourth Gospel's

---

49. For this critique, see Greg Carey, "Moving Things Ahead: A Lukan Redactional Technique and Its Implications for Gospel Origins," *BibInt* 21, no. 3 (2013): 302–19.
50. In response to Carey's "Moving Things Ahead," see Keith, "Social Memory Theory and the Gospels," forthcoming: "The argument that Carey forwards for understanding Lukan redaction is not contrary to social memory theory properly understood." For the relevance of redaction-critical conclusions for the application of social memory theory, see especially Le Donne, *Historiographical Jesus*, 83, 89.
51. Regarding the invention of traditions and the manufacturing of memories (although not in relation to redaction criticism), see Crook, "Collective Memory Distortion," 66–75.
52. Jacob L. Wright, *David, King of Israel, and Caleb in Biblical Memory* (New York: Cambridge University Press, 2014), 136, 149, 239 n. 9.
53. Regarding the ways John recast Lukan traditions, see Philip F. Esler and Ronald A. Piper, *Lazarus, Mary and Martha: Social-Scientific Approaches to the Gospel of John* (Minneapolis: Fortress Press, 2006).
54. Hans Windisch, *Johannes und die Synoptiker: wollte der vierte Evangelist die Älteren Evangelien ergänzen oder ersetzen?* (UNT 12; Leipzig: J.C. Hinrichs, 1926).
55. E.g., David C. Sim, "Matthew's Use of Mark: Did Matthew Intend to Supplement or to Replace His Primary Source?," *NTS* 57, no. 2 (2011): 176–92.

originality, unity, and sufficiency.[56] His fullest expression of Johannine self-sufficiency runs as follows:

> The *result* of our critical investigations can be clearly and easily summarized. The Fourth Gospel is no collection of paralipomena; it wants neither to supplement older accounts nor to be supplemented by them. Instead it is explicable all by itself, self-contained, sufficient, and—pushing all older, earlier writings to the side—provides description of the story of Jesus. Nowhere have there been detected positive references to the older writings and to the more abundant underlying tradition within them; in sharper focus, all observations of the way [John purportedly references the Synoptics] go up in smoke. Nowhere are there gaps in which one can insert the synoptic narratives John skipped over. Every attempt at harmonization and combination pits the Fourth Evangelist in the greatest opposition. Not one instance of specified recognition can be read. The opinion that John had the intention to correct the older tradition where it was necessary—that he thus wanted to validate everything else in them—has still up to now nowhere been proven with certainty. The few comments that *could* be understood as corrections to the synoptic narratives stand in the way of important cases where a clearer reference would have been required, but was spurned by the evangelist. And every place that one could understand as allusions to the Synoptics—so long as they are not glosses—can be completely explained much better based purely on the very structure of the Johannine narrative. The Fourth Gospel is a self-contained narrative; it presents a continuous narrative; much less is it open to anything so artificial as a harmony or a Diatessaron; it is *autonomous* and *sufficient*. Of the four explanations listed above . . . , the first [the supplemental theory] must in any case already be rejected based on the proofs thus far. The second theory [the independence theory] at least has the right understanding of the composition of John; only already its historical presupposition, that John presents a faithfully remembered historical report, has become doubtful to us. This reservation becomes unnecessary for the third hypothesis [the interpretation theory], regarding which the difficulty has already been emphasized that the older writings, which John should supposedly interpret, apparently do not appear at all on his horizon. So let us now push all observations to the elimination hypothesis already.[57]

According to Windisch, then, the Fourth Gospel's self-sufficiency

---

56. Windisch, *Johannes und die Synoptiker*, 126–27.
57. Ibid., 87–88; regarding that quotation, Smith (*John among the Gospels*, 25 n. 39) noted, "One could scarcely imagine a stronger statement of the Fourth Gospel's independence, in the sense of self-sufficiency, than is found on pp. 87–88."

entails that John disregarded the Synoptics and desired to replace them.[58]

To test Windisch's claim, I highlight the relationships among extracanonical and canonical gospels as an analogy to John and the Synoptics. Several scholars have countenanced similar possibilities. In what follows, I review their proposals, and then I adduce infancy gospels as self-standing narratives that both supplement and correct the nativity stories in the Gospels of Matthew and Luke. These extracanonical gospels cannot have been written independently of their canonical counterparts, and yet the extracanonical stories cannot replace the canonical nativity stories. In my view, the composition of the eventually extracanonical gospels provides a working model for John's relationship to Matthew.

D. Moody Smith observes that Matthew and Luke's close correspondence to Mark creates the phenomenon of Synoptic Gospels.[59] Since John does not correspond to the Synoptics in the same way, Smith asks whether—in a sense—the fourth canonical gospel could be considered the first apocryphal gospel.[60] He develops this analogy as it pertains to methodology: apocryphal gospels might have accessed independent Jesus traditions that were still developing, or the apocryphal gospels might have used canonical gospels to supplement them and align with them.[61] Smith ultimately leaves this question open, and he mainly discusses the *Gospel of Peter*, Egerton Papyrus 2, the *Gospel of Thomas*, and the *Secret Gospel of Mark*. By raising the question, though, Smith makes a breakthrough in reconfiguring John's relation to the Synoptics.

Ulrich Wilckens adopts a similar reading strategy in his commentary on the Fourth Gospel. Wilckens draws an analogy between John and "apocryphal" gospels that construct new gospel narratives by reworking and harmonizing preexisting ones;[62] according to Wilckens,

---

58. Windisch, *Johannes und die Synoptiker*, 134.
59. D. Moody Smith, "The Problem of John and the Synoptics in Light of the Relation between Apocryphal and Canonical Gospels," in *John and the Synoptics*, ed. Adelbert Denaux (BETL 101; Leuven: Leuven University Press, 1992), 147–62, here 156.
60. Ibid., 156–62.
61. Ibid., 152.

John expected his readers' familiarity with corresponding synoptic accounts. Thomas Kazen also pointed out that the Gospel of John, had it been lost in antiquity and rediscovered in the twentieth century, would seem "foreign" when compared to the Synoptics.[63] And in a highly significant, recent study, Francis Watson urges that the gospels "initially be read as though the distinction between canonical and noncanonical did not exist."[64] These scholars have thus joined Koester in an effort to overcome canonical prejudice,[65] the ahistorical tendency to presuppose and privilege the fourfold gospel canon as though the composition and reception of eventually extracanonical gospels were somehow different, derivative processes.

Windisch clearly knew about apocryphal gospels that fill in gaps in the life of Jesus, and Windisch mentions stories of Mary's and Jesus' childhood in particular.[66] He adds that "here the canonical gospels were acknowledged from the start, and the new writings were actually written for *supplementation*."[67] These extracanonical gospels do not show extended verbatim agreements with the canonical gospels, and the extracanonical gospels do not make any explicit references to the canonical gospels. This is significant because, in Windisch's estimation, the Fourth Gospel's failure to mention the Synoptics indicated John's intention to replace—rather than supplement—the Synoptics. In other

---

62. Ulrich Wilckens, *Das Evangelium nach Johannes* (NTD 4; Göttingen: Vandenhoeck & Ruprecht, 2000), 4.
63. Thomas Kazen, "Sectarian Gospels for Some Christians? Intention and Mirror Reading in the Light of Extra-Canonical Texts," *NTS* 51, no. 4 (2005): 561–78, here 566 n. 25. Kazen wrote in response to the measurable absence of apocryphal gospels in Richard Bauckham, ed., *The Gospels for All Christians: Rethinking the Gospel Audiences* (Grand Rapids: Eerdmans, 1998); the same critique would apply to Bauckham's *Jesus and the Eyewitnesses*.
64. Francis Watson, *Gospel Writing: A Canonical Perspective* (Grand Rapids: Eerdmans, 2013), 406; see also 609–11.
65. For "apocryphal and canonical gospels" and "the prevailing prejudice," see Helmut Koester, *Ancient Christian Gospels: Their History and Development* (Philadelphia: Trinity Press International; London: SCM, 1990), 43–44.
66. Windisch, *Johannes und die Synoptiker*, 166n1.
67. Ibid., 166; Windisch earlier cited Otto Bardenhewer (*Geschichte der altkirchlichen Litteratur, bd. 1* [2d ed.; Freiburg: Herder, 1913], 503), who writes, "The so-called *Protevangelium of James* wants to narrate the earlier life of the mother of God and in this regard constitutes a supplement to the canonical Gospels." On the following page Bardenhewer classifies the *Gospel of Peter* as gnostic and places it in a different group than those that "fill in the gaps of the canonical gospels," such as Jesus' childhood. *Inter alia* Windisch does not discuss the *Protevangelium of James*, which was nonetheless available to him in Tischendorf's collection (Constantin von Tischendorf, *Evangelia Apocrypha* [Leipzig: Hermann Mendelssohn, 1876]), as cited by Bardenhewer.

words, Windisch's canonical prejudice assumes a different writing process for the Fourth Gospel, as compared to apocryphal gospels. I argue to the contrary that John fits neatly within the compositional conventions of the extracanonical gospels.

*Protevangelium of James* comprises independent traditions, especially ones about Mary. These stories narrate Mary's birth and childhood, proofs of her virginal conception and post-partum virginity, and clarification that she did not give birth to Jesus' supposed siblings. In these regards, *Protevangelium of James* intentionally supplements the canonical nativity stories. Quintessentially, *Prot. Jas.* 22 harmonizes Matthew and Luke to explain how the baby John the Baptist escaped Herod's slaughter of infants.[68] Only Luke makes Jesus and John blood relatives born within six months of each other, and only Matthew has Herod slaughter the Bethlehem children two years and younger shortly after Jesus' birth. When read alongside one another, the question arises as to how John the Baptist survived Herod's slaughter. *Protevangelium of James* resolves the seeming contradiction by constructing the angelic mountain rescue of the baby John the Baptist and his mother Elizabeth.[69]

Readers of the *Protevangelium* are by no means required to know Matthew or Luke or their seeming contradiction.[70] However, the story of Elizabeth and John's miraculous deliverance only originates from an author's self-conscious attempt to resolve the tension between the

---

68. See Ronald F. Hock, *The Infancy Gospels of James and Thomas* (The Scholars Bible 2; Santa Rosa, CA: Polebridge, 1995), 9; idem, ed., *The Life of Mary and the Birth of Jesus: The Ancient Infancy Gospel of James* (Berkeley, CA: Ulysses Press, 1997), 15.
69. One could argue topographically that no real contradiction exists between Matthew and Luke. Herod commands the slaughter "in Bethlehem and in all its regions/boundaries/districts" (ἐν Βηθλέεμ καὶ ἐν πᾶσαι τοῖς ὁρίοις αὐτῆς; Matt. 2:16); Bethlehem's boundaries go unspecified. To visit Elizabeth, though, Mary goes "into the hill country . . . into a city of Judah" (εἰς τὴν ὀρεινὴν . . . εἰς πόλιν Ἰούδα; Luke 1:39). Luke's reference to the hill country would most likely locate John's birthplace in a city such as Hebron, which lies farther south of Bethlehem than Bethlehem lies south of Jerusalem. In other words, Luke's hill country was likely far enough from Matthew's boundaries of Bethlehem for baby John to have stayed safe from Herod's henchmen. However, considering that Elizabeth flees with John into the hill country to avoid the slaughter (*Prot. Jas.* 22.3), the author of the *Protevangelium* likely had no detailed knowledge of Judean geography. Thus, considering Matthew and Luke contradictory, the author constructed the harmonization.
70. Similarly Bauckham ("John for Readers of Mark," in *Gospels for All Christians*, 147–71, here 158) points out that readers of John can understand the gospel even if they have not read Mark; Bauckham nevertheless assumes that the Fourth Gospel "presupposes that many of its readers/hearers will know Mark and will expect to be able to relate John's narratives to Mark's" (p. 159).

two. *Contra* Windisch's reasoning, such self-sufficiency does not imply the author's intention that the *Protevangelium* be read in isolation from the other gospels. Just as the Gospels of Matthew and Luke had to be read alongside one another within the circle that produced the *Protevangelium*, so too the *Protevangelium* placed itself alongside Matthew and Luke as a supplement, not as a replacement.

The intentions of the *Infancy Gospel of Thomas* are similar to those of the *Protevangelium of James*. The conclusion to the longer recension of the *Infancy Gospel of Thomas* overlaps with Luke's narrative of the twelve-year-old Jesus in Jerusalem (2:41–52). The shorter version of the *Infancy Gospel* narrates events transpiring when Jesus was five, six, and eight years old. Accordingly, the *Infancy Gospel of Thomas* fills in the gaps of Luke's gospel, which skips from Jesus' day of birth (2:7) and his circumcision on day eight (2:21) to Jesus' return to the temple at age twelve (2:42). Vernon Robbins describes this infancy gospel as "grounding" its narrative with Luke's, combining the familiar Lukan story with the new or unfamiliar infancy material.[71] At the same time, the *Infancy Gospel's* episodes do not require knowledge of Luke, and in no way could the *Infancy Gospel of Thomas* replace Luke's gospel.

Simply put, extracanonical infancy gospels stand on their own, but they do not stand alone. Windisch argued that since John's gospel does not require knowledge of the Synoptics, John did not intend to be read alongside them.[72] Along the same lines, Smith asked, "If the Fourth Gospel is intended to be supplemented by the Synoptics and to supplement them, why should it contain narratives that are parallel to the Synoptics at all?"[73] The infancy gospels reveal the answer: Matthew and Luke must have been read alongside one another in the same reading circles, and the *Protevangelium of James* gained credibility by sidling up to Matthew and Luke and resolving a contradiction between them. Similarly, the *Infancy Gospel of Thomas* positioned itself beside

---

71. Vernon K. Robbins, *Who Do People Say I Am? Rewriting Gospel in Emerging Christianity* (Grand Rapids: Eerdmans, 2013), 185–86.
72. Windisch, *Johannes und die Synoptiker*, 96: "Not a single one of the synoptic parallels in John is composed such that the synoptic account must be compared for its explanation and supplementation."
73. Smith, *John among the Gospels*, 25–26.

the Gospel of Luke as a supplement to its stories of Jesus' birth and childhood. These extracanonical gospels could be *read* and understood without knowledge of their canonical counterparts, but the extracanonical gospels could not have been *written* independently of the canonical ones.[74] I propose a similar relationship between John and Matthew.[75]

The phenomenon of "interlocking" coheres with John's intended supplementation, not replacement.[76] As Neirynck explained, Mary grabs Jesus' feet in Matthew (28:9), and Jesus tells Mary to let go in John (20:17). John's use of the imperfect tense (μή μου ἅπτου) signifies that Mary had indeed touched Jesus,[77] and so John's narrative invites comparison with Matthew's. An even stronger example of interlocking comes when Jesus says, "Destroy this temple, and in three days I will raise it" (John 2:19). In Matthew (26:61) and Mark (14:58), false-witnesses testify before the Sanhedrin that Jesus said something like this, but neither gospel ever depicts Jesus doing so. If John had included both Jesus' temple saying and the witnesses' accusation, then readers would not need to compare with Matthew or Mark, and this might count as evidence for replacement. Once again, though, John's detail supplements Matthew or Mark, but John's narrative does not replace either of theirs.

I have found Benedict Viviano's study of "John's hypothetical but

---

74. See Paul Foster, "Memory, Orality, and the Fourth Gospel," 209: "Consideration of second-century non-canonical Gospels and Acts shows how authors who clearly betray knowledge of written canonical counterparts in parts of their new works can be independently creative in their handling of the tradition elsewhere. The first point to remember is that we are not dealing with scribes making accurate copies of their exemplar texts, but with authors who wish to redeploy and recast traditions that they already know."
75. The notion of John's positioning itself alongside one or more Synoptics is not unprecedented, but scholars usually attribute such a Johannine intention to later redactional stages; e.g., conformity with the Synoptics is a characteristic of Bultmann's ecclesiastical redactor, Boismard's John II-B, Baum-Bodenbender's later Johannine redaction, and von Wahlde's third and final edition of John; cf. Raymond Brown, *An Introduction to the Gospel of John*, ed. Francis J. Moloney (ABRL; New York: Doubleday, 2003), 104; Ismo Dunderberg, *Johannes und die Synoptiker: Studien zu Joh 1–9* (AASF Dissertationes Humanarum Litterarum 69; Helsinki: Suomalainen Tiedeakatemia, 1994).
76. On John's interlocking with the Synoptics, see D. A. Carson, *The Gospel according to John* (Pillar New Testament Commentary; Grand Rapids: Eerdmans, 1991), 51–55; see also Leon Morris, *Studies in the Fourth Gospel* (Grand Rapids: Eerdmans, 1969), 40–63.
77. Harold W. Attridge, "'Don't Be Touching Me': Recent Feminist Scholarship on Mary Magdalene," in *A Feminist Companion to John* (ed. Amy-Jill Levine with Marianne Blickenstaff; 2 vols.; Sheffield: Sheffield Academic Press, 2003), 2:140–66.

probable use of Matthew" to be especially illuminating.[78] Viviano considers Windisch's replacement hypothesis tempting but improbable,[79] and he proposes a more complex relationship between John and Matthew. Viviano's case studies show John's varying levels of disagreement with Matthew. For example, Jesus' heavenly origins in John 1 are different from, yet compatible with, Jesus' human origins in Matthew 1.[80] In Mark, Jesus defends healing on the Sabbath because it is permissible to do good on the Sabbath (3:4); Matthew adds that priests work on the Sabbath (12:5), and John supplements Matthew by claiming that even God works on the Sabbath (5:17).[81] Whereas Matthew depicts Jesus riding two donkeys into Jerusalem (21:7), John improves Matthew by including only one donkey (12:14).[82] Compared with Matthew, John demotes Peter but does not demonize him.[83] According to the Fourth Gospel, John the Baptist says that he is not Elijah (1:21), thereby contradicting Matthew's identification of the Baptist as Elijah (11:14).[84] Viviano refers to John's "subtle nuance and refinement" as well as "restrained criticism" of Matthew.[85]

A source-critical demonstration of John's dependence on Matthew lay beyond the scope of Viviano's article. Instead, Viviano constructed a working hermeneutic for John's relationship to Matthew. Viviano did exceptionally well to explain John's differences from Matthew and to avoid Windisch's false dichotomies. According to Viviano, sometimes John supplemented Matthew, and at other times John reinterpreted or even contradicted Matthew, but at no time did John intend to replace Matthew. Viviano's findings have been highly influential for my own understanding of John's complex relationship to Matthew.

---

78. Benedict T. Viviano, "John's Use of Matthew: Beyond Tweaking," *RB* 111, no. 2 (2004): 209–37, here 235; similarly in his abstract Viviano "presupposes direct Johannine knowledge of the synoptics" (p. 209).
79. Ibid., 212. Jörg Frey ("Das Vierte Evangelium auf dem Hintergrund der älteren Evangelientradition: Zum Problem: Johannes und die Synoptiker," in *Johannesevangelium—Mitte oder Rand des Kanons? Neue Standortbestimmungen*, ed. Thomas Söding, et al. [QD 203; Freiburg: Herder, 2003], 60–118, here 114–16) similarly rejected Windisch's replacement hypothesis.
80. Viviano, "John's Use of Matthew," 213–15.
81. Ibid., 222–23.
82. Ibid., 230–31.
83. Ibid., 223–29.
84. Ibid., 217–19.
85. Ibid., 235–36.

Viewing John as both in continuity and in competition with Matthew fits well within the context of Greco-Roman compositional practices.[86] A particularly important practice is known as *oppositio in imitando*, whereby a subsequent text imitates and reinterprets—but does not replace—a predecessor. Vergil's use of Homer is quintessential.[87] For example, Aeneas's trip to the underworld in book 6 of the *Aeneid* parallels Odysseus's trip to Hades in book 11 of the *Odyssey*. At the same time, Vergil could repeat, recast, and relocate particular scenes. During Odysseus's trip to Hades, he tries three times to hug the ghost of his mother (*Od.* 11.204-209). During Aeneas's trip to the underworld, he tries three times to hug the ghost of his father (*Aen.* 6.700-701). Long before then, during the Battle of Troy, Aeneas had tried three times to hug the ghost of his wife (*Aen.* 2.790-794); moments earlier, he had seen her alive. Perhaps Vergil aspired to surpass Homer, but Vergil could hardly imagine supplanting Homer. On the contrary, Vergil's imitation of Homer presupposes some readers' familiarity and comparisons with Homer's epics.[88] By way of analogy, John could imitate and reinterpret Matthew, but John's gospel could hardly replace Matthew's.

Finally, I view my methodology and hermeneutic as compatible with

---

86. For ancient compositional practices and the gospels, see James W. Barker, "Ancient Compositional Practices and the Gospels: A Reassessment," *JBL*, forthcoming; Alex Damm, *Ancient Rhetoric and the Synoptic Problem: Clarifying Markan Priority* (BETL 252; Leuven: Peeters, 2013); R. A. Derrenbacker, Jr., *Ancient Compositional Practices and the Synoptic Problem* (BETL 186; Leuven: Peeters, 2005); F. Gerald Downing, "Compositional Conventions and the Synoptic Problem," *JBL* 107, no. 1 (1988): 69–85; Anne M. O'Leary, *Matthew's Judaization of Mark: Examined in the Context of the Use of Sources in Graeco-Roman Antiquity* (LNTS 323; New York: T&T Clark, 2006). For arguments that the evangelists imitated Homer and Vergil, see Dennis R. MacDonald, *The Homeric Epics and the Gospel of Mark* (New Haven: Yale University Press, 2000); idem, *The Gospels and Homer: Imitations of Greek Epic in Mark and Luke-Acts* (Lanham, Md.: Rowman & Littlefield, 2015); idem, *Luke and Vergil: Imitations of Classical Greek Literature* (Lanham, Md.: Rowman & Littlefield, 2015). For arguments that Luke imitated and rewrote Elijah–Elisha narratives, see Thomas L. Brodie, *The Birthing of the New Testament: The Intertextual Development of the New Testament Writings* (New Testament Monographs 1; Sheffield: Sheffield Phoenix Press, 2004).
87. For an introduction to Vergilian intertextuality, see Joseph Farrell, *Vergil's Georgics and the Traditions of Ancient Epic: The Art of Allusion in Literary History* (New York: Oxford University Press, 1991), 3–25; other influential studies include Alessandro Barchiesi, *Homeric Effects in Vergil's Narrative*, trans. Ilaria Marchesi and Matt Fox (Princeton: Princeton University Press, 2015); Gian Biagio Conte, *The Rhetoric of Imitation: Genre and Poetic Memory in Virgil and Other Latin Poets*, trans. Charles Segal (Cornell Studies in Classical Philology 44; Ithaca: Cornell University Press, 1986); Georg Nicolaus Knauer, *Die Aeneis und Homer: Studien zur poetischen Technik Vergils mit Listen der Homerzitate in der Aeneis* (Hypomnemata 7; Göttingen: Vandenhoeck & Ruprecht, 1964).
88. For Vergil's use of Homer, see O'Leary, *Matthew's Judaization of Mark*, 25–38; see p. 35 for an example of *oppositio in imitando*.

Watson's notion of "gospel production . . . as interpretative rewriting."[89] Watson retains the language of Matthean and Johannine redaction, but his project ranges more widely. In particular, Watson identifies redaction as one characteristic found along multiple steps in the process of reception.[90] Watson focuses on the effects of the eventual fourfold gospel canon, and he sidesteps the question of the Evangelists' intentions. According to Watson, even if Matthew intended to correct or contradict Mark, the fourfold collection "can *override* whatever may have been the intentions or expectations of individual evangelists."[91] I hope that my findings will fill in a gap and show that, although Matthew might have intended to supplant Mark,[92] John did *not* intend to replace Matthew. According to my thesis, the eventual, canonical complementarity of the Fourth Gospel and the Gospel of Matthew was simply the actualization of John's original intent.

---

89. Watson, *Gospel Writing*, 288. On the topic of rewriting, see also Steven A. Hunt, *Rewriting the Feeding of the Five Thousand: John 6.1–15 as a Test Case for Johannine Dependence on the Synoptic Gospels* (StBibLit 125; New York: Peter Lang, 2011). Also, Jean Zumstein (*Kreative Errinerung: Relecture und Auslegung im Johannesevangelium*, 2d ed. [ATANT 84; Zürich: Theologischer Verlag, 2004], esp. 15–30) uses the term *Relecture* to describe the process of composition, reinterpretation, and revision of the Gospel and Epistles of John, but Zumstein does not argue that John was rewriting one or more of the Synoptics.
90. Watson, *Gospel Writing*, 353–55.
91. Ibid., 90–91, his emphasis; along similar lines, specifically the function of the Fourth Gospel's canonical placement, see George C. Heider, "The Gospel according to John: The New Testament's Deutero-Deutronomy?," *Bib* 93, no. 1 (2012): 68–85.
92. See Sim, "Matthew's Use of Mark."

# 3

# Ecclesial Authority

According to Matthew, Jesus authorizes disciples to bind and loose: "Whatever you bind on earth will have been bound in heaven, and whatever you loose on earth will have been loosed in heaven" (Matt. 18:18b; cf. 16:19).[1] According to John, the risen Jesus tells disciples, "If you forgive anyone's sins, (the sins) have been forgiven them; if you retain anyone's [sins], (the sins) have been retained" (John 20:23).[2] The Matthean and Johannine logia evince syntactical similarities,[3] and ever since the patristic era the sayings have been interpreted in light of one another.[4] The scholarly consensus explains the sayings as independent,

---

1. ὅσα ἐὰν δήσητε ἐπὶ τῆς γῆς ἔσται δεδεμένα ἐν οὐρανῷ, καὶ ὅσα ἐὰν λύσητε ἐπὶ τῆς γῆς ἔσται λελυμένα ἐν οὐρανῷ (Matt. 18:18b).
2. ἄν τινων ἀφῆτε τὰς ἁμαρτίας ἀφέωνται αὐτοῖς, ἄν τινων κρατῆτε κεκράτηνται (John 20:23).
3. The formal similarities between Matt. 18:18 and John 20:23 are as follows. Each saying contains two clauses, each of which depicts future more vivid conditions. Introducing the subjunctives are ἄν [ᾶ] (John 20:23), which is equivalent to ἐάν (Matt. 18:18; cf. 16:19). In each condition the same verb appears in the protasis and apodosis; the protases use the active voice, and the apodoses use the (divine) passive. Whereas Matthew's apodoses use periphrastic future perfects, John's use only the perfect, which are nonetheless understood as future perfects since they involve future conditions.
4. Regarding "history of interpretation" and "similar syntactic patterns" as criteria for discerning textual echoes, see Richard B. Hays, *Echoes of Scripture in the Letters of Paul* (New Haven: Yale University Press, 1989), 30–31. Matthew 18:18//John 20:23 appears in Kurt Aland, *Synopsis Quattuor Evangeliorum* (15th ed.; Stuttgart: Deutsche Bibelgesellschaft, 1996), 252, ch. 170; of course, the synopsis merely presents parallels rather than implying literary dependence.

orally transmitted variants of an original Aramaic saying. Another possibility is secondary orality, the notion that sayings from Matthew's written gospel entered into ongoing oral transmission, thereby influencing the writing of John's gospel.

This chapter divides into two parts. The first part shows that the previously adduced arguments for oral tradition do not hold. The second part demonstrates John's dependence on Matthew.[5] John knows Matthew's second binding and loosing saying (18:18) embedded within an extended discussion of sin and forgiveness (18:15–35). Matthew's redactional transition from Jesus' saying about binding and loosing (18:18) to Peter's question about forgiving sin (18:21) explains how John adopted the *form* of the Matthean logion and inserted the *content* of forgiveness and non-forgiveness. As a corrective to Matthew, John emphasized the disciples' responsibility not to forgive in every instance. I also offer a supporting argument that the first Johannine epistle harmonizes the binding and loosing saying in Matt. 18:18 and the forgiving and retaining sins saying in John 20:23. First John thus reveals traces of the Gospels of Matthew and John being read alongside one another, which was most likely John's original intent.

## Arguments for Oral Tradition

John's forgiving and retaining sins passage has long been considered an independent variant of Matthew's binding and loosing saying. There are two prevailing arguments, both of which posit an original Aramaic saying that could have engendered Matthew's and John's sayings. One idea is that the original saying described opening and shutting, which morphed into Matthew's binding and loosing as well as John's forgiving and retaining sins. Another idea is that that the concepts of binding and loosing can convey the same meaning as forgiving and retaining sins because in Aramaic (שרי) and in Greek (λύω) the same word can mean both *loosen* and *forgive*. Yet another possibility is secondary

---

5. Pace J. H. Bernard (*A Critical and Exegetical Commentary on the Gospel according to St. John* [2 vols.; ICC 29; Edinburgh: T&T Clark, 1928], 2:680), who concluded that Matthew more likely depended on John.

orality, the idea that someone quoted Matthew's written gospel and indirectly influenced the writing of John's gospel. In this section, I reassess the lexical semantics underlying these arguments, and I find the arguments invalidated by misunderstandings of the key Aramaic terms.

## An "Open and Shut" Case

John Emerton posits a single Aramaic saying about opening and shutting that could underlie the Matthean and Johannine sayings.[6] Emerton's argument has strongly influenced scholars who connect John's and Matthew's sayings through oral tradition.[7] Until now, though, Emerton's philological evidence has gone largely unchecked, so herein I reveal its semantic implausibility. In particular, the crux of Emerton's argument stretches the meaning of the verb פתח (open) beyond what it can bear in Aramaic.

Since Matt. 16:19 mentions a set of keys and a pair of opposites, Emerton suggests Isa. 22:22 as an Old Testament parallel: "I will put the key of the house of David upon his shoulder: he will open, and no one will shut; he will shut, and no one will open." Emerton proposes the following as Jesus' original saying: "whatsoever thou shalt shut shall be shut: and whatsoever thou shalt open shall be opened."[8] Emerton claims that the terminology of opening and shutting later shifted to the rabbinic concept of binding and loosing found in the Mishnah and in

---

6. John A. Emerton, "Binding and Loosing—Forgiving and Retaining," *JTS* 13, no. 2 (1962): 325-31.
7. E.g., C. K. Barrett, *The Gospel according to St. John: An Introduction with Commentary and Notes on the Greek Text* (2d ed.; Philadelphia: Westminster, 1978), 571; Raymond E. Brown, *The Gospel according to John* (2 vols.; AB 29-29A; Garden City, NY: Doubleday, 1966-70), 2:1039-40; F. F. Bruce, *The Gospel of John: Introduction, Exposition, and Notes* (Grand Rapids: Eerdmans, 1983), 392, 397 n. 19; W. D. Davies and Dale C. Allison, *A Critical and Exegetical Commentary on the Gospel according to Saint Matthew* (3 vols.; ICC; Edinburgh: T&T Clark, 1988-97), 2:640; Donald A. Hagner, *Matthew* (2 vols.; WBC 33A-33B; Dallas: Word Books, 1993-95), 2:473; Craig Keener, *The Gospel of John: A Commentary* (2 vols.; Peabody, Mass.: Hendrickson, 2003), 2:1207-8; Andreas Köstenberger, *John* (BECNT; Grand Rapids: Baker, 2004), 575; Barnabas Lindars, *The Gospel of John* (New Century Bible Commentary; London: Marshall, Morgan & Scott, 1972; repr. Grand Rapids: Eerdmans, 1982), 612-13; Francis Moloney, *The Gospel of John* (SP 4; Collegeville, Minn.: Liturgical Press, 1998), 535-36. Others argue against related oral tradition by claiming that on different occasions Jesus likely uttered the related Matthean and Johannine logia; e.g., D. A. Carson, *The Gospel according to John* (Pillar New Testament Commentary; Grand Rapids: Eerdmans, 1991), 655; Craig S. Keener, *A Commentary on the Gospel of Matthew* (Grand Rapids: Eerdmans, 1999), 430n93.
8. Emerton, "Binding and Loosing—Forgiving and Retaining," 328.

Matt. 16:19 and 18:18. Although John 20:23 does not mention keys at all, Emerton thinks that keys are implied insofar as the kingdom is open to people whose sins are forgiven as opposed to the unforgiven who are shut out of the kingdom.[9] In this way, Emerton attempts to show how opening and shutting shifted to binding and loosing in Matthew as well as forgiving and retaining sins in John.

In Isa. 22:22, the Hebrew words for *open* and *shut* are פתח and סגר respectively. However, Emerton focuses on the Aramaic cognates פתח and אחד (Tg. J. Isa. 22:22) because Jesus spoke Aramaic and because אחד (Aram.)—unlike סגר (Heb.)—can mean both *shut* and *hold*.[10] Emerton considers "keeping sins" an odd expression, and so he posits אחד—in the sense of holding—as the best explanation of John's use of κρατέω for holding onto sins (John 20:23).[11] Emerton does not notice that "holding onto sins" is attested in Aramaic: "Is it not [the case that] if your work is good in this world, (your sin) will be remitted [שרי] and forgiven [שבק] you in the world that is coming, and if your work is not good in this world, your sin is kept [נטר] for the day of great judgment?" (Tg. Neof. Gen. 4:7). Thus John's expression is less problematic than Emerton realizes.

In attempting to explain how a generic statement about "opening" came to signify forgiveness of sins, Emerton overextends the meaning of פתח (Aram.). He lists instances of פתח as *loose* or *release* in Hebrew, and he suggests that those who transmitted the Aramaic Jesus saying

---

9. Ibid., 328.
10. Ibid., 328. Emerton's preference for shutting/holding in the second half of John 20:23 (p. 329) results in part from F. Crawford Burkitt's (*Evangelion da-Mepharreshe: The Curetonian Version of the Four Gospels, with the readings of the Sinai Palimpsest and the early Syriac Patristic evidence* [2 vols.; Cambridge: Cambridge University Press, 1904], 1:529) mistranslation of John 20:23 according to the Old Syriac Sinaiticus: "and whom ye shall shut *your door* against—it is shut;" Burkitt italicizes "your door" to signify that the words do not appear in the text; cf. "and he whom ye shall shut up, he is shut up" (Burkitt, *Evangelion da-Mepharreshe*, 2:316). A more accurate rendering would be: "Whom you forgive him his sins, they are forgiven to him; and whom you hold [his sins] against him, he holds fast". "Hold fast" indeed sounds strange, but that is the meaning of the Pael of ܐܚܕ, which Sinaiticus, the Peshitta, and the Harklean all use at this point in John 20:23. The only difference from Sinaiticus is that the Peshitta and the Harklean make "sins," rather than the sinner, the subject (3 f. pl.) of "hold fast," and in those versions "shut" would not make sense.
11. Emerton, "Binding and Loosing—Forgiving and Retaining," 329. Emerton dismisses the long held explanation that John simply used κρατέω (hold onto) as the literal opposite of ἀφίημι (let go; forgive); see, e.g., Walter Bauer, *Das Johannesevangelium* (3d ed.; HNT 6; Tübingen: Mohr Siebeck, 1933), 232; Brown, *Gospel according to John*, 2:1024.

relied upon such Old Testament usage.¹² Emerton's appeal to the Hebrew cognate of פתח is problematic insofar as he earlier insisted on an original Aramaic saying because he needed the double meaning of אחד. Emerton does attempt to explain the nuances of Aramaic פתח on its own terms, but this argument also has its difficulties. He cites two Targumic texts, namely Tg. Job 12:14b and Tg. Ps. 105:20, both of which plausibly render פתח as *to be released*.¹³ The problem is that both texts simply reproduce פתח from their Hebrew *Vorlagen*, and neither Targum likely predates the fourth century CE.¹⁴

Emerton claims additional evidence in that ܦܬܚ twice signifies *release* in John 18:39, where Pilate would have set Jesus free. For these instances, Emerton relies on Friedrich Schulthess's dictionary of Christian Palestinian Aramaic (CPA).¹⁵ Although the dialect of CPA reaches back much earlier, the texts that read ܦܬܚ in John 18:39 are lectionary codices A (Vatican) and C (Sinai, 1893), which date to the eleventh and twelfth centuries respectively.¹⁶ Christa Müller-Kessler distinguishes early (fifth- to seventh-century) and middle period (eighth- to ninth-century) CPA manuscripts from late-period (tenth- to thirteenth-century) ones, which contain numerous "corrupted and doubtful forms."¹⁷ Accordingly, the lectionary texts are not simply late copies of CPA texts: these lectionary texts only emerged at a very late

---

12. Emerton, "Binding and Loosing—Forgiving and Retaining," 329.
13. Targum Job 12:14b could read either of two ways: "[If] he shuts [יסגר] a man in a grave, then it [i.e. the grave] will not be opened [יתפתח];" also, "[If] he shuts [יסגר] a man in a grave, then he will not be released [יתפתח]." The MT lacks the specific location of a "grave" and could refer either to the man not being released or to whatever encloses the man not being opened; the Greek translation favors the containment vessel: "If he shuts out people, who will open [τίς ἀνοίξει]?," Targum Ps. 105:20 reads, "The king sent and released [שרא; cf. נתר Hithpael in the MT] him; the ruler among the peoples set him free [פתח; cf. פתח in the MT]."
14. Based partly on the reference to Rome and Constantinople in Tg. Ps. 108:11 David M. Stec (*The Targum of Psalms* [ArBib 16; Collegeville, Minn.: Liturgical Press, 2004], 2) tentatively dates Targum Psalms between the fourth and sixth centuries; Raphael Weiss did not date Targum Job earlier than Bavli (Frederick E. Greenspahn, review of Raphael Weiss, *The Aramaic Targum of Job*, JAOS 101, no. 4 [1981]: 452–53).
15. Emerton, "Binding and Loosing—Forgiving and Retaining," 329; see Friedrich Schulthess, *Lexicon Syropalestinum* (Berlin: Georgii Reimer, 1903; repr., Amsterdam: APA, 1979), 165.
16. Agnes Smith Lewis and Margaret Dunlop Gibson, eds., *The Palestinian Syriac Lectionary of the Gospels: Re-edited from two Sinai MSS. and from P. de Lagarde's edition of the "Evangeliarium Hierosolymitanum"* (London: Kegan Paul, Trench, Trübner & co., 1899), 197.
17. Christa Müller-Kessler, "Christian Palestinian Aramaic and Its Significance to the Western Aramaic Dialect Group," JAOS 119, no. 4 (1999): 631–36, here 632.

stage of CPA as a dialect.¹⁸ Earlier Syriac texts do not read ܫܒܩ at John 18:39; the Peshitta gives ܫܪܐ and the Harklean uses ܐܫܪܐ.¹⁹ Simply put, Emerton's case is based on פתח (Aram.) signifying *release* in the first century, when שרי would have been the normal term, and he is unable to demonstrate any early attestation.

Emerton nevertheless rests on the supposition that פתח could mean *release* in first-century Aramaic, and he further suggests that "the idea of releasing or setting free led to the thought of releasing or setting free from sin, and hence of forgiveness."²⁰ *Inter alia* he cites Rev. 1:5, which refers to setting free (λύω) from sin (ἁμαρτία), to show that Greek verbs for *release* come to mean *forgive*. Without a doubt λύω can signify forgiveness, but in instances such as Rev. 1:5 the direct object *sin* is clearly marked. By contrast, Emerton's reconstructed saying about opening/releasing and shutting lacks an object, and only by circular reasoning can one claim the connotation of sin. Emerton also points out that שרי (Aram.), which signifies both *loosening* and *forgiving*,²¹ sometimes stands for פתח (Heb.). That too is true, but it is again circular to cite an attested usage of שרי (Aram.) as a corollary to an unattested usage of פתח (Heb. and Aram.)—especially considering that Emerton began by rejecting אסר and שרי as the terms underlying the Matthean and Johannine sayings. On their own, then, Emerton's terms פתח and אחד simply do not convey the meanings his argument requires because פתח is nowhere attested as *forgive* in Hebrew or Aramaic.

For the Matthean logia, Emerton claims that the concept of opening

---

18. Müller-Kessler ("Christian Palestinian Aramaic and Its Significance to the Western Aramaic Dialect Group," 633) similarly criticizes Alain Desreumaux (*Codex sinaiticus Zosimi rescriptus: Description codicologique des feuillets araméens melkites des manuscrits Schøyen 35, 36 et 37 (Londres-Oslo) comprenant l'édition de nouveaux passages des Évangiles et des Catéchèses de Cyrille* [HTB 3; Lausanne: Éditions du Zèbre, 1997]) for intermingling readings from late-period lectionary texts in a reconstruction of the early-period Codex Sinaiticus Rescriptus.
19. George Anton Kiraz, ed., *Comparative Edition of the Syriac Gospels: Aligning the Sinaiticus, Curetonianus, Peshitta and Harklean Versions* (4 vols.; NTTS 21–24; Leiden: Brill, 1996), 4:326; John 18:39 is not extant in Old Syriac: Curetonianus preserves nothing past "And now, look..." (ܗܐ ܘܗܫܐ) in John 14:29, and Sinaiticus is broken from John 18:31–19:40 (E. Jan Wilson, ed., *The Old Syriac Gospels: Studies and Comparative Translations* [2 vols.; Eastern Christian Studies 1–2; Piscataway, NJ: Gorgias Press, 2002]).
20. Emerton, "Binding and Loosing—Forgiving and Retaining," 329.
21. Ibid., 330.

and shutting gave rise to rabbinic sayings about binding and loosing. As supporting evidence, he appeals to Strack-Billerbeck: Sipre Deut. 32:25 (Pisqa 321) quotes 2 Kgs. 24:16, which mentions engravers and locksmiths.[22] The Midrash plays on the word *engraver* (חָרָשׁ) as being *silent* (cf. חֵרֵשׁ, deaf) in face of authoritative teaching, and the word *locksmith* (מסגר) derives from the verb *shut* (סגר), which prompts a quotation of the saying in Isa. 22:22. Strack-Billerbeck also cites a chain of wordplay based on 2 Kgs. 24:16 (b. Sanh. 38a; b. Giṭ. 88a; Tanḥ. Noah 3), but—as Herbert Basser observes—only at the latest stage is there any association with rabbinic declarations of what is permissible.[23] Rabbinic sayings about binding and loosing were already well established in the Mishnah, which Sipre Deuteronomy cites, and so there is no evidence that opening and shutting was an earlier formulation for declaring authoritative rabbinic teaching.

In summary, Emerton's supporting evidence is far too late to establish first-century usage. He posits opening and shutting (Aram. פתח and אחד) in place of binding and loosing (Aram. אסר and שרי) as explaining the sayings in Matt. 16:19 and 18:18 as well as John 20:23. However, Emerton supposes that particular meanings of שרי also extended to פתח without ever demonstrating his thesis that פתח (open) morphed into Matthew's λύω (loose) and John's ἀφίημι (forgive).

## Is Binding and Loosing Synonymous with Begrudging and Forgiving Sins?

Matthew's binding and loosing sayings use δέω and λύω, the equivalents of אסר and נתר (Hiphil) in Hebrew and אסר and שרי, which is also spelled שרא, in Aramaic. Since the verbs שרי and λύω can mean both *loose* and *forgive*, a host of scholars understand Matthew's saying as synonymous with begrudging and forgiving sins.[24] This purported

---

22. Ibid., 330, there citing Str-B 1:741.
23. Herbert W. Basser, "Derrett's 'Binding' Reopened," *JBL* 104, no. 2 (1985): 297–300, here 298–99; following Basser closely is John Nolland, *The Gospel of Matthew: A Commentary on the Greek Text* (NIGTC; Grand Rapids: Eerdmans, 2005), 680.
24. E.g., George R. Beasley-Murray, *John* (WBC 36; Waco: Word Books, 1987), 383; Brown, *The Gospel according to John*, 2:1044–45; Hans von Campenhausen, *Ecclesiastical Authority and Spiritual Power in*

synonymy constitutes the basis for many arguments that John's forgiving and retaining sins saying (20:23) represents an independent variant of Matthew's binding and loosing saying (16:19; 18:18).[25] I argue to the contrary that a proper understanding of binding and loosing rules out the meaning of forgiveness.

By extension of *loosening* bonds, λύω and נתר can signify a person's being released from prison, and λύω and שרי can also signify forgiveness of sin. Regarding forgiveness, Hillel says that Israel should not expect the Messiah since the Messiah already came during the days of Hezekiah; Yosef replies, "May his master [that is, God] forgive [שרא] Rabbi Hillel" (b. Sanh. 99a). The LXX says that the Lord forgave [λύω] Job's three friends' sin on account of Job (42:9), and the next verse reiterates, "concerning (Job's) friends, (the Lord) forgave [ἀφίημι] them the sin" (42:10).[26] On the supposition that λύω could signify forgiveness in Matt. 16:19 and 18:18, the antonym δέω would signify the disciples' lack of forgiveness.

The interpretation of δέω and λύω as withholding and granting

---

the Church of the First Three Centuries, trans. J. A. Baker (Stanford: Stanford University Press, 1969), 139 n. 72; Davies and Allison, *Matthew*, 2:636; C. H. Dodd, *Historical Tradition in the Fourth Gospel* (Cambridge: Cambridge University Press, 1963), 348; Robert H. Gundry, *Matthew: A Commentary on His Literary and Theological Art* (Grand Rapids: Eerdmans, 1982), 369; Daniel J. Harrington, *The Gospel of Matthew* (SP 1; Collegeville, MN: Liturgical Press, 1991), 248, 269; Köstenberger, *John*, 575; Hans Kvalbein, "The Authorization of Peter in Matthew 16:17-19: A Reconsideration of the Power to Bind and Loose," in *The Formation of the Early Church*, ed. Jostein Ådna (WUNT 183; Tübingen: Mohr Siebeck, 2005), 145-74, here 158; Ulrich Luz, *Matthew*, trans. James E. Crouch (3 vols.; Hermeneia; Minneapolis: Fortress Press, 2001-7), 2:454; Leon Morris, *The Gospel according to John* (rev. ed.; NICNT; Grand Rapids: Eerdmans, 1995), 750. Similarly, binding and loosing means "convicting and acquitting" rather than prohibiting and permitting according to Craig A. Evans, *Matthew* (NCBC; New York: Cambridge University Press, 2012), 334. Cf. J. Duncan M. Derrett, "Binding and Loosing (Matt. 16:19; 18:18; John 29:23 [sic])," *JBL* 102, no. 1 (1983): 112-17, here 116: Matt. 16:19; 18:18 do "not necessarily" pertain to forgiveness.

25. See esp. Dodd, *Historical Tradition in the Fourth Gospel*, 347-49; those citing Dodd approvingly include Barrett, *Gospel according to St. John*, 571; Brown, *Gospel according to John*, 2:1039; Rudolf Bultmann, *The Gospel of John: A Commentary*, trans. G. R. Beasley-Murray (Oxford: Basil Blackwell, 1971), 693n2; Davies and Allison, *Matthew*, 2:639-40; Tobias Hägerland, *Jesus and the Forgiveness of Sins: An Aspect of His Prophetic Mission* (SNTSMS 150; Cambridge: Cambridge University Press, 2012), 81; Rudolf Schnackenburg, *The Gospel according to St. John*, trans. Kevin Smyth et al. (3 vols.; HTKNT 4; New York: Herder & Herder; Seabury; Crossroad, 1968-82; repr. New York: Crossroad, 1990), 3:473 n. 87; Urban C. von Wahlde, *The Gospel and Letters of John* (3 vols.; Eerdmans Critical Commentary; Grand Rapids: Eerdmans, 2010), 2:856-57. For John's "forgiving and retaining sins" as the original form of the saying, which Matthew changed to "binding and loosing," see Michael Theobald, *Herrenworte im Johannesevangeliums* (Herder's Biblical Studies 34; Freiburg: Herder, 2002), here 193-94.

26. Davies and Allison, *Matthew*, 2:636; Job 42:9, 10 MT lack explicit reference to sin or forgiveness.

forgiveness unravels upon closer inspection. In Job 42:9 LXX, λύω clearly means *forgive* because it takes *sin* as a direct object and stands in parallel with ἀφίημι. The Matthean saying does not mention sin, and so it is questionable whether a connotation of forgiveness pertains. Moreover, another explanation proves satisfactory. As has long been noted,[27] Matthew's binding and loosing denote respectively rabbinic prohibition and permission of certain actions, and the cognates אסר and נתר (Hiphil) in Hebrew as well as אסר and שרי in Aramaic are widely attested among the Tannaim. For example, the house of Shammai permits [נתר Hiphil] levirate marriages of deceased brothers' co-wives to the surviving brothers, but the house of Hillel prohibits [אסר] such marriages (m. Yebam. 1:4). This meaning in fact precludes any understanding of λύω in terms of forgiveness, for *there is no transgression in doing what is permitted*. Regarding levirate marriage, Shammai would not forgive men who marry their deceased brothers' co-wives; instead Shammai declares such marriages permissible, and so there is no sin to forgive.

Persons who engaged in prohibited behavior could be expelled from the community, and sages would sound a horn when readmitting someone who previously had been expelled: "a toot binds, and a toot releases" (טוט אסר וטוט שרי; b. Moʿed Qat. 16a).[28] The verb for *expel* is נדה (Piel), and the state of expulsion or separateness is מנודה; the verb for *release* or *readmit* is שרי. For example, in b. Moʿed Qat. 16a, a butcher was expelled for insulting Tobai ben Mattena; the expulsion held for thirty days, even though the butcher made peace with the rabbi in the meantime. When someone was expelled and readmitted, שרי would not denote forgiveness: a sinner was not being forgiven a sin

---

27. E.g., BDAG, 222; Gustaf Dalman, *The Words of Jesus: Considered in the Light of Post-Biblical Jewish Writings and the Aramaic Language,* trans. D. M. Kay (Edinburgh: T&T Clark, 1902; repr. Eugene, OR: Wipf & Stock, 1997), 213–17; Str-B 1:738–41. I concur with Davies and Allison (*Matthew*, 2:635–39) that in Matt. 16:19; 18:18 δέω and λύω do not pertain to exorcism, eternal judgment, vows, "totality," magic, or the consummation of the kingdom.

28. In b. Moʿed Qat. 16a, rabbis delineate a seven-day rebuke (נזיפה) and a thirty-day separation (נידה); the ban is imposed (חרם Pael) after successive separations of sixty days total. For comparison, the concept of expulsion and readmission is also common in the Dead Sea Scrolls, but the terminology differs; see, e.g., the verbs *banish* (שלח Piel) and *separate* (בדל Hiphil) as well as *return* (שוב) in 1QS 8.20–9.2.

or (metaphorically) a debt; a sinner would have done just the opposite, namely to repay his or her debt.²⁹

It is fair to question how much of the Mishnaic and Talmudic terminology would have been in use during the first century, but Josephus shows that binding and loosing was established. Josephus juxtaposes bind and loose (δέω and λύω) with banish and recall (διώκω and κατάγω) in a discussion of the Pharisees' political influence over Alexandra Salome, who ruled Judea 78–69 BCE: "(the Pharisees) were also presently becoming administrators of everything—to banish and recall whom they want, to loose and bind" (B.J. 1.111).³⁰

In summary, λύω means *forgive* when it takes ἁμαρτία (sin) as its object (for example, Job 42:9 LXX). Since Matthew's saying does not mention sin, I think it questionable that binding and loosing be interpreted as withholding and granting forgiveness. In rabbinic usage, the Hebrew and Aramaic cognates of the word pair δέω and λύω adequately explain the Matthean logia as distinguishing prohibited beliefs and practices from permitted ones; in all likelihood, the expulsion of people who indulge in such prohibitions would pertain as well. Accordingly, there would be no denotation of forgiveness, for nobody sins when doing that which is permitted. So far, then, there is an unstable foundation for this argument that John's saying about forgiving and retaining sins represents an independent variant of Matthew's binding and loosing sayings.

## The Possibility of Secondary Orality

Paul Anderson proposes an interfluential model, whereby a mixture of oral and written sources allowed the Gospel of John to be influenced by the synoptic tradition even as the Johannine tradition influenced the Synoptics.³¹ The interrelation of Matt. 16:19 and 18:18 and John

---

29. For the metaphor of debt as sin and for remittance as the opposite of repayment in matters of debts/sins, see Gary A. Anderson, *Sin: A History* (New Haven: Yale University Press, 2009), esp. 31–33.
30. Matthew chose a fundamental Greek political term to signify the church (ἐκκλησία), and so Josephus's reference to political banishment could be related to Matthew's notion of binding and loosing.
31. Paul N. Anderson, *The Christology of the Fourth Gospel: Its Unity and Disunity in the Light of John 6*

20:23 provides an important test case.³² In the Gospel of Mark (8:27–30), Peter's confession at Caesarea Philippi lacks the blessing of Peter and his receiving the "keys of the kingdom" and authority to bind and loose (16:17–19), which constitute Matthean redaction. Anderson argues that the Fourth Gospel reflects knowledge of this redacted Matthean passage. In line with previous arguments for oral tradition, Anderson considers binding and loosing equivalent to retaining and forgiving sins, and he stops short of arguing for John's direct use of Matthew. At the same time, Anderson has made a significant advancement by positing a plausible, close relationship between Matthean and Johannine traditions undergoing the process of textualization.

According to Anderson, the original tradition of Peter individually holding the power to bind and loose (Matt. 16:19) influenced continuing Johannine preaching. Anderson reconstructs a specific historical event. Around 95 CE the Johannine community had a negative interaction with Diotrephes, who loves his primacy and does not accept the Johannine community (3 John 9–10). Anderson envisions Diotrephes explicitly claiming Petrine authority. John's church members knew what Diotrephes said (John 20:23 thus evinced close structural parallels with the Matthean logion), but John's church did not necessarily know that Diotrephes was quoting a written gospel. In other words, the Johannine community directly encountered Diotrephes and indirectly encountered Matt. 16:19.³³ Then, in opposition to rising ecclesial institutionalization as personified by Diotrephes, the final edition of John's gospel granted a wider group of disciples egalitarian authority to forgive and retain sins (John 20:23). Since Anderson accepts that binding and loosing is equivalent to forgiving and retaining sins, Matt. 18:18 would serve essentially the same function as John 20:23, namely to authorize a group of disciples—rather than an individual—to forgive sins.

Anderson originally suggested that John's egalitarian formulation

---

(WUNT 78; Tübingen: Mohr Siebeck, 1996; repr. with a new introduction, outlines, and epilogue, Eugene, OR: Cascade, 2010); citations refer to the 2010 edition.
32. Ibid., 235–40, 244.
33. Ibid., xli, 244, 346.

might have influenced Matthew's second "binding and loosing" saying (18:18), which was likewise addressed to the wider group of disciples. However, Anderson has backed away from John's reciprocal influence on Matthew.[34] Anderson now claims that the dialogue between John and Matthew more likely involved secondary orality than direct contact with a written text.[35] The model is still interfluential because John and Matthew remain in dialogue, yet there are no specific examples of Johannine texts or traditions embedded in Matthew's written gospel.[36] More particularly, Anderson presumes that both binding and loosing sayings stood in Matthew from the beginning because Diotrephes might have rejected the elder of 3 John for abrogating the process of Matthew 18 by addressing the entire church (18:17) without first having met one-on-one in private (18:15).[37]

Anderson makes a significant contribution by placing the Matthean and Johannine churches—along with their processes of textualization—in closer proximity. Yet he still focuses too much on Matt. 16:19 to the neglect of Matt. 18:18, and he retains the misperception that binding and loosing is equivalent to retaining and forgiving sins. Anderson proposes secondary orality, and he denies John's direct knowledge of Matthew's written text. I will argue that an even closer acquaintance with Matthew's text can resolve the tensions Anderson highlights in John's gospel.

To conclude this section, I recall the tendency in studies of John

---

34. Paul N. Anderson, *The Fourth Gospel and the Quest for Jesus: Modern Foundations Reconsidered* (T&T Clark Biblical Studies; New York: T&T Clark, 2006), 126. According to Anderson, the written Gospel of Mark (70 CE) influenced the written Gospel of Matthew (90 CE). John's written gospel appeared in two editions: the first edition (80–85 CE) was independent of all Matthean oral and written traditions; the second edition postdated Matthew (100 CE). In the meantime there was continuous oral preaching based on the first edition of John's gospel. In association with this preaching, the Johannine epistles appeared in five-year increments: 1 John (85 CE), 2 John (90 CE), and 3 John (95 CE). The ongoing Johannine preaching (80/85–100 CE) not only influenced but also was influenced by the written Gospel of Matthew (90 CE). If Anderson were to reassert that John 20:23 represents a reaction to Matt. 18:18, then his new model would require modification—perhaps a second edition of Matthew's gospel (after 100 CE).
35. Anderson, *Christology of the Fourth Gospel*, xli; elsewhere Anderson (*Fourth Gospel and the Quest for Jesus*, 187) defines secondary orality as "what was heard about what was written or said about what was heard or written."
36. Anderson, *Christology of the Fourth Gospel*, 119–25.
37. Paul N. Anderson, "'You have the words of eternal life!' Is Peter Presented as *Returning* the Keys of the Kingdom to Jesus in John 6:68?," *Neotestamentica* 41, no. 1 (2007): 6–41, here 26.

and the Synoptics to claim oral tradition by default whenever sayings do not agree verbatim. The relation of Matthew's binding and loosing to John's forgiving and retaining sins provides a refreshing example, insofar as previous studies have attempted to demonstrate semantically how one saying engendered another. Nevertheless, I have concluded that the prevailing arguments for oral tradition rely on inapplicable meanings of key terms and thereby fail to establish that John's saying is an independent variant of Matthew's. The same semantic problem recurs in the argument for secondary orality, which nonetheless succeeds in reconstructing a closer affinity between the texts of Matthew and John. At the same time, an even closer textual relationship can be demonstrated.

## John's Dependence on Matthew

I have reaffirmed the interpretation of Matthew's binding and loosing in terms of rabbinic prohibition and permission. I have also advanced the argument that such an understanding precludes the connotation of forgiveness in Matthew's binding and loosing sayings (16:19; 18:18). My purpose is to correct the widespread misperception that Matthew's binding and loosing essentially expresses the same idea as John's forgiving and retaining sins. This misperception underlies the prevailing attempts to explain the relationships among the Matthean and Johannine logia—whether in terms of independent oral tradition or secondary orality. In what follows, I offer an alternative explanation according to which the saying about forgiving and retaining sins reveals John's knowledge of Matthean redaction, specifically Matthew's redacted chapter 18—not chapter 16. In a single saying (20:23), John effectively rewrote an entire Matthean discourse (chapter 18) to offer a corrective theology of forgiveness.

### Binding and Loosing according to Matt. 16:19 and 18:18

The first of Matthew's two binding and loosing sayings attains almost no explication from the surrounding context. In Matthew 16, the disciples come to Caesarea Philippi, and Jesus asks them about the identity of the Son of Man (16:13). Jesus also asks who the disciples say he is, and Simon Peter answers that Jesus is "the Christ, the Son of the living God" (16:15-16). Jesus then blesses Simon and calls him Peter, the rock upon whom he will build the church (16:17-18). Jesus promises to give Peter "the keys of the kingdom" and the power to bind and loose (16:19). Finally, Jesus orders the disciples not to tell people that he is the Christ (16:20). Neither Jesus nor the narrator explains the meaning or the object of Peter's binding and loosing.

The second binding and loosing saying occurs in Matthew 18, which comprises a carefully arranged unit.[38] In Matt. 18:1-14, Jesus warns the disciples against causing anyone to stumble, and he commends the disciples to seek and save anyone who falls away from the church. The remainder of the chapter concerns sin and forgiveness. When a church members sins, the disciples are to convict each sinner and to expel sinners who disregard the admonishment of the disciples and the church (18:15-17). Jesus then gives the disciples the authority to bind and loose (18:18), and he emphasizes that the disciples must agree on matters of church discipline (18:19-20). Peter asks how many opportunities he should give a sinner to respond in obedience (18:21), and Jesus says to forgive seventy times seven (18:22). The ensuing parable serves as a cautionary tale for disciples who would withhold forgiveness from a penitent sinner (18:23-35).

Chapter 18 provides more context than chapter 16, but the precise meaning of binding and loosing is more implicit than explicit. As indicated earlier in this chapter, Matthew's binding and loosing denote respectively rabbinic prohibition and permission of certain beliefs and actions; the Greek terms are δέω and λύω, cognates of אסר and נתר (Hiphil) in Hebrew as well as אסר and שרי in Aramaic. By extension, persons who persist in prohibited behavior can be expelled and readmitted. The schools of Hillel and Shammai give binding and loosing pronouncements in the Mishnah (for example, m. Yebam. 1:4),

---

38. For a more detailed description of the structure of Matthew 18, see Davies and Allison, *Matthew*, 2:750-51.

and Josephus uses the same terms to describe the Pharisees' authority to expel and readmit people (*B.J.* 1.111).

In Matthew 18, then, Jesus teaches the disciples how to regulate the church (ἐκκλησία). First, one must go and convict a church member—literally a brother—who sins (18:15).[39] If the sinner listens (ἀκούω), in the sense of obeying, then she or he is regained or benefited (κερδαίνω). If the sinner refuses reproof, then the disciplinarian should enlist another disciple or two as confirming witnesses (18:16). If the sinner still shows disregard (παρακούω), then the matter goes before the church; if the sinner refuses to listen to the church, then Jesus says to expel him or her from the church "just like a Gentile and a tax collector" (18:17). Jesus adds, "Truly I say to you: whatever you bind on earth will have been bound in heaven, and whatever you loose on earth will have been loosed in heaven" (Matt. 18:18), and then he reiterates the principle of having two disciples agree (συμφωνέω) in matters of church discipline (18:19-20). Peter then asks, "Lord, how many times will a brother sin against me and I forgive him? Up to seven times?" (18:21b). Jesus says not seven but seventy times seven (18:22), and then he tells a parable about an unforgiving slave (18:23-35).

In the context of Matthew 18, the power to bind and loose indeed relates to the concept of sin, but the terms themselves do not denote withholding and granting forgiveness when someone sins. Instead, binding and loosing mean that the disciples have the authority to determine what counts as sin in the first place.[40] To regulate the church, the disciples individually convict sinners (18:15), but a supposed sinner could resist reproof by claiming that his or her actions are not in fact sinful. In such instances, another disciple must concur that the church member really has committed a sin (18:16), for a conviction only holds if two or three disciples stand in agreement.[41]

---

39. Based on *lectio brevior* and *difficilior*, the qualification of sinning "against you" (εἰς σέ) in Matt. 18:15—included in KJV, NIV, RSV, and NRSV but omitted in NASB and NJB—is a Western interpolation taken from Peter's specification "against me" (εἰς ἐμέ) in 18:21.
40. According to Tertullian, God had given Israel the Torah, but Peter was free to decide how much of Torah would be binding for Gentiles, and God would accept whatever Peter decided (*Pud.* 21; cf. Matt. 16:19; Acts 15).
41. The difference between Matt. 16:19 and Matt. 18:18 is that Jesus initially grants Peter the sole

Conversely, an accused sinner could agree that a given action is wrong but deny having committed the act, in which case a second witness must confirm the misdeed. Recalcitrant sinners are expelled from the church.[42] If a sinner were expelled and later readmitted, this person would not be forgiven a sin or (metaphorically) a debt; reintegrated sinners would have done exactly the opposite, namely to repay their debts or to atone for their sins.[43] Matthew's binding and loosing refers to the process of discerning what counts as sin. The terms binding and loosing do not denote withholding and granting forgiveness.

Matthew's goal in church discipline is the sinner's repentance, whether mediated by an individual, small group of disciples, or the entire church (18:15–17). Matthew considers obedience—depicted as imploring the master's forbearance (18:32)—a prerequisite to forgiveness. In the parable, the first slave falls down and begs for more time to repay the debt. At this point, the master surprisingly grants forgiveness (18:26–27). The forgiven slave then calls his co-slave to account for a debt (18:28). Even though the co-slave likewise falls down and asks for more time, the forgiven slave refuses to offer more time or to grant forgiveness (18:29–30). As punishment, the master revokes his pardon and orders the unforgiving slave to be tortured (18:31–34). Jesus concludes the parable, "And likewise [οὕτως] my heavenly father will do to you [plural] if each of you does not forgive his brother from your hearts" (18:35). Torture imagery would have encouraged Matthew's church to err on the side of caution by forgiving the penitent.

The tortured slave illustrates Matthew's theology of forgiveness, which involves people's authority and obligation to forgive. Regarding the human authority to forgive, all three Synoptics regard Jesus'

---

authority to determine permissible behavior, and only later does Jesus explain the necessity of at least two disciples' concord in such determinations.

42. The connection between prohibiting an action and expelling a person already held in the early church; e.g., Origen applied Matt. 18:18 to a "bound" person ("such a one who is bound;" ὁ τοιοῦτος δεδεμένος; *Comm. Matt.* 13.31.12-17). I agree with Friedrich Büchsel ("δέω [λύω]," *TDNT* 2:60–61) and Joachim Gnilka (*Das Matthäusevangelium* [HTKNT 1; 2 vols.; Freiburg: Herder, 1986], 2:66), pace Davies and Allison (*Matthew*, 2:639), that binding and loosing in Matthew could already be applied to people.

43. Pace Hägerland, *Jesus and the Forgiveness of Sins*, 80.

healing of the paralyzed man (Matt. 9:1–8; Mark 2:1–12; Luke 5:17–26) as proof that the Son of Man has authority to forgive sins (Matt. 9:6; Mark 2:10; Luke 5:24). Yet only in Matthew's redaction does the miracle story extend such authority to other people: upon seeing the formerly paralyzed man walking, "the crowds . . . glorified the God who gives such authority to humans" (Matt. 9:8).[44] Regarding the disciples' obligation to forgive, Jesus elsewhere teaches them to pray, "forgive us our debts, just as we forgive our debtors" (Matt. 6:12). After the prayer concludes, Matthew reads, "For if you [plural] forgive people their transgressions, your heavenly father will also forgive you; but if you do not forgive people, neither will your father forgive your transgressions" (Matt. 6:14–15). Debts are metaphoric for sins,[45] and one whose sins are not forgiven must repay the debt, which the Parable of the Unforgiving Slave depicts as physical torture.[46]

### Forgiving and Retaining Sins according to John 20:23

If binding and loosing do not mean retaining and forgiving sins, then the language in John 20:23 requires another explanation. My solution is quite simply that John knows the context of Matthew 18, particularly the redactional transition from instructions for convicting a sinner (18:15) to the binding and loosing saying (18:18) and then to Peter's question about forgiveness of sins (18:21).[47] My thesis requires jettisoning the notions that in this instance *loosen* (λύω) is synonymous with *forgive* and that John is reacting against Peter's authority as depicted in Matt. 16:19. I argue that John 20:23 amounts to a reinterpretation of the entire redacted chapter of Matthew 18. Whereas Matthew admonishes disciples not to withhold forgiveness

---

44. . . . οἱ ὄχλοι . . . ἐδόξασαν . . . τὸν θεὸν τὸν δόντα ἐξουσίαν τοιαύτην τοῖς ἀνθρώποις (Matt. 9:8); I agree with Luz (*Matthew*, 2:28–29) and Davies and Allison (*Matthew*, 2:96) that Matthew's point in 9:8 is that the authority to forgive sins will pass from Jesus to the church/his followers.
45. See Anderson, *Sin: A History*, 27–39.
46. Ibid., 32–33.
47. Regarding the transition from Matt. 18:18 to v. 21, Dodd (*Historical Tradition in the Fourth Gospel*, 348–49) once raised this very possibility, but he immediately rejected it as "far-fetched" and concluded instead that John had independent access to a special—i.e., variant—form of synoptic oral tradition.

from the penitent, John reminds disciples of their authority and responsibility not to grant blanket forgiveness.

The Johannine saying occurs after Jesus' resurrection when he first appears to a group of disciples. Despite the doors being shut, he stands in their midst and greets them with a word of peace (20:19). Jesus then shows them his hands and his side to identify the marks of his crucifixion, and the disciples rejoiced (20:20). John writes: "So he said to them again, 'Peace to you; as the Father sent me, even I send you.' And having said this, he breathed on them, and he says, 'Receive the Holy Spirit.' If you forgive anyone's sins, (the sins) have been forgiven them; if you retain anyone's [sins], (the sins) have been retained'" (20:21–23). In the forgiveness saying, the (divine) passive voice conveys that God concurs with the disciples' decisions, and the perfect aspect signifies the enduring significance of the disciples' decisions.[48]

John agree with Matthew that humans have the authority to forgive sins. However, John leaves out Matthew's *proviso* that God will only forgive the disciples' sins inasmuch as the disciples forgive other people's sins. In other words, Matthew 18 focuses on what happens to the disciples if they do not forgive, and John 20:23 focuses on what

---

48. The passive verbs in Matt. 16:19; 18:18; John 20:23 are rightly understood as divine passives, but there is a persistent misunderstanding of the meaning of the perfect tense/aspect. Julius Mantey ("The Mistranslation of the Perfect Tense in John 20:23, Mt 16:19, and Mt 18:18," *JBL* 58, no. 3 [1939]: 243–49; idem, "Evidence That the Perfect Tense in John 20:23 and Matthew 16:19 Is Mistranslated," *JETS* 16, no. 3 [1973]: 129–38; idem, "Distorted Translations in John 20:23; Matthew 16:18-19 and 18:18," *RevExp* 78, no. 3 [1981]: 409–16) argued that the perfect tense—generally a past action, the result of which endures to the present—means that God has already decided whom or what to bind, loose, forgive, or retain and that disciples must simply adhere to God's prior declarations. Others (see esp. Henry J. Cadbury, "The Meaning of John 20:23, Matthew 16:19, and Matthew 18:18," *JBL* 58, no. 3 [1939]: 251–54, here 252) have corrected Mantey by pointing out that all three verses constitute conditional sentences and in each one the (future) perfect tense appears in the apodosis; the action described in the apodosis does not precede the action of the protasis. Although in Matt. 16:19; 18:18; John 20:23 a future perfect such as "will have been bound/loosed" constitutes formal equivalence, it is not a mistranslation to use the dynamically equivalent present or future. As Raymond Brown (*Gospel according to John*, 2:1024) observed, scribes in antiquity readily interpreted the perfect in such ways, for variant readings of John 20:23 use ἀφίενται (e.g., B², W, and 𝔐) and ἀφεθήσεται (ℵ). The aspect of the perfect conveys the continuing significance of whatever the disciples would determine, and the passive voice implies divine sanction. Brown accurately paraphrases, "When you forgive men's sins, at that moment God forgives those sins and they remain forgiven" (John 20:23). *Contra* Mantey, the syntax of Matt. 16:19; 18:18; John 20:23 does mean that God is the one who concurs—just as John Chrysostom commented, "whatever the priests work out below, these things God above ratifies; the master confirms the verdict of the slaves" (*Sac.* 3.5).

happens to the sinners whom the disciples do not forgive. Table 3.1 illustrates this contrast.

Table 3.1 Forgiveness of Sins according to Matthew and John

If Peter does not forgive Andrew's sins, then God does not forgive *Peter's* sins. (Matt. 18:21–35).

If Peter does not forgive Andrew's sins, then God does not forgive *Andrew's* sins. (John 20:23).

According to my thesis, John copied the structure of Matthew's binding and loosing saying while knowing that binding and loosing refer to declarations of prohibited and permissible beliefs and actions. John would not merely have encountered a free-floating, orally transmitted saying. John must know Matthew's redactional transition from the binding and loosing saying to the discussion about forgiveness and the consequences of withholding forgiveness. In other words, the wider context of Matthew 18—not the Aramaic term שרי or its Greek cognate λύω—accurately and sufficiently explains how John turned Matthew's binding and loosing into forgiving and retaining sins. John's logion intimates a concern that unrestrained permissiveness toward sinners in the church in effect declares their sins permissible. Read in this light, the operative concern in John 20:23 is not Matthean authoritarianism, as Anderson characterizes Diotrephes. In John's estimation, church authorities were not too strict; church authorities were too lenient. John's primary intent was to correct Matthew by reasserting the church's authority and responsibility to withhold forgiveness in some instances.[49]

John's relocation of the saying to a resurrection appearance likely reveals an additional corrective. Matthew's binding and loosing saying turns out to be embarrassing because Judas Iscariot is included among the disciples who are authorized to determine what counts as sin.[50] John intentionally eliminates this embarrassment by excluding Judas

---

49. For an excellent contemporary study along these lines, see Maria Mayo, *The Limits of Forgiveness: Case Studies in the Distortion of a Biblical Ideal* (Minneapolis: Fortress Press, 2015).
50. A similarly embarrassing Matthean saying places Judas on a throne judging one of the Israelite tribes when the Son of Man comes (Matt. 19:28; cf. Luke 22:30).

from the disciples who receive the authority to forgive sins. Similar to Judas's suicide in Matthew's gospel (27:5), John presupposes that Judas is destroyed and no longer to be counted among the disciples (17:12). Thomas was also absent when Jesus bestowed the Spirit and the authority to forgive (20:24), and his exclusion arguably indicates rivalry between Johannine and Thomasine communities.[51]

In summary, the prevailing consensus has assumed that John's forgiving and retaining sins and Matthew's binding and loosing are independent sayings that mean the same thing. On the contrary, I have shown that the sayings mean different things and yet that John directly depends on Matthew. John emphasizes the disciples' authority and responsibility to withhold forgiveness, even though Matthew seems to caution against doing so. Matthew's and John's respective theologies of forgiveness are nonetheless complementary. The main tension is not between Matt. 18:18 and John 20:23. The main tension stands already in Matthew 18. Prior to the Parable of the Unforgiving Slave (18:23–35), Jesus authorizes the expulsion of recalcitrant sinners (18:15–17). In practice, though, the imagery of torturing unforgiving disciples (18:34–35) could have undermined strict church discipline. As a reinterpretation of Matthew 18, then, John 20:23 would represent an effort to balance Jesus' commands to forgive penitent sinners and to expel unrepentant sinners.

## Matthew's and John's Sayings in the Light of the First Johannine Epistle

Thus far I have demonstrated that existing arguments for oral tradition cannot adequately explain the shift in language from binding and loosing to forgiving and retaining sins. I have shown that the Johannine terminology depends on knowledge of Matthean redaction,

---

51. Regarding possible rival between Johannine and Thomasine communities, see e.g. April D. DeConick, *Voices of the Mystics: Early Christian Discourse in the Gospels of John and Thomas and Other Ancient Christian Literature* (JSNTSup 157; Sheffield: Sheffield Academic Press, 2001), 77–85; cf. Ismo Dunderberg, *The Beloved Disciple in Conflict? Revisiting the Gospels of John and Thomas* (Oxford: Oxford University Press, 2006); Christopher W. Skinner, *John and Thomas—Gospels in Conflict? Johannine Characterization and the Thomas Question* (Princeton Theological Monograph Series 115; Eugene, Oreg.: Pickwick, 2009).

specifically the transition from the binding and loosing authorization (Matt. 18:18) to the question whether to forgive sins or to withhold forgiveness (18:21). In my estimation, this argument stands on its own. In this section, I offer a supporting argument that John intended his gospel to be read alongside—not instead of—Matthew's. Undoubtedly, these Matthean and Johannine sayings were interpreted in light of one another by the early third century (for example, Tertullian *Pud.* 21.9-10 and Hippolytus *Trad. ap.* 3.4). I propose that 1 John provides evidence that Matthew and John were read alongside one another even earlier.

I accept 1 John as coming from the same circle—although not necessarily the same author—that produced the Fourth Gospel.[52] Some scholars consider 1 John as independent of the written Gospel of John,[53] whereas others argue that 1 John preceded the final form of the Fourth Gospel, which added the saying about forgiving and retaining sins.[54] On the contrary, I concur with Raymond Brown regarding the priority of the gospel, for the first epistle "concretized" the gospel's insights.[55]

The Johannine saying about forgiving and retaining sins attains greater clarity in light of 1 John. John 4:2 unequivocally depicts Jesus' disciples performing baptisms, and so there is no reason to doubt the performance of the ritual in the Johannine church. I also accept "water and blood" in 1 John 5:6 as an allusion to baptism.[56] Some scholars object that the references in 1 John would be too obscure; however, possible Johannine references to sacraments are nothing if not obscure—for example, baptism in John 3:3, 5 and Eucharist in John

---

52. For an excellent review of recent scholarship, see R. Alan Culpepper, "The Relationship between the Gospel of John and 1 John," in *Communities in Dispute: Current Scholarship on the Johannine Epistles*, ed. R. Alan Culpepper and Paul N. Anderson (SBLECL 13; Atlanta: SBL Press, 2014), 95-119.
53. E.g., Judith Lieu, *I, II, & III John: A Commentary* (NTL; Louisville: Westminster John Knox, 2008), 18.
54. E.g., Anderson, *Fourth Gospel and the Quest for Jesus*, 126; von Wahlde, *Gospel and Letters of John*, 1:376-85.
55. Raymond Brown, *The Epistles of John* (AB 30; New York: Doubleday, 1982), 35; for a similar view, see Rudolf Bultmann, *The Johannine Epistles*, trans. R. Philip O'Hara with Lane C. McGaughy and Robert W. Funk (Hermeneia; Philadelphia: Fortress Press, 1973), 1.
56. In addition to 1 John 5:6, 1 John 2:20, 27 refer to "anointing oil" (χρῖσμα). Scholars favoring sacramental interpretations of 1 John include Wolfgang Nauck (*Die Tradition und Charakter des ersten Johannesbriefes* [WUNT 3; Tübingen: Mohr Siebeck, 1957], 147-82) and Rudolf Schnackenburg (*The Johannine Epistles: A Commentary*, trans. Reginald and Ilse Fuller [New York: Crossroad, 1992], 236); scholars opposing sacramental interpretations include Brown (*Epistles of John*, 344) and Lieu (*I, II, & III John*, 211).

6:53.⁵⁷ Read alongside the first Johannine epistle, then, John 20:23 most likely pertains to pastors who have performed baptisms and subsequently question whether to forgive certain post-baptismal sins.

Neither the Gospel of Matthew, the Gospel of John, nor 1 John explicitly associates baptism with forgiveness of sins. In the Gospels, Matthew and John align against Mark (1:4) and Luke (3:3) by eliminating the description of John as "preaching a baptism of repentance for the forgiveness of sins."⁵⁸ Matthew has the Baptist object to baptizing Jesus (3:14), and Tom Blanton has argued persuasively that—according to Matthew—Jesus' saving his people from their sins (1:21b) simply means to stop sinning and to obey the commandments of Torah (5:17–20, for example).⁵⁹ John's gospel omits the description of Jesus' baptism altogether, and Jesus' disciples were baptizing immediately after the first of three Passovers (4:2), that is, two years before Jesus authorized the disciples to forgive sins (20:23). Aligning with Matthew and John, the overarching concerns of 1 John are keeping the commandments and not sinning as well as receiving forgiveness whenever sin does occur. The Matthean and Johannine churches thus share an uneasiness with baptism for the forgiveness of sins because baptized Christians struggled to keep the commandments and hence still needed forgiveness when they inevitably sinned.⁶⁰

John 20:23 is the sole reference to forgiveness of sins in the Fourth Gospel,⁶¹ yet the concept appears several times in 1 John (1:7, 9; 2:2, 12; 3:5; 4:10). I argue that John wanted his gospel to be read alongside—not instead of—Matthew, and I claim 1 John as evidence that this happened

---

57. See, e.g., Makayla Marinack, "Searching for Baptism in the Gospel of John," paper presented at the Annual Meeting of the Upper Midwest Region of the SBL, Saint Paul, Minn., 18 April 2015.
58. Matthew 3:6 merely acknowledges that John's baptizands confessed their sins, and—as a gloss of Mark 14:24—Matt. 26:28 clarifies that Jesus' blood, signified in the Eucharist, forgives sins.
59. Thomas R. Blanton IV, "Saved by Obedience: Matthew 1:21 in Light of Jesus' Teaching on the Torah," *JBL* 132, no. 2 (2013): 393–413.
60. The problem of post-baptismal sin predated the gospels (e.g., Rom. 6:1–2) and continued thereafter in the development of the Sacrament of Penance. The Roman Catholic position holds that John 20:23 concerns post-baptismal sins, and according to Raymond Brown (*Gospel according to John*, 2:1044) the Johannine community could be forgiving sins through baptism or penance.
61. In John 1:29, John the Baptist identifies Jesus as "the lamb of God who takes away [αἴρω] the sin of the world."

very early on. Specifically, 1 John 5:16 harmonizes John 20:23 and Matthew 18.

> If someone should see his or her brother [or sister] having sinned a sin not unto death, she or he will ask and give him [or her] life—to those sinning not unto death. There is sin unto death; I do not say that she or he should ask about that. All injustice is sin, and there is sin not unto death. (1 John 5:16–17)

The protases of 1 John 5:16 and Matt. 18:15 closely resemble one another: "if someone should see his brother having sinned" (1 John 5:16) and "if your brother should sin" (Matt. 18:15). The apodosis of 1 John 5:16 resembles John 20:23 by granting the authority to forgive and not to forgive. The epistle affirms that God would grant one person's request for another person's forgiveness, and the epistle introduces the concept of "sin unto death" to clarify which sins not to forgive. I have argued that in some ways John 20:23 intentionally contradicted Matt. 18:18, and I consider it probable that 1 John 5:16 represents an early attempt to reconcile these teachings. Table 3.2 illustrates this thesis, antithesis, and synthesis. Most significantly, since the same circle produced the Gospel of John and the first Johannine epistle, 1 John 5:16 provides evidence that the Gospel of Matthew remained an authoritative text within the circle that produced a subsequent, corrective gospel.

Table 3.2 Conviction and Forgiveness of Sin according to 1 John

Thesis: If one church member sins, then another church member must convict the sin; if the sinner repents, then the one who convicted the sin must grant forgiveness; if one withholds forgiveness, then one's own sins are not forgiven (Matt. 18:15–35).

Antithesis: The Paraclete will come to the disciples to convict the world of sin (John 16:7–8); the disciples receive the Spirit along with the authority to discriminate whose sins to forgive and whose sins not to forgive (John 20:22–23).

Synthesis: If one church member sees another commit a sin not unto death, then the witness should ask for the sinner's forgiveness, which will be granted (1 John 5:16).

Finally, the power to withhold forgiveness immediately raised the question of which sins not to forgive, and 1 John introduced categories of sins unto death and sins not unto death. A century later, Tertullian took the next step. His treatise *De pudicitia* quotes the binding and loosing saying in Matt. 16:19 (*Pud.* 21.9–10) after having alluded to John 20:23 and quoting 1 John 5:16 (*Pud.* 2.13–14). According to Tertullian, getting angry and swearing exemplify sins not unto death (*Pud.* 19.24), while adultery and fornication exemplify sins unto death (*Pud.* 19.28).[62] I do not presume that Tertullian's list coincides precisely with whatever sins the author of 1 John had in mind. I simply posit a plausible snowballing trajectory whereby John reinterprets Matthew; 1 John synthesizes Matthew and John; and Tertullian harmonizes Matthew, John, and 1 John. It is undeniable that Matthew and John were read alongside one another in the early church. I find it most plausible that this was the very intention of the Evangelist John.

## Conclusions

John's forgiving and retaining sins logion (20:23) closely resembles Matthew's binding and loosing logion (16:19; 18:18), but previous scholarship has inaccurately explained the sayings' interrelation. The idea of an original saying about opening and shutting fails to demonstrate that Aramaic פתח (open) could have become Matthew's λύω (loose) and John's ἀφίημι (forgive). Another line of interpretation rightly identifies the Aramaic terms אסר and שרי as cognates of Matthew's δέω and λύω, both pairs meaning *bind* and *loose* respectively. However, the corresponding argument for oral tradition errs by claiming that "bind and loose" independently morphed into "retain and forgive sins," given that שרי and λύω can both mean *forgive*. Since "bind and loose" refer to rabbinic authority to discriminate prohibited from permitted actions, it is inherently contradictory to claim the connotation of forgiveness, because rabbis do not need to forgive

---

62. An edict claiming the right to forgive penitent adulterers and fornicators prompted Tertullian's treatise (*Pud.* 1.6); his full list of specific unforgivable sins is murder, idolatry, fraud, apostasy, blasphemy, adultery, and fornication (*Pud.* 19.25).

someone for doing something deemed permissible. Paul Anderson makes a significant contribution by placing the Matthean and Johannine churches—along with their processes of textualization—in closer proximity. Yet he retains the misperception that binding and loosing is equivalent to begrudging and forgiving sins, and Anderson denies John's direct knowledge of Matthew's written text.

I have advanced a new argument that binding and loosing changed to forgiving and retaining sins because of Matthew's redactional placement of his second binding and loosing saying within the discussion of church discipline in Matthew 18. The disciples' authority to bind and loose pertains particularly to convicting sin, but the discourse transitions to the question of forgiving sinners who repent after having been convicted. According to Matthew, if a church leader refuses to forgive penitent sinners, then God will not forgive the church leader's own sins. Reinterpreting this teaching, John reasserts the right to withhold forgiveness in order to guard against laxity, which could ensue from Matthew's insistence on practically limitless forgiveness. John also shows an uneasiness with baptism guaranteeing forgiveness of sins, and the question of withholding forgiveness likely related particularly to post-baptismal sins. John issued a sharp corrective to Matthew, and yet—in terms of reception history—the tension between Matt. 18:18 and John 20:23 attenuated relatively quickly, due to the harmonizing efforts of texts such as 1 John and Tertullian's *De pudicitia,* both of which inscribed greater specificity regarding the forgiveness of post-baptismal sins.

## 4

## Proof from Prophecy

In all four gospels, Jesus sits on a young animal when he enters Jerusalem at the beginning of passion week (Matt. 21:1-9; Mark 11:1-10; Luke 19:29-38; John 12:12-19). Mark and Luke mention that the animal had never been ridden. Matthew and John do not include that detail, but they do specify that the animal was a donkey and that Jesus was fulfilling the prophecy from Zechariah (9:9) about Israel's king coming on a donkey. Nearly a century ago, B. H. Streeter reached the following conclusion:

> Seeing that Christians were in the habit of ransacking the Old Testament for Messianic prophecies, concurrence in such an obvious instance proves nothing. What is significant is that the words as quoted by John are so different from Matthew that they must either represent a different translation of the Hebrew or be free quotations from memory.[1]

In response to Streeter, I raise three simple questions: How did John know that Jesus rode a donkey? How did John know that Jesus' riding a donkey related to Zechariah's prophecy? And what was John's source

---

1. Burnett Hillman Streeter, *The Four Gospels: A Study in Origins: Treating of the Manuscript Tradition, Sources, Authorship and Dates* (London: Macmillan, 1925), 411.

for Zech. 9:9? I argue that the answer to all three questions is John's knowledge of the redacted gospel of Matthew.

This chapter divides into four parts. First, I discuss the meaning of the word πῶλος, which occurs in Zech. 9:9 and in all four gospels for the animal on which Jesus sits. Contrary to popular opinion, the word does not in itself specify a donkey, and so Mark and Luke may not allude to Zech. 9:9 at all. Since Matthew and John do specify a donkey (ὄνος), these gospels evince a closer connection than is usually acknowledged. Second, I examine the testimony-book hypothesis, which claims that early Christians collected Old Testament proof texts to prove that Jesus was the Messiah. It is widely held that Zech. 9:9 stood in such *testimonia*, and so Matthew and John could have accessed the prophecy independently. However, I review all first- and second-century texts purported to attest *testimonia* and find no evidence for this claim. Third, I follow Edwin Freed in reconstructing John's quotation of Zech. 9:9 out of Matthew's narrative and not from any extant Old Testament text.[2] For John's differences from Matthew, I follow Benedict Viviano in saying that John corrects Matthew by placing Jesus on one donkey instead of two.[3] Finally, John supplements Matthew by explaining that Jesus' disciples could not have understood the prophetic significance of Jesus' entry into Jerusalem until they received the Holy Spirit after Jesus' resurrection.

### Jesus' Entry into Jerusalem: Mark and Luke's *Pōlos*

Mark and Luke record that Jesus rode into Jerusalem on a πῶλος, which most scholars understand as denoting a *donkey*.[4] Most frequently in Greek literature, the word is associated with horses, but in five of its seven LXX instantiations, it stands in for the Hebrew term עִיר, meaning

---

2. Edwin D. Freed, "The Entry into Jerusalem in the Gospel of John," *JBL* 80, no. 4 (1961): 329–38.
3. Benedict T. Viviano, "John's Use of Matthew: Beyond Tweaking," *RB* 111, no. 2 (2004): 209–37, here 230–31.
4. A survey of key lexicons yields the following definitions of πῶλος. BDAG: 1) "young animal, *foal*"; 2) "horse"; *GELS:* "*any young animal*" (the final edition of Muraoka's *GELS* corrected earlier editions' definitions, which were restricted to an ass); LEH: "colt of a horse Jgs 10,4; foal of an ass Gn 32,16;" *LSJ:* a) "*foal*, whether *colt* or *filly*" [vis-à-vis horses]; b) "*any young animal;*" et al.; MM: "'foal,' 'colt' of an ass."

ass.⁵ Based on this handful of attestations, LXX lexicons have occasionally rendered πῶλος inaccurately as *young ass*.⁶ Similarly, studies of Mark and Luke have often assumed that Mark's πῶλος denotes a donkey. This interpretation results from a sequence of publications by Walter Bauer, H. W. Kuhn, and Otto Michel in the 1950s. They adduced evidence that could have correctly established the sense of πῶλος as *young animal* (of any number of species), and yet each scholar claimed a more restrictive meaning.

In what follows, I show that Mark and Luke's πῶλος does not necessarily identify the animal's species, and so Matthew and John's specification that Jesus rode a donkey is a stronger agreement than is usually admitted. Irrespective of the meaning of πῶλος, scholars make several other arguments as to why a donkey is more likely the species Mark and Luke intended—for example, that donkeys were more common than horses. I find no supporting evidence for these claims, and I question whether Mark and Luke even intended to allude to Zech. 9:9. By stripping away unarticulated harmonizations of the four gospels, it becomes apparent that Matthew and John evince close similarities that are not found in Mark and Luke.

### Walter Bauer's Argument: *Pōlos* = Horse

Bauer rightly begins by questioning whether Mark's πῶλος (11:2, 4, 5, 7) had to be an ass, as identified by Matthew and John based on their use of Zech. 9:9. Rather than harmonize the Gospels, Bauer points out that "in fact, (Mark) does not even allude to (Zech. 9:9) in any way that would be understandable to anyone who did not already know Matt(hew) and John."⁷ Bauer intends to show that πῶλος carried

---

5. Gen. 32:16; 49:11; Judg. 10:4; 12:14; Zech. 9:9; see also πῶλος τῆς ὄνου, "young of an ass," for בן אתון "offspring of a she-ass" (Gen. 49:11), and πῶλος for אילה, meaning "doe" (Prov. 5:19).
6. The relation between Semitic terms and their Greek cognates is a major methodological concern in LXX lexicography. LEH (xxi) presumes that the LXX translators intended fidelity to their Semitic *Vorlagen*, and so this lexicon is sometimes defining an underlying Hebrew or Aramaic term rather than the Greek word appearing in the LXX; the lexicographers try not to do so "all too quickly" (LEH, xvi). By contrast, *GELS* works from the perspective of ancient Greek-readers/hearers who did not need to know Hebrew or Aramaic in order to understand the LXX; these lexicographers nonetheless consult Semitic *Vorlagen* when translating the Greek (*GELS*, viii).
7. Walter Bauer, "The 'Colt' of Palm Sunday (Der Palmesel)," *JBL* 72, no. 4 (1953): 220–29, here 220; as

two meanings, either a young animal of no particular species or a horse of no particular age.⁸ For the generic rendering *young animal*, Bauer provides good examples of πῶλος either juxtaposed with, or in close proximity to, the words for elephant, cattle, horse, donkey, gazelle, dog, dove, swallow, and grasshopper.⁹ These zoological terms designate the species of the young animal, and without such designation Bauer admits that the species would be indeterminable.¹⁰ For example, Bauer cites P.Oxy. 1222.1, a fourth-century private letter in which a man requests that his son send a πῶλος; the son most likely knew the intended animal, but Bauer says that "we must remain ignorant of what is meant."¹¹

Bauer further argues that "πῶλος is also used without any more specific zoological designation" and that such instances refer to a horse, not particularly a young one.¹² Bauer typically selects references to πῶλοι (for which I would prefer the generic rendering *young animals*) that occur in proximity to ἵπποι (horses). As examples, I discuss here his references to the term πωλευτής and to Pausanias's *Description of Greece*, and I submit a reference from Philo that Bauer does not discuss. A full semantic analysis of the lexeme πῶλος lies beyond the scope of this section,¹³ and my purpose is simply to caution against making strong claims for the species of an undesignated πῶλος. Bauer is correct that the term is most commonly associated with horses, but in my estimation his examples do not prove that the term itself means *horse*.

Bauer claims that πωλευτής (adding -της to πωλεύω) necessarily has "something to do with the horse."¹⁴ Indeed this is usually the case (for example, Xenophon *Eq. mag.* 2.1), but I point out that the term elsewhere refers to someone who trains elephants (Aelian *Nat. an.*

---

supporting evidence, Bauer (p. 220) mentions that Luke uses ὄνος elsewhere (13:15; 14:5 v.l.) and yet repeats Mark's fourfold πῶλος in this pericope; see also BDAG, 900.
8. Bauer, "'Colt' of Palm Sunday," 221.
9. Ibid., 220–21.
10. Ibid., 222–23.
11. Ibid., 222.
12. Ibid..
13. Regarding the Hebrew terms, see Kenneth C. Way, "Donkey Domain: Zechariah 9:9 and Lexical Semantics," *JBL* 129, no. 1 (2010): 105–14.
14. Bauer, "'Colt' of Palm Sunday," 225.

8.17.20). Just as πῶλος can refer to multiple species, πωλευτής could refer to someone working with a species other than a horse. Without describing the scene, Bauer cites Pausanias's *Descr.* 5.8.10 as an instance wherein "πῶλος used alone means *horse*."[15] *Description of Greece* 5.8 gives an overview of innovations to the Olympian Games. The twenty-fifth Olympiad included "a (chariot) race of full-grown horses" (ἵππων τελείων δρόμον; 5.8.7). Eight festivals later came the "riding-horse" race (κέλης; 5.8.8). The ninety-third games initiated a race where "a pair of full-grown horses" (δύο ἵππων τελείων; 5.8.10) pulled each chariot. The ninety-ninth games introduced "chariots (pulled by) colts" (πώλων ἅρμασιν; 5.8.10), with a single horse pulling each chariot. Later still came the chariot race for a "pair of colts" (συνωρίδα πώλων) and the "riding-colt" race (πώλων κέλητα; 5.8.11). I maintain that the πῶλοι in these passages can only be understood as horses because ἵπποι stands in close proximity.

Pausanias's immediately ensuing section mentions races for "wagon-carts" (ἀπήνη) pulled by "a pair of mules as opposed to horses" (συνωρίδα ἡμιόνους ἀντὶ ἵππων; 5.9.1–2), which ran from the seventieth to the eighty-fourth games. The mule-cart races were short-lived and, according to Pausanias, not a pretty sight. Had there been innovations to the mule races, though, one would expect subdivisions for colts and full-grown mules just as there were for horses. In Pausanias's references, then, πῶλος only stands in apposition with horses, but such apposition does not entail that πῶλος means *horse* exclusively. Furthermore, Pausanias contrasts πῶλος with τέλειος, thereby showing clearly that πῶλος denotes neither a foal, which would be too young to be ridden or to pull a chariot, nor a fully matured animal. This observation refutes Bauer's insistence that πῶλος does not denote youth.[16]

---

15. Ibid., 224.
16. Ibid.; Pausanias similarly describes the Pythian games at Delphi: the first "horse race" (ἵππων δρόμος) involved "chariots" (ἅρμη; 10.7.6); later "they yoked colts to a chariot" (πώλους ἔλευξαν ὑπὸ ἅρματι; 10.7.7), with one horse per chariot; later still came the chariot race of "a pair of colts" (συνωρίς πωλικός) and the "riding colt" (πῶλος κέλης; 10.7.8).

In a passage that escapes Bauer's notice, Philo once uses the word πῶλος:

> Some prefer mules [ὀρεύς] over all other beasts of burden, since their bodies are sturdy and very muscular. And where horses are kept and in horse stables they raise huge donkeys [ὄνος], which they refer to as stallions, so that they will cover the fillies [θηλείαις . . . πώλοις]; and they foal a hybrid animal, a mule [ἡμίονος; literally a half-ass]. Knowing their genesis to be contrary to nature, Moses strongly forbade [the practice] in a more general commandment not to breed between unlike species. (*Spec. Laws* 3.47)

Literally Philo refers simply to "female young animals" (ταῖς θηλείαις πώλοις). The term indeed designates a horse in this instance, but the species is known only because this particular πῶλος produces a mule when covered by an ass.

In summary, I agree with Bauer that tacit harmonization of Matthew and John leads to the supposition that Mark and Luke's πῶλος designates a donkey. Accordingly, Bauer rightly takes issue with Liddell-Scott for designating the πῶλος in Mark 11:2 as referring to the young of an ass.[17] However, Bauer overstates his case in concluding, "The word πῶλος in Mark and Luke can be understood only as *horse*, and it was nothing else either for these evangelists or for their readers."[18] I prefer to read the πῶλος in Mark 11:2, 4, 5, 7 and Luke 19:30, 33, 35 more like the πῶλος in P.Oxy. 1222.1 and thus to leave open the possibility of a species other than a horse. Bauer's article hardly went unnoticed, but the respondents did not offer accurate correctives.

## H. W. Kuhn's Counterargument:
### To Non-Greeks, *Pōlos* = Young Ass

H. W. Kuhn begins by reviewing the seven occurrences of πῶλος in the Septuagint. He admits that in Gen. 49:11aβ πῶλος simply means *young animal* (Tierjunges),[19] and he marvels that יַעְלָה—which Koehler

---

17. Bauer, "'Colt' of Palm Sunday," 225.
18. Ibid., 229.
19. Heinz W. Kuhn, "Das Reittier Jesu in der Einzugsgeschichte des Markusevangeliums," *ZNW* 50, no. 1 (1959): 82–91, here 83.

rendered as "female ibex" (Steinbockweibchen)—is translated simply as πῶλος in Prov. 5:19.[20] In the five remaining instances (Gen. 32:16; 49:11aα; Judg. 10:4; 12:14; Zech. 9:9), Kuhn says that πῶλος stands alone as "the translation of the Hebrew word 'male ass.'"[21] He avers that the word is not restricted to this meaning, and he agrees with Bauer's conclusion that πῶλος was at times a last resort (Verlegenheitsübersetzung),[22] given translators' occasional uncertainty regarding עִיר/עַיִר.[23]

Referring to a gloss in Jerome's commentary on Isaiah, Kuhn supposes that Matthew and John's usage influenced an understanding of πῶλος as *young of an ass* among people who did not regularly speak Greek.[24] Kuhn claims second-century evidence based on Justin Martyr's comment that "it is possible for the name πῶλος to signify the young [πῶλος] both of an ass and of a horse" (*1 Apol.* 54.7).[25] Kuhn says that Justin could not have meant "that the bare πῶλος could mean the young of a horse as well as that of an ass" because in *1 Apol.* 32.6 Justin used πῶλος by itself to signify a young ass. The problem with Kuhn's argument is that in *1 Apol.* 32.1–5 Justin is discussing Gen. 49:11, and he explicitly designates the young animal as an ass. In other words, this is not an example of a "bare πῶλος." *Contra* Kuhn, the statement in *1 Apol.* 54.7 presents clear evidence that for Justin the term πῶλος did not *ipso facto* denote a species. Thus Kuhn errs in delineating a non-Christian usage of πῶλος as "(young) horse" and a Christian meaning of πῶλος as "foal of an ass."[26]

### Otto Michel's Response: In Egypt, *Pōlos* = Ass

Otto Michel responded to Bauer and Kuhn. Arguing that in Egyptian and Palestinian usage πῶλος simply means *ass*, Michel points out that עַיִר was translated πῶλος in Judg. 10:4 and 12:14. Michel says that both

---

20. Ibid., 83.
21. Ibid.
22. Bauer, "'Colt' of Palm Sunday," 227.
23. Ibid., 228–29; Kuhn, "Reittier Jesu," 84. In Isa. 30:24, e.g., עִיר/עַיִר is rendered βοῦς, meaning "cow."
24. Kuhn, "Reittier Jesu," 84–85.
25. καὶ τὸ τοῦ πώλου ὄνομα καὶ ὄνου πῶλον καὶ ἵππου σημαίνειν ἐδύνατο (*1 Apol.* 54.7).
26. Kuhn, "Reittier Jesu," 91.

references have in mind a "young, strong ass" as opposed to a "foal of an ass."[27] The most problematic lexicographical issue is that Michel presupposes one-to-one correspondence between עַיִר (also עִילָא) and πῶλος based on translation patterns in the LXX.[28]

One piece of Michel's evidence does show the considerable overlap between עַיִר and πῶλος, and yet that evidence actually contradicts Michel's argument that עִילָא means "young strong ass." Michel cites b. Šabb. 155a–b, which contains two references to עילי זוטרי. Contra Michel, I would translate the phrase as "young small animals," not "young strong ass."[29] The Mishnah states, "They crush neither young grain nor carob pods in front of livestock, whether small or large" (m. Šabb. 24:2); that is, making fodder is prohibited on the Sabbath. The Bavli questions whether soft (fresh) or hard (dried) grain or carobs are meant, and Rabbi Huna is supposed to have in mind hard grain for use with young small animals (עילי זוטרי). The next line elaborates, "Rabbi Judah permits [crushing] with regard to carobs with small [livestock]" (m. Šabb. 24:2). The antecedent of "small" (דקה) is "livestock" (בהמה), and the ensuing sections (24:3–4) discuss the permissibility of certain types of feeding for various creatures—for example, a camel, young cow, chicken, beehive, dove, goose, and dog. Neither the Mishnaic nor the Talmudic passage has specifically equine animals in view. In this case, Michel's argument is contradictory: if he is correct that עַיִר and πῶλος convey the same basic meaning (as I think he is), then he is incorrect in defining עַיִר as *young, strong ass*.

Also refuting Michel's claim for a specific Egyptian usage of πῶλος as *ass* is Philo of Alexandria, who—as mentioned above—used a

---

27. Otto Michel, "Eine philologische Frage zur Einzugsgeschichte," *NTS* 6, no. 1 (1959): 81–82; see also idem, "πῶλος," *TDNT* 6:959–61.
28. The relation of עיל/עיר is hardly unexpected given the "mutation" of ר < ל from Hebrew to Aramaic; see M. H. Segal, *A Grammar of Mishnaic Hebrew* (Oxford: Clarendon, 1927; repr., Eugene, OR: Wipf & Stock, 2001), 34 (ch. 54).
29. The term זוטר can mean "small" or "young," and עיל here simply refers to a young animal; Jastrow renders עיל (p. 1069) and עיר (p. 1075) as "foal." If זוטר is understood as "young," then the construction would be redundant or perhaps emphatic: "very young animals;" cf. "very young foals" (Jastrow, 1069). The context favors reading זוטר as "small," corresponding to דק in the Mishnah tractate—young small animals (e.g., sheep and goats) as opposed to young large animals (e.g., cows and horses).

standalone πῶλος to refer to a horse (*Spec. Laws* 3.47). While Philo's literary Greek would unlikely reveal Egyptian regionalisms, Michel's only evidence for understanding πῶλος as *ass* in Egypt is the LXX. In summary, in Bauer's favor, the earliest usage of πῶλος (prior to Aristotle) pertained exclusively to horses, and even thereafter the word's most common referent was a horse. I fully agree with Bauer that apart from harmonization with Matthew and John, Mark and Luke's πῶλος would hardly signify a donkey. For early Christian understandings of the term, though, I place more weight on Justin's description in *1 Apol.* 54.7, whereby πῶλος refers to both horses and asses. Accordingly, I stop short of Bauer's insistence that Mark and Luke's readers would necessarily have envisioned a horse. At the same time, Michel and Kuhn are also incorrect to insist that Mark and Luke necessarily intended a donkey. I conclude that Mark and Luke actually leave the species undesignated, and so should their readers.

### A Mistaken Consensus Regarding Mark's *Pōlos*

In spite of the semantically unstable basis for considering an unqualified πῶλος an ass, the vast majority of Markan commentators—often citing Kuhn and/or Michel as authoritative—assume this meaning.[30] Some even say that Jesus specifically fetched a donkey rather than a horse, and there are frequent claims that πῶλος meant *ass* in Palestine.[31] The notion is that Jesus rode a donkey because that species was more common than the horse.[32] J. Duncan Derrett even claims, "The ordinary villager would

---

30. E.g., Adela Yarbro Collins, *Mark: A Commentary* (Hermeneia; Minneapolis: Fortress Press, 2007), 517; R. T. France, *The Gospel of Mark* (NIGTC; Grand Rapids: Eerdmans, 2002), 431; Joel Marcus, *Mark* (2 vols.; AB 27–27A; New York: Doubleday; New Haven: Yale University Press, 2000–09), 2:772, 778; Francis J. Moloney, *The Gospel of Mark: A Commentary* (Peabody, Mass.: Hendrickson, 2002), 217 n. 8; see also David R. Catchpole, "The 'triumphal' entry," in *Jesus and the Politics of His Day*, ed. Ernst Bammel and C. F. D. Moule (Cambridge: Cambridge University Press, 1984), 319–34, here 323; Brent Kinman, *Jesus' Entry into Jerusalem: In the Context of Lukan Theology and the Politics of His Day* (AGJU 28; Leiden: Brill, 1995), 92 n. 3; Claus-Peter März, "*Siehe, dein König kommt zu dir . . .*": *eine traditionsgeschichtliche Untersuchung zur Einzugsperikope* (FTS 43; Leipzig: St. Benno, 1980), 36; Jacques Nieuviarts, *L'Entrée de Jésus à Jérusalem (Mt 21,1-17)* (LD 176; Paris: Cerf, 1999), 68.
31. E.g., P. M.-J. Lagrange, *Évangile selon Saint Marc* (EBib; Paris: J. Gabalda, 1947), 288; Robert Gundry, *Mark: A Commentary on His Apology for the Cross* (Grand Rapids: Eerdmans, 1993), 626; France, *Gospel of Mark*, 431; Ulrich Luz, *Matthew: A Commentary*, trans. James E. Crouch (3 vols.; Hermeneia; Minneapolis: Fortress Press, 2001–7), 3:7n30.

not know how to look after (horses)."[33] Unfortunately no one provides supporting evidence for such claims.

The literary and material evidence show that assertions concerning horses' scarcity are overstated. Regarding literary sources, the Mishnah incontrovertibly shows the use of horses, asses, and mules in Palestinian agriculture (m. Kil. 8:4–5).[34] Since Josephus is often preoccupied with military details, he unsurprisingly mentions horses far more than asses, mules, or camels.[35] His attestations by no means imply that horses existed in greater abundance in first-century Palestine (in all likelihood they did not), but Josephus's abundant references should at least guard against claiming the rarity of horses.

Regarding archaeozoology, it is difficult to distinguish among horses, asses, their hybrids, and onagers, but all were present in first-century Palestine. Hesban, in modern-day Jordan, yields the most evidence for equids.[36] Stratum 14 dates to 63 BCE–130 CE, when Hesban was a small village.[37] There were ten finds of equids at this stage, three of which were identified as asses; by comparison there were seven finds of camels.[38] Horses and mules were identified in the preceding stratum.[39] For the Hellenistic/Roman periods, the ratio of equids to camels was almost exactly 2:1;[40] however, the 2:1 ratio misleadingly includes an influx of equids as Hesban was rapidly growing into a temple town in the period after the bar Kokhba revolt.[41] More

---

32. See, e.g., Collins, *Mark*, 517; Gundry, *Mark*, 629; Marcus, *Mark*, 2:772; Moloney, *Gospel of Mark*, 217n8.
33. J. Duncan M. Derrett, "Law in the New Testament: The Palm Sunday Colt," *NovT* 13, no. 4 (1971): 241–58, here 248.
34. By my count, there are six occurrences of horses (סוס), seven of asses (חמור), and two of mules (פרד) in m. Kil'ayim.
35. According to the *TLG* database for Josephus's writings, there are approximately eighty passages involving horses (ἵππος; excluding eight references to the city Hippos), twenty-three of asses (ὄνος), thirteen of mules (ἡμίονος [8x]; ὀρεύς [5x]), and fifteen of camels (κάμηλος); the passages involving horses would increases dramatically if including common chariotry and other horsemanship terminology.
36. I extend special thanks to Guy Bar-Oz and Ram Bouchnik for sharing preliminary data from the Archaeozoological Digitized Database of Israel, a project of the Laboratory of Archaeozoology at Haifa University's Zinman Institute of Archaeology.
37. Øystein Sakala LaBianca et al., *Faunal Remains: Taphonomical and Zooarchaeological Studies of the Animal Remains from Tell Hesban and Vicinity* (Hesban 13; Berrien Springs, Mich.: Andrews University Press, 1995), 70, Table 5.6.
38. Ibid., 72, Table 5.9.
39. Ibid., 84, Table 5.20.
40. Ibid., 72, Table 5.10.

accurately, then, Strata 15–14 (198 BCE–130 CE) reveal a camels to equids ratio of 3:2.⁴² Granting for the sake of argument that Jesus would have ridden the more common animal, he actually would have ridden a camel rather than a horse, ass, or mule. The term πῶλος could refer to the young of any of these species, and all of these species were present in first-century Palestinian villages.

Another way of getting Jesus on a donkey—according to Mark and Luke—is to claim that travelers could procure one at a donkey pool.⁴³ However, there is no evidence for such pools. Michael Rostowzew discussed the state-run donkey-driver position (δημοσία ὀνηλασία; BGU 1.15) and inferred that there might have been guilds of ass-drivers in Egypt.⁴⁴ Citing Rostowzew, Derrett then assumed not only that there were such guilds in first-century Palestine but also that the Palestinian guilds formed in reaction to Roman requisition so that no one's business suffered too much when compelled to state service such as hauling grain.⁴⁵ To the contrary, in Palestine even one's rented ass could be requisitioned (m. B. Meṣiʿa 6:3; אנגריא; cf. ἀγγαρεία), and so Derrett's assumed situation is unfounded and unlikely.

Even if πῶλος be defined generically as *young animal*, the catchword still appears in Zech. 9:9, and many interpreters claim that Mark intended this allusion. David Nineham begins his exposition of Jesus' entry into Jerusalem by saying, "In studying this story it is particularly important to do two things which the original readers will have done automatically; to have in mind certain Old Testament and later Jewish expectations, and *not* to have at the back of one's mind impressions derived from the accounts of the incident in the other Gospels."⁴⁶ He adds, though, that the original readers would have assumed Zech. 9:9.⁴⁷

---

41. Ibid., 70, Table 5.6; following the bar Kokhba revolt, finds of pig bones increase dramatically: forty-three in Stratum 14 (63 BCE–130 CE) as compared with 183 in Strata 11–13 (130–365 CE), which includes nearly a century of inoccupation due to an earthquake (Stratum 12: 193–284 CE).
42. Ibid., 72, Table 5.9.
43. Derrett, "Law in the New Testament," 244; Darrell Bock, *Luke* (2 vols.; BECNT; Grand Rapids: Baker, 1994–96), 2:1553; Gundry, *Matthew*, 407; idem, *Mark*, 627–28.
44. M. Rostowzew, "Angariae," *Klio* 6 (1906): 249–58, here 253; see Derrett, "Law in the New Testament: The Palm Sunday Colt," 243.
45. Derrett, "Law in the New Testament," 244.
46. D. E. Nineham, *Saint Mark* (Pelican; London: SCM, 1963), 291–93; Eduard Schweizer, *The Good News according to Mark*, trans. Donald H. Madvig (Atlanta: John Knox, 1970), 291.

I see that as a contradiction, for it is only by harmonizing with Matthew or John that one most easily reads Zech. 9:9 into Mark's narrative. Nonetheless the allusion to Zech. 9:9 is widely claimed among Markan commentators;[48] the same goes for Lukan commentators,[49] and Matthean commentators often state that Matthew simply makes Mark's scriptural allusion explicit.[50] Mark's young animal had never been ridden before, but this element is by no means implied in Zech. 9:9.[51]

Some scholars suggest that Matthew's foal is the same thing Mark had in mind with a young animal that had never been ridden.[52] Yet this suggestion reveals a lack of understanding about raising livestock. It is true that Matthew's πῶλος would never have been ridden, but this is because the animal would have been too young. Matthew's narrative necessarily depicts a foal—not just a colt—because the animal is still tethered to its mother; tethering most likely implies that the foal is still unweaned and thus younger than six months old. Such animals have grown nowhere near the physical maturity required to bear a load, which usually comes at two years of age. This remains true in

---

47. Nineham, *Saint Mark*, 291.
48. E.g., M. Eugene Boring, *Mark: A Commentary* (NTL; Louisville: Westminster John Knox, 2006), 314; John R. Donahue and Daniel J. Harrington, *The Gospel of Mark* (SP 2; Collegeville, MN: Liturgical Press, 2002), 321–22; France, *Gospel of Mark*, 429; Richard B. Hays, *Reading Backwards: Figural Christology and the Fourfold Gospel Witness* (Waco: Baylor University Press, 2014), 17–18; Marcus, *Mark*, 2:778; Nieuviarts, *L'Entrée de Jésus à Jérusalem*, 68; Nineham, *Saint Mark*, 291–92.
49. E.g., Bock, *Luke*, 2:1546; R. Alan Culpepper, *Luke* (NIB 9; Nashville: Abingdon, 1994), 367; Joel Green, *The Gospel of Luke* (NICNT; Grand Rapids: Eerdmans, 1997), 682–85.
50. E.g., W. D. Davies and Dale C. Allison, *A Critical and Exegetical Commentary on the Gospel according to Saint Matthew* (3 vols.; ICC; Edinburgh: T&T Clark, 1988–97), 3:118; Daniel J. Harrington, *The Gospel of Matthew* (SP 1; Collegeville, Minn.: Liturgical Press, 1991), 294; John Nolland, *The Gospel of Matthew* (NIGTC; Grand Rapids: Eerdmans, 2005), 835n62; Rudolf Schnackenburg, *The Gospel of Matthew*, trans. Robert R. Barr (Grand Rapids: Eerdmans, 2002), 200.
51. Pace J. Blenkinsopp, "The Oracle of Judah and the Messianic Entry," *JBL* 80, no. 1 (1961): 55–64, here 55; Craig A. Evans, "Zechariah in the Markan Passion Narrative," in *Biblical Interpretation in Early Christian Gospels, Vol. 1*, ed. Thomas Hatina (LNTS 304; London: T&T Clark, 2006), 64–80, here 70; France, *Gospel of Mark*, 431; März, "Siehe, dein König kommt zu dir," 36; Nineham, *Saint Mark*, 295; George M. Soares-Prabhu, *The Formula Quotations in the Infancy Narrative of Matthew: An Enquiry into the Tradition History of MT 1-2* (AnBib 63; Rome: Biblical Institute Press, 1976), 141; W.J.C. Weren, "Jesus' Entry into Jerusalem," in *The Scriptures in the Gospels*, ed. C. M. Tuckett (BETL 131; Leuven: Leuven University Press, 1997), 117–41, here 119–20.
52. E.g., Donald A. Hagner, *Matthew* (2 vols.; WBC 33A-33B; Dallas: Word Books, 1993–1995), 2:594–95; Craig S. Keener, *A Commentary on the Gospel of Matthew* (Grand Rapids: Eerdmans, 1999), 491; Barnabas Lindars, *New Testament Apologetic: The Doctrinal Significance of the Old Testament Quotations* (London: SCM, 1961), 114; Charlene McAfee Moss, *The Zechariah Tradition and the Gospel of Matthew* (BZNW 156; Berlin: Walter de Gruyter, 2008), 87.

the present day, and it was well known in antiquity; for example, m. B. Meṣiʿa 5:4 specifically refers to raising the foal (סייח) of an ass (חמור) until it can bear a load (שתהא טוענת).[53] In common parlance, Mark's animal would be called a "colt" (or "filly" had it been female), but it would definitely not be called a "foal."

Even though the English term *foal* is derived etymologically from πῶλος, I reiterate that an actual foal would lack the physical maturity to be ridden or to carry or pull a load.[54] I readily admit that Matthew derived his young animal from Mark's young animal that had never before been ridden, but it is essential to understand that Matthew has recast Mark's narrative by envisioning a much younger animal. According to Mark, Jesus wants to ride the animal, and so the disciples would have understood that he wanted an animal at least capable of being ridden. By specifying that the animal had never been ridden, Mark actually depicts a nature miracle, whereby Jesus tames the unbroken animal.[55] Luke follows Mark in describing an unridden colt, but Luke seems to shift the miraculous aspect to Jesus' foreknowledge, since Luke emphasizes that the disciples "found [the young animal] just as (Jesus) said to them" (19:32).

Matthew leaves out entirely Mark's description of Jesus' miraculous taming of the young animal. Instead, Matthew introduces Jesus' fulfillment of Zech. 9:9. I agree with those scholars who doubt that Mark has Zech. 9:9 in mind.[56] And even if Mark does echo the Old Testament, the options are hardly limited to Zechariah's text. Since πῶλος is not restricted to donkeys, Mark's text could just as easily—if not more easily—evoke David's mule upon which Solomon rode at his

---

53. Regarding πῶλος, Bauer ("'Colt' of Palm Sunday," 222) refers to "an animal something like the one referred to in the language of horse-racing as having passed its 'two-year test.'"
54. E.g., three-year-olds in the Kentucky Derby are colts and fillies—not foals; three-year-old horses are full-grown, in a sense, but they will continue to develop physically for approximately three more years.
55. A rough parallel to Mark and Luke's never before ridden animal could be Plutarch's story of Alexander the Great mounting and breaking the very expensive and spirited horse Bucephalus, whom Alexander had observed to be afraid of his own shadow (*Alex.* 6).
56. Evans, "Zechariah in the Markan Passion Narrative," 70 (Evans does, however, think that Jesus intended a fulfillment of Zech. 9:9); Keener, *Matthew*, 493; Luz, *Matthew*, 3:5n11; Moloney, *Gospel of Mark*, 220n21; Kelli S. O'Brien, *The Use of Scripture in the Markan Passion Narrative* (LNTS 384; New York: T&T Clark, 2010), 123n29.

accession (1 Kgs. 1:33, 38, 44). Jesus reenacting Solomon's coronation would fit especially well with Mark's crowd saying, "blessed is the coming kingdom of our father David" (11:10).[57] I conclude that the identification of Jesus' mount as a donkey constitutes a minor agreement between Matthew and John against Mark and Luke, an agreement that would not have arisen necessarily from the traditional element that Jesus rode a πῶλος into Jerusalem.

## Did Matthew and John Independently Find Zech. 9:9 in a *Testimonium*?

A number of scholars have concluded that Zech. 9:9 constituted a mainstay within hypothetical early Christian *testimonia*, collections of Old Testament proof texts showing Jesus to be the Messiah and Son of God.[58] If this conclusion stands, then John need not have depended on Matthew for the Zechariah prophecy. In addition to Matthew and John, Justin Martyr and Irenaeus cite the donkey prophecy, and these citations serve as crucial evidence for an early *testimonium* containing Zech. 9:9.[59] In this section, I show that Justin utilized Matthew and John as well as the LXX and its earliest recension; I also show that Irenaeus drew directly on Matthew and John. By isolating these actual sources, I dispel the need for hypothetical ones. The consequence of my study is that there is no evidence for the inclusion of Zech. 9:9 in *testimonia* up through the second century. *Testimonia* should therefore not be admitted as possible sources for Matthew's and John's quotations of Zech. 9:9.

Table 4.1 shows the transmission of Zech. 9:9 down to the early

---

57. Marcus (*Mark*, 2:779) and Nolland (*Luke*, 3:928) claim such an echo, but they misidentify Solomon's mount as a donkey rather than a mule; cf. Gundry's (*Mark*, 626) claim that Jesus rode a donkey in contrast to Solomon's mule. Regarding the influence of 1 Kgs. 1:32–40 on Jesus' temple procession, see Anthony Le Donne, *The Historiographical Jesus: Memory, Typology, and the Son of David* (Waco: Baylor University Press, 2009), 201–2.
58. For a Forschungsbericht of the testimony-book hypothesis, see Martin Albl, "*And Scripture Cannot Be Broken*": *The Form and Function of the Early Christian* Testimonia *Collections* (NovTSup 96; Boston: Brill: 1999), 7–69.
59. E.g., Albl, "*And Scripture Cannot Be Broken*," 101–6; Craig D. Allert, *Revelation, Truth, Canon and Interpretation: Studies in Justin Martyr's* Dialogue with Trypho (Supplements to Vigiliae Christianae 64; Boston: Brill, 2002), 160–61; Helmut Koester, *Ancient Christian Gospels: Their History and Development* (Philadelphia: Trinity Press International; London: SCM, 1990), 378, 396.

third century when Origen preserved the witnesses to LXX recensions by Aquila, Symmachus, Theodotion, and the *quinta* (*Comm. Matt.* 16.16.180–193).[60] I have retroverted Irenaeus's quotation from Armenian into Greek.[61] I also include a line each from Isaiah and Zephaniah: Irenaeus and Justin respectively attribute Zech. 9:9 to Isaiah and Zephaniah, which is somewhat understandable given the parallels of Isa. 62:11//Matt. 21:5 and Zeph. 3:14//Zech. 9:9 in the LXX; also, the misattribution to prophets is part of the criteria for detecting a *testimonium* source text.

Table 4.1 Transmission of Zech. 9:9

| | |
|---|---|
| Cf. Zeph. 3:14a LXX | χαῖρε σφόδρα θύγατερ Σιων• κήρυσσε θύγατερ Ιερουσαλημ |
| Cf. Zeph. 3:14a MT | רני בת־ציון הריעו ישראל |
| Zech. 9:9aα MT | גילי מאד בת־ציון הריעי בת ירושלם |
| Zech. 9:9aα LXX | χαῖρε σφόδρα θύγατερ Σιων• κήρυσσε θύγατερ Ιερουσαλημ |
| Justin *Dial.* 53.3b | χαῖρε σφόδρα θύγατερ Σιων• ἀλάλαξον κήρυσσε θύγατερ Ιερουσαλημ |
| Justin *1 Apol.* 35.11b | χαῖρε σφόδρα θύγατερ Σιων• κήρυσσε θύγατερ Ιερουσαλημ |
| John 12:15a | μὴ φοβοῦ θυγάτηρ Σιών |
| Matt. 21:5a | εἴπατε τῇ θυγατρὶ Σιών |
| Irenaeus *Epid.* 65 | εἴπατε τῇ θυγατρὶ Σιών |
| Cf. Isa. 62:11αβ LXX | εἴπατε τῇ θυγατρὶ Σιών |
| Cf. Isa. 62:11αβ MT | אמרו לבת־ציון |

---

60. Erich Klostermann, ed., *Origenes Werke, vol. 10: Matthäuserklärung, vol. 1* (GCS 40; Leipzig: J.C. Hinrichs, 1935). The *quinta* is the "fifth" Greek version (besides the LXX, Aquila, Symmachus, and Theodotion) occasionally preserved in Origen's Hexapla; for Zech. 9:9, the *quinta* is identical to the *kaige* recension of the LXX.

61. *asacʿēkʿ dstern Siovni • aha tʿagawor gay kʿez hez ew nsteal ï veray išoy yawanaki ordwoy išoy* (*Epid.* 65). For the Armenian text, see Karapet Ter Mekerttschian and S. G. Wilson, eds., "The Proof of the Apostolic Preaching," in PO 12 (Paris, 1919), 653–731.

| | |
|---|---|
| Cf. Isa. 62:11aγ LXX | ἰδού σοι ὁ σωτὴρ παραγίνεται |
| Cf. Isa. 62:11aγ MT | הנה ישעך בא |
| Zech. 9:9aβ MT | הנה מלכך יבוא לך צדיק ונושע הוא |
| Zech. 9:9aβ LXX | ἰδοὺ ὁ βασιλεύς σου ἔρχεταί σοι δίκαιος καὶ σῴζων αὐτός |
| Justin *Dial.* 53.3c | ἰδοὺ ὁ βασιλεύς σου ἥξει σοι δίκαιος καὶ σῴζων αὐτός |
| Justin *1 Apol.* 35.11c | ἰδοὺ ὁ βασιλεύς σου ἔρχεταί σοι |
| John 12:15b | ἰδοὺ ὁ βασιλεύς σου ἔρχεταί |
| Matt. 21:5b | ἰδοὺ ὁ βασιλεύς σου ἔρχεταί σοι |
| Irenaeus *Epid.* 65 | ἰδοὺ ὁ βασιλεὺς ἔρχεταί σοι |
| | |
| Zech. 9:9b MT | עני ורכב על־חמור ועל־עיר בן־אתנות |
| Zech. 9:9b LXX | πραῢς καὶ ἐπιβεβηκὼς ἐπὶ ὑποζύγιον καὶ πῶλον νέον |
| Aquila | πραῢς καὶ ἐπιβεβηκὼς ἐπὶ ὄνου καὶ πώλου υἱοῦ ὀνάδων |
| Symmachus | πτωχὸς καὶ ἐπιβεβηκὼς ἐπὶ ὄνον καὶ πῶλον υἱὸν ὀνάδος |
| Theodotion | ἐπακούων καὶ ἐπιβεβηκὼς ἐπὶ ὄνον καὶ πῶλον υἱὸν ὄνου |
| *Quinta* | πτωχὸς καὶ ἐπιβεβηκὼς ἐπὶ ὑποζύγιον καὶ πῶλον υἱὸν ὄνων |
| Justin *Dial.* 53.3c | καὶ πραῢς καὶ πτωχὸς ἐπιβεβηκὼς ἐπὶ ὑποζύγιον καὶ πῶλον ὄνου |
| Justin *1 Apol.* 35.11c | πρᾶος ἐπιβεβηκὼς ἐπὶ πῶλον ὄνον υἱὸν ὑποζυγίου |
| John 12:15b | καθήμενος ἐπὶ πῶλον ὄνου |
| Matt. 21:5b | πραῢς καὶ ἐπιβεβηκὼς ἐπὶ ὄνον καὶ ἐπὶ πῶλον υἱὸν ὑποζυγίου |
| Matt. 21:5b [Bezae] | πραῢς ἐπιβεβηκὼς ἐπὶ ὄνον καὶ πῶλον υἱὸν ὑποζυγίου |
| Irenaeus *Epid.* 65 | πραῢς καὶ καθήμενος ἐπὶ ὄνον πῶλον υἱὸν ὄνον [or ὑποζυγίου] |

## Justin Martyr's Transmission of Zech. 9:9 in *1 Apol.* 35.11

Of the extant renditions of Zech. 9:9 down to the time of Origen, Justin's quotation in *1 Apology* most easily derives from the LXX, Matt. 21:5, and John 12:15.[62] Matthew's quotation begins, "Say to the daughter Zion,"

---

62. Justin's combination of Zech. 9:9 LXX and Matt. 21:5 has long been recognized; see, e.g., Helmut Köster, *Septuaginta und Synoptischer Erzählungsstoff im Schriftbeweis Justins des Märtyrers*, Habilitationsschrift, Heidelberg, 1956, 93 n. 4; Édouard Massaux, *The Influence of the Gospel of Saint Matthew on Christian Literature before Saint Irenaeus*, trans. Norman J. Belval and Suzanne Hecht (3 vols.; New Gospel Studies 5; Macon, Ga.: Mercer University Press, 1990–93), 3:37–38; M.J.J. Menken, *Matthew's Bible: The Old Testament Text of the Evangelist* (BETL 173; Leuven: Leuven University Press,

as compared with John's "Do not fear, daughter Zion." I posit that Justin encountered these different opening lines in the gospels and then turned to the LXX for clarification. Finding that neither evangelist quoted Zechariah accurately, Justin reproduced the correct wording, "Rejoice greatly, daughter Zion;" he also included the ensuing parallel phrase "proclaim, daughter Jerusalem," which Matthew and John had omitted. In the next line Justin says, "Look, your king comes to you," and—as did Matthew and John—Justin leaves out Zechariah's description "righteous and salvific is he."

Justin's sharpest divergence from the LXX concerns faunal terminology. Justin has the rider mounted upon "a colt of an ass, an offspring of a yoke animal." The phrase "a colt of an ass" (πῶλον ὄνου) occurs neither in Zech. 9:9 nor in Matt. 21:5, but the phrase does appear in John 12:15. I posit that Justin simply combined John's "a colt of an ass" with Matthew's "an offspring of a yoke animal." Justin juxtaposes these animal word pairs without a conjunction, thereby signifying a single ass as in John's account. John and Justin's lone donkey erases an embarrassing exegetical problem: Matthew presents Jesus riding on two donkeys, a dam and her foal.[63] In other words, Justin intentionally includes all of Matthew and John's animal words, yet Justin follows John in envisioning only one donkey.

Finally, Justin's misattribution to Zephaniah most likely arose because Zeph. 3:14a LXX and Zech. 9:9aα LXX read verbatim, "Rejoice greatly, daughter Zion; proclaim, daughter Jerusalem."[64] It is even possible that Justin read from the Book of the Twelve and arrived at Zephaniah 3 prior to Zechariah 9. After copying as far as "daughter Jerusalem," Justin could have relied on Matthew and John without further recourse to any Old Testament text. In any case, Justin intended the donkey prophecy, which occurs in Zechariah rather than Zephaniah.

---

2004), 106n2; Krister Stendahl, *The School of St. Matthew and Its Use of the Old Testament* (Philadelphia: Fortress Press, 1968), 120.

63. There is indeed a ו/καί separating the animal words in the MT and LXX, so Zech. 9:9 could literally signify two animals; however, the *waw* is considered explicative rather than coordinative; see GKC ch. 154: p. 484 n. 1 (b).

64. Lindars, *New Testament Apologetic*, 115.

## Justin Martyr's Transmission of Zech. 9:9 in *Dial.* 53.3

In *Dial.* 53.3, Justin has looked up the text in the book of Zechariah, and this quotation differs from the earlier one in *1 Apology*. Here in the *Dialogue,* Justin correctly identifies the prophet as "Zechariah, one of the Twelve," and Justin includes the phrase "righteous and salvific is he." Justin also includes καί (and) to depict two donkeys as in Zechariah's prophecy and in Matthew's narrative; according to Justin, though, Jesus only rode upon the saddled (ὑποσαγή) dam,[65] not the unsaddled (ἀσαγή) colt.[66] Elsewhere I have demonstrated that in *Dial.* 53.3 Justin himself combined the LXX, the *kaige* recension of the Dodekapropheton,[67] and the wording from John 12:15.[68] Here I will summarize that argument to show that Justin was not quoting from a *testimonium*.

The *kaige* recension of the LXX is long established as one of Justin's sources in the *Dialogue*. In 1952 Bedouin discovered the Greek Minor Prophets Scroll from Naḥal Ḥever (8ḤevXIIgr),[69] a late first century BCE text that had been hidden during the bar Kokhba revolt. Soon after the scroll's discovery, Dominique Barthélemy classified the text as *kaige*;[70] for example, 8ḤevXIIgr translates וגם (also) as καίγε (even; at least) in Zech. 9:2. Based on Justin's agreements with 8ḤevXIIgr against the LXX, Barthélemy identified the *kaige* as Justin's source for the quotation of Mic. 4:1–7 in *Dial.* 109.2–3.[71]

---

65. I.e., padded with the disciple's clothes; cf. Matt. 21:7.
66. Justin's understanding reflects the Western text of Matt. 21:7; e.g., Codex Bezae uses the singular pronouns αὐτόν and αὐτοῦ such that the disciples only put their clothes and Jesus on one donkey, not on both of them (αὐτῶν) as in Codices Sinaiticus and Vaticanus.
67. For the *kaige,* see Leonard Greenspoon, "The *Kaige* Recension: The Life, Death, and Postmortem Existence of a Modern—and Ancient—Phenomenon," in *XII Congress of the International Organization for Septuagint and Cognate Studies: Leiden, 2004*, ed. Melvin K. H. Peters (SCS 54; Atlanta: Society of Biblical Literature, 2006), 1–16; Natalio Fernández Marcos, *The Septuagint in Context: Introduction to the Greek Versions of the Bible,* trans. Wilfred G. E. Watson (Leiden: Brill, 2000), 142–54; Tim McLay, "*Kaige* and Septuagint Research," *Textus* 19 (1998): 127–39.
68. James W. Barker, "The Reconstruction of *Kaige/Quinta* Zechariah 9,9," *ZAW* 126, no. 4 (2014): 584–88.
69. See now Emanuel Tov, *The Greek Minor Prophets Scroll from Naḥal Ḥever (8ḤevXIIgr)* (DJD 8; Oxford: Clarendon, 1990).
70. Dominique Barthélemy, "Redécouverte d'un chaînon manquant de l'histoire de la Septante," *RB* 60 (1953): 18–29.
71. Barthélemy, "Redécouverte d'un chaînon manquant," 20–21; see also idem, *Les Devanciers d'Aquila:*

Justin also relies on the *kaige* for his quotation of Zech. 9:9 in *Dial.* 53.3. Justin's differences from the LXX are as follows: (1) ἥξει (he will be present or will have come) rather than ἔρχεται (he comes); (2) the "doublets" ἀλαλάζω (shout) and κηρύσσω (proclaim) as well as πραΰς (humble) and πτωχός (poor); (3) πῶλον ὄνου (a colt of an ass) rather than πῶλον νέον (a young colt).

Justin puts ἥξει in place of ἔρχεται. Morphologically ἥκω is in the present tense (I am here), but the sense is that of a perfect (I have come). In effect, Justin's use of the future ἥξει has Zechariah predict that the king "will have come." The *kaige* does not appear to have changed the LXX's ἔρχομαι to ἥκω, but Justin himself does make this change in another scriptural quotation in the *Dialogue*.[72] Justin also conflated the imperatives "proclaim" (κήρυσσε) in the LXX and "shout" (ἀλάλαξον) in the *kaige*. Likewise "meek" (πραΰς) would have come from the LXX and "poor" (πτωχός) from the *kaige*. The *kaige* would not have contained any conflations, for it represents the earliest known recension of the LXX. Regarding animal words, Zech. 9:9 MT placed the king upon "a he-ass" (חמור), and "a male ass, a son of she-asses" (עיר בן־אתנות), which the LXX translated loosely as "a yoke animal and a young colt" (ὑποζύγιον καὶ πῶλον νέον).[73] Although Matthew, Aquila, Symmachus, and Theodotion changed ὑποζύγιον to ὄνος (ass), the *kaige* would have maintained ὑποζύγιον for חמור (ass). Finding no disagreement between the LXX and the *kaige*, Justin too wrote ὑποζύγιον. Then, as was the case in 1 *Apology*, Justin looked up (or remembered) John 12:15 for "a colt of an ass" (πῶλον ὄνου), which occurs in no other extant rendition of Zech. 9:9 down to the time of Origen. Justin himself thus redacted multiple, extant Old Testament and New Testament texts

---

*première publication intégrale du texte des fragments du Dodécaprophéton trouvés dans le désert de Juda* (Leiden: Brill, 1963), 210–11.

72. Justin calls John the Baptist a prophet who cried out that someone stronger than he "will have come" (ἥξει; *Dial.* 49.3); Justin's *Vorlage(n)* would have said either that someone "comes" (ἔρχεται; Mark 1:7b; Luke 3:16c) or "is coming" (ἐρχόμενος; Matt. 3:11a; John 1:27).

73. For a recent analysis of the animal words in *Dial.* 53.3, see Felix Albrecht, "Das Zwölfprophetenbuch und seine Rezeption im frühen Christentum am Beispiel Justins des Märtyrers," in *Textual History and the Reception of Scripture in Early Christianity*, ed. Johannes de Vries and Martin Karrer (SCS 60; Atlanta: Society of Biblical Literature, 2013), 349–57, here 353–55.

for this particular quotation. Therefore, there is no reason to assume a hypothetical *testimonium*.

### Irenaeus's Transmission of Zech. 9:9 in *Epid.* 65

Some arguments for the inclusion of Zech. 9:9 in a *testimonium* cite Irenaeus, *Demonstration [Epideixis] of the Apostolic Preaching* 65, which survives only in Armenian: "Say to the daughter Zion: look, the king comes to you, meek and sitting on an ass, a colt, a son of an ass." In all likelihood the text has been preserved intact since it has not been assimilated to the Armenian versions of Matt. 21:5 or John 12:15 (see Table 4.2).[74] Irenaeus's quotation derives from his own combination of Matt. 21:5 and John 12:15, and there is no evidence that he drew from a *testimonium*.

Table 4.2 The Armenian Versions of Matt. 21:5; Irenaeus *Epid.* 65; John 12:15

| | |
|---|---|
| Matt. 21:5 | *asac͑ ēk͑ dster Siovni •* |
| *Epid.* 65 | *asac͑ ēk͑ dstern Siovni •* |
| John 12:15 | *mí erknč͑ir dowstr Siovni •* |
| Matt. 21:5 | *aha t͑agawor gay k͑ez hez ew heceál y-ēš ew ï yawanaki išoy* |
| *Epid.* 65 | *aha t͑agawor gay k͑ez hez ew nsteal ï veray išoy yawanaki ordwoy išoy* |
| John 12:15 | *ahawadik [variant: aha] t͑agawor k͑o gay nsteal ï veray yawanaki išoy* |

Irenaeus begins with Matthew's phrase "say to the daughter Zion," which also occurs in Isa. 62:11aβ; this explains Irenaeus's misattributing the prophecy to Isaiah. Irenaeus's variant reading "the king comes to you," rather than "your king comes to you," also occurs in the Armenian and the Bohairic versions of Matt. 21:5.[75] Irenaeus

---

74. E.g., the Armenian of Matt. 21:5 omits "son" (as in ℵ[c], L, Origen *Comm. Jo.* 10.124), but Irenaeus includes *ordi*. For the Armenian of the Gospels, see Beda O. Künzle, *Das Altarmenische Evangelium* (2 vols.; Europäische Hochschulschriften, Reihe XXI, Linguistik und Indogermanistik, bd. 33; New York: Peter Lang, 1984).

75. In Matt. 6:4, 6, 18, 23; 12:47; 15:28, "your" (*k͑o*) and "to you" (*k͑ez*) correspond exactly with σου and σοι respectively, and so *k͑ez* should not be thought a dative of possession in Irenaeus's quotation, *pace* the Eng. translations by Bishop Karapet and S. G. Wilson (PO 12.5, 709) and John Behr (*On the Apostolic Preaching* [Popular Patristics Series; Crestwood, N.Y.: St. Vladimir's Seminary Press, 1997], 82); Joseph P. Smith (*Proof of the Apostolic Preaching* [ACW 16; New York: Paulist, 1978], 90) translates accurately, "a king cometh to thee." For the Bohairic, see George Horner, *The Coptic*

follows Matthew in calling the king "meek." At this point, Irenaeus diverges from Matthew's "riding on" (*heceál* with the locative) and says instead "sitting on" (*nsteal ï veray* with the genitive).[76] Although Latin texts almost always use "sitting" (*redens*) in both Matt. 21:5 and John 12:15, "sitting" and "riding" are clearly distinguishable in Greek and Armenian. Accordingly, Irenaeus most likely took "sitting" from John's καθήμενος.[77] Irenaeus's phrase "an ass, a colt, a son of an ass" uses all of Matthew's terms in exactly Matthew's order.[78] At the same time, Irenaeus omits "and" (*ew*), thereby signifying only one donkey as in John's rendition. In summary, Irenaeus's quotation derives from Matthew and John without any recourse to Zechariah's text. At the same time, Irenaeus's quotation is not identical to any of his predecessors, whether Matthew, John, or Justin Martyr.

### The Dearth of Evidence for an Early *Testimonium* Containing Zech. 9:9

In a classic statement of the testimony-book hypothesis, Rendel Harris established criteria for determining authors' use of *testimonia*. His criteria included recurring peculiar Old Testament quotations and recurring misattribution of authorship.[79] Regarding peculiarity, the five earliest Christian citations—including Matt. 21:5 and John 12:15—diverge from all known Jewish *Vorlagen* in Hebrew and Greek;[80] however, each of the Christian versions also differs from all the others,

---

*Version of the New Testament in the Northern Dialect, otherwise called Memphitic and Bohairic* (4 vols.; Oxford: Clarendon, 1898–1905).

76. One of the limitations of Armenian is that this participle is built from the aorist stem, which does not imply an aorist participle in the Greek *Vorlage*; for *nsteal* as "sitting," see Robert W. Thomson, *An Introduction to Classical Armenian* (Delmar, N.Y.: Caravan Books, 1975), 70.

77. Codex d—i.e., the Latin page facing the Greek pages of Codex Bezae—at Matt. 21:5 (*ascendens*) and Ambrose *ep.* 74.9 (*ascendit*) use the verb "mount" (cf. ἐπιβεβηκώς in Matthew), but all other Latin occurrences use a verb for "sitting" (i.e., riding); it is almost always the present participle sedens, which corresponds to John's καθήμενος. In other words, Matt. 21:5 is indistinguishable from John 12:15 in Latin vis-à-vis the participle *sedens*.

78. Here I consider the possibility that the final ἴσον represents ὑποζύγιον, as does ܥܒܕܐ in the Syro-Hexapla.

79. Rendel Harris, *Testimonies* (2 vols.; Cambridge: Cambridge University Press, 1916–20), 1:8.

80. Compared with the Hebrew text, the Aramaic (Tg. J. Zech. 9:9) reads "assembly" (כנ) rather than "daughter" (בת); "in your midst" (לגויך) rather than "to you" (לך); and "rescuing/redeeming" (פריק) as corresponding to "salvific" (נו). Since none of the distinctive Aramaic renderings have affected the Greek transmission, I exclude it from my analysis.

and so there is no recurrence of a peculiar reading. Misattribution indeed occurs, but it does not recur: Justin mentions Zephaniah (*1 Apol.* 35.10), whereas Irenaeus mentions Isaiah (*Epid.* 65). To maintain the *testimonium* hypothesis, then, scholars are forced to relax their own criteria.[81] The problem is that in absence of recurring distinctive elements, the testimony-book hypothesis necessitates a different *testimonium* for each author quoting Zech. 9:9, thereby violating the principle of parsimony. Aside from Matthew's and John's quotations of Zech. 9:9, Justin and Irenaeus provide the only evidence that the donkey prophecy stood in a *testimonium* anytime in the first and second centuries. Having shown the ways Justin and Irenaeus combined actual sources for their quotations, I have eliminated the need to appeal to hypothetical *testimonia*.[82] John's quotation of Zech. 9:9 must therefore be explained in some other way.

## John's Quotation of Zech. 9:9 via Matthew

Because John and Matthew quote Zech. 9:9 so differently, the consensus holds that the two gospels must have worked independently.[83] I begin with a word of caution against drawing conclusions of literary dependence based on gospels' divergent Old Testament quotations. The Synoptics shows numerous such differences. For example, however one solves the Synoptic Problem, there is no doubt of literary dependence in the account of the rich man

---

81. So Harry Y. Gamble, *Books and Readers in the Early Church* (New Haven: Yale University Press, 1995), 27; so too Smith, *St. Irenaeus: Proof of the Apostolic Preaching*, 33–34.
82. Scholars who deny Matthew and John's use of *testimonia* include Menken, *Matthew's Bible*, 107–8; Soares-Prabhu, *Formula Quotations*, 158; Stendahl, *School of St. Matthew*, 215.
83. E.g., Brown, *The Gospel according to John* (AB 29–29A; Garden City: Doubleday, 1966-70), 1:460–61; C. H. Dodd, *According to the Scriptures: The Sub-structure of New Testament Theology* (London: James Nisbet & Co., 1952), 49; Luz, *Matthew*, 3:5; M.J.J. Menken, "The Quotations from Zech. 9,9 in Mt 21,5 and in Jn 12,15," in *John and the Synoptics*, ed. A. Denaux (BETL 101; Leuven: Leuven University Press, 1992), 571–78, here 578; idem, *Old Testament Quotations in the Fourth Gospel: Studies in Textual Form* (CBET 15; Leuven: Peeters, 1996), 79–97; Günter Reim, *Studien zum alttestamentlichen Hintergrund des Johannesevangeliums* (SNTSMS 22; Cambridge: Cambridge University Press, 1974), 29–32; Wilhelm Rothfuchs, *Die Erfüllungszitate des Matthäus-Evangeliums: Eine biblisch-theologische Untersuchung* (BWANT 88; Stuttgart: W. Kohlhammer, 1969), 165; Rudolf Schnackenburg, *The Gospel according to St. John*, trans. Kevin Smyth et al. (3 vols.; HTKNT 4; New York: Herder & Herder; Seabury; Crossroad, 1968-82; repr. New York: Crossroad, 1990), 2:376; Stendahl, *School of St. Matthew*, 120.

who asks Jesus about eternal life (Matt. 19:16–30; Mark 10:17–31; Luke 18:18–30). The story quotes from the Decalogue, and below I isolate just three of the commandments listed (see Table 4.3).

Table 4.3 Partial Quotations of the Decalogue in the Synoptics

| | | |
|---|---|---|
| Exod. 20:13–15 MT | kill, adultery, steal | לא תרצח לא תנאף לא תגנב |
| Deut. 5:17–19 MT | kill, adultery, steal | לא תרצח לא תנאף לא תגנב |
| Matt. 19:18c | kill, adultery, steal | οὐ φονεύσεις οὐ μοιχεύσεις οὐ κλέψεις |
| Mark 10:19b | kill, adultery, steal | μὴ φονεύσῃς μὴ μοιχεύσῃς μὴ κλέψῃς |
| Deut. 5:17–19 LXX | adultery, kill, steal | οὐ μοιχεύσεις οὐ φονεύσεις οὐ κλέψεις |
| Luke 18:20b | adultery, kill, steal | μὴ μοιχεύσῃς μὴ φονεύσῃς μὴ κλέψῃς |
| Exod. 20:13–15 LXX | adultery, steal, kill | οὐ μοιχεύσεις οὐ κλέψεις οὐ φονεύσεις |

Matthew (19:18c) and Mark (10:19b) use the same sequence of prohibiting killing, adultery, and stealing, which appears in Exodus (20:13–15 MT) and Deuteronomy (5:17–19 MT). Luke (18:20b) uses a different sequence, namely adultery, killing, and stealing, which appears in Deuteronomy (5:17–19 LXX). None of the synoptists utilizes yet another attested sequence, namely adultery, stealing, and killing (Exod. 20:13–15 LXX). Grammatically, Matthew and the LXX use οὐ with the future tense throughout, which corresponds more literally to the imperfect aspect of the Hebrew. Conversely, Mark and Luke always use μή with subjunctive, which does not appear in the LXX. Within a single verse, then, each of the synoptists presents three successive commandments in a different order. On the supposition of Markan priority, Matthew and Luke easily could have reproduced their source text of Mark. Matthew and Luke also could have copied the LXX identically, as they do on other occasions. Instead, Matthew and Luke produced idiosyncratic readings of the Ten Commandments, but the divergent Old Testament quotations in no way call into question Matthew's and Luke's dependence on Mark in this pericope.

That John quotes Zech. 9:9 differently than Matthew does not indicate *ipso facto* John's independence of Matthew. The differences do need to be explained, though (see Table 4.4).[84]

Table 4.4 Quotations of Zech. 9:9 in Matthew and John

| | |
|---|---|
| Zech. 9:9 | Χαῖρε σφόδρα θύγατερ Σιών, κήρυσσε θύγατερ Ιερουσαλήμ |
| Matt. 21:5 | εἴπατε τῇ θυγατρὶ Σιών |
| John 12:15 | Μὴ φοβοῦ θυγάτηρ Σιών |
| Zech. 9:9 | ἰδοὺ ὁ βασιλεύς σου ἔρχεταί σοι δίκαιος καὶ σώζων αὐτός |
| Matt. 21:5 | ἰδοὺ ὁ βασιλεύς σου ἔρχεταί σοι |
| John 12:15 | ἰδοὺ ὁ βασιλεύς σου ἔρχεταί |
| Zech. 9:9 | πραΰς καὶ ἐπιβεβηκὼς ἐπὶ ὑποζύγιον καὶ πῶλον νέον |
| Matt. 21:5 | πραΰς καὶ ἐπιβεβηκὼς ἐπὶ ὄνον καὶ ἐπὶ πῶλον υἱὸν ὑποζυγίου |
| John 12:15 | καθήμενος ἐπὶ πῶλον ὄνου |

A half-century ago, Edwin Freed called John 12:15 "a free artistic creation on the basis of Matt(hew)," and he rightly observed that John is closer to Matthew than to the Hebrew or Greek text of Zechariah.[85] I also agree with Benedict Viviano's more recent explanation of John's lone donkey as an improvement to Matthew's embarrassing, seeming misunderstanding of Zechariah's synonymous parallelism.[86] Despite John's differences from Matthew, Matthew's text best explains John's quotation of Zech. 9:9.

The only similarity between John's and Matthew's opening lines is that neither matches Zech. 9:9, which begins, "Rejoice exceedingly,

---

84. Jaime Clark-Soles (*Scripture Cannot Be Broken: The Social Function of the Use of Scripture in the Fourth Gospel* [Boston: Brill, 2003], 264) suggests, "Perhaps the author is (mis)quoting from memory or perhaps he is working from an alternative text of the LXX passage." Scholars who appeal to hypothetical sources (e.g., *testimonia* and the pre-Johannine passion narrative) frequently fail to explain why the authors/compilers of the source texts would have altered Zechariah's prophecy. Those appealing to *testimonia* include Dodd, *According to the Scriptures*, 49; Judith M. Lieu, "Justin Martyr and the Transformation of Psalm 22," in *Biblical Traditions in Transmission: Essays in Honour of Michael A. Knibb*, ed. Charlotte Hempel and Judith M. Lieu (Supplements to the Journal for the Study of Judaism 3; Boston: Brill, 2006), 195–211, here 200–201; D. Moody Smith, "John 12:12ff. and the Question of John's Use of the Synoptics," *JBL* 82, no. 1(1963): 58–64, here 63. Scholars positing a pre-Johannine passion narrative include Rudolf Bultmann, *The Gospel of John: A Commentary*, trans. G. R. Beasley-Murray (Oxford: Basil Blackwell, 1971), 417–18; Robert Tomson Fortna, *The Fourth Gospel and Its Predecessor: From Narrative Source to Present Gospel* (Philadelphia: Fortress Press, 1988), 146–48; Menken, *Old Testament Quotations in the Fourth Gospel*, 85; Frank Schleritt, *Der vorjohanneische Passionsbericht: Eine historisch-kritische und theologische Untersuchung zu Joh 2,13–22; 11:47–14,31 und 18,1–20,29* (BZNW 154; Berlin: Walter de Gruyter, 2007), 218; Schnackenburg, *Gospel according to St. John*, 2:376, 379; Smith, "John 12:12ff.," 63.
85. Freed, "The Entry into Jerusalem in the Gospel of John," 337–38.
86. Viviano, "John's Use of Matthew," 230–231.

daughter Zion." Matthew's quotation begins with the phrase, "Say to the daughter Zion," a parallel to Isa. 62:11a, which speaks of the arrival of Israel's "salvation" (ישׁע) or "savior" (σωτήρ).[87] John provides yet another introduction, "Do not fear, daughter Zion." To account for "Do not fear," Barnabas Lindars suggested that John deliberately combined Zephaniah and Zechariah.[88] Problematically, though, extant sources do not put the commands to rejoice and not to fear in proximity to one another: "rejoicing" appears in Zech. 9:9aα LXX = Zeph. 3:14a LXX, but "not fearing" is only in the Hebrew (Zeph. 3:16b MT; cf. θάρσει in the LXX). Since "do not fear" is such a common phrase (occurring more than sixty times in the MT and more than seventy in the LXX), I suggest that that John did not use an Old Testament text at all when "quoting" Zechariah's prophecy.

The LXX, Matthew, and John agree verbatim, "Look, your king comes"; John is the only one of the three to omit "to you" at this point, and he likely considered it redundant. John also chooses not to describe the king as meek (πραΰς). Matthew and John's strongest similarity in these verses is the shared omission of "righteous and salvific is he." The phrase is lacking in no other extant source for Zechariah, and I argue that such a conspicuous absence presents a problem for those who claim Johannine independence.[89] For example, Krister Stendahl and M.J.J. Menken consider the LXX the middle term between Matthew and John,[90] yet neither scholar can explain how the evangelists made the same omission independently.[91]

From this point on, John uses terms synonymous with Matthew's surrounding narrative. John characteristically avoids reduplicated prepositional constructions,[92] and so it is unsurprising that he

---

87. Matthias Konradt (*Israel, Church, and the Gentiles in the Gospel of Matthew*, trans. Kathleen Ess [Baylor-Mohr Siebeck Studies in Early Christianity; Waco: Baylor University Press, 2014], 97) suggests that Zechariah's command to rejoice "does not fit with Jerusalem's role in the Matthean story of conflict."
88. Lindars, *New Testament Apologetic*, 26n2; similarly Menken, *Old Testament Quotations in the Fourth Gospel*, 84; Menken considers it likely equally likely that Isa. 40:9 figured into John's exegesis.
89. E.g., Stendahl, *School of St. Matthew*, 162.
90. Ibid., 120; Menken, *Old Testament Quotations in the Fourth Gospel*, 82n13; there in response to Frans Neirynck, "John and the Synoptics: 1975–1990," in *John and the Synoptics*, ed. Adelbert Denaux (BETL 101; Leuven: Leuven University Press, 1992), 3–62, here 26–28.
91. Stendahl, *School of St. Matthew*, 119; Menken, *Old Testament Quotations in the Fourth Gospel*, 79.

disregards ἐπιβαίνω ἐπί, which Matthew used for getting Jesus atop the donkeys.⁹³ John instead uses the participle καθήμενος to signify Jesus' sitting or riding on the ass. As Freed explained, Matthew's narrative says that Jesus sat on (ἐπικαθίζω) the ass and colt,⁹⁴ and John had already used καθίζω ἐπί immediately before his quotation of Zech. 9:9 (12:14). Freed rightly observes, "John frequently uses synonyms instead of repeating the same word."⁹⁵

For John's animal terms, Menken concludes that John's anarthrous "a colt of an ass" (πῶλος ὄνου) come from Gen. 49:11 LXX, which includes definite articles (τὸν πῶλον τῆς ὄνου).⁹⁶ Menken's full argument requires John to have drawn upon Gen. 49:11; 1 Kgs. 1:38, 44; Isa. 40:9; Zeph. 3:16; Zech. 9:9—mostly in Greek but occasionally in Hebrew as well.⁹⁷ I have found no evidence that John looked up any Old Testament Scripture for the quotation in John 12:15, and so I propose a simpler solution. Among the Synoptics, only Matthew names the animal's species.⁹⁸ Having introduced the animal by the diminutive (ὀνάριον; John 12:14), John uses "a colt of an ass" (πῶλος ὄνου) in the quotation. The word choice in John's quotation most easily derives from Matt. 21:2, 7, the verses surrounding Matthew's quotation of Zechariah.⁹⁹ Matthew has Jesus

---

92. Reduplicated prepositions with compound verbs appear less frequently in the Fourth Gospel than in the Synoptics. E.g., when the crown of thorns is put on Jesus' head (another John–Matthew parallel), John uses ἐπιτίθημι without reduplicating ἐπί (19:2) as compared with Matthew's ἐπιτίθημι ἐπί (27:29); in the Fourth Gospel, see especially ἔρχομαι πρός [27x] rather than προσέρχομαι πρός.
93. To mount Jesus upon the ass, Homeric usage could have separated the preposition ἐπί from the verb βαίνω; however, in koine βαίνω ἐπί would have sounded as though Jesus were standing beside or stepping on the donkey.
94. In Matt. 21:7, even if "atop them" (ἐπάνω αὐτῶν) refers to the clothes, the clothes are already on both animals (ἐπ᾽ αὐτῶν).
95. Freed, "Entry into Jerusalem in the Gospel of John," 333n23, vis-à-vis ὀνάριον and ὄνος in John 12:14-15; see also p. 338 re καθίζω and κάθημαι. Freed also points out that "sitting" shows up in Isa. 19:1 as "riding" (רכב > κάθημαι); the idea is that the rider simply sits while the vehicle moves.
96. Menken, *Old Testament Quotations in the Fourth Gospel*, 95.
97. Ibid., 97. Cf. Bruce G. Schuchard, *Scripture within Scripture: The Interrelationship of Form and Function in the Explicit Old Testament Citations in the Gospel of John* (SBLDS 133; Atlanta: Scholars Press, 1992), 84; Schuchard argues that John took "fear not" from Isa. 44:2 and "colt of an ass" from Gen. 49:11. Cf. also Andreas Obermann, *Die christologische Erfüllung der Schrift im Johannesevangelium: Eine Untersuchung zur johanneischen Hermeneutik anhand der Schriftzitate* (WUNT 2/83; Tübingen: Mohr Siebeck, 1996), 207, 208, 213; Obermann argues that John took "colt of an ass" from Gen. 49:11, but Obermann does not think that John took "fear not" from any particular Old Testament text.
98. Neither Freed ("Entry into Jerusalem in the Gospel of John," 333) nor Smith ("John 12:12ff.," 62) notes this point, and Smith claims ὀνάριον as proof John uses a non-Synoptic source.
99. See Freed, "Entry into Jerusalem in the Gospel of John," 338; he cites only Matt. 21:2, 5.

tell two disciples to get him an ass (ὄνος) and a colt (πῶλος) with her (21:2), and so the disciples bring both animals (21:6), on which Jesus sits (21:7). The strangest detail in Matthew's story is that Jesus rides on two donkeys at once in order to fulfill Zechariah's prophecy, which literally depicted a king riding "upon" (עַל) one donkey "and upon" (וְעַל) another one (Zech. 9:9b). To correct Matthew's seeming misunderstanding of Zechariah's synonymous parallelism, John subtracted a donkey. In other words, John borrowed Matthew's πῶλος and ὄνος (Matt. 21:2, 7), but John used the two terms to depict only one animal.

I conclude that the sole source for the quotation of Zech. 9:9 in John 12:15 was Matt. 21:2, 5, 7. Apart from that, John simply had to know that Zech. 9:9 did not begin with the word "say" (εἴπατε), and so he picked a generic introduction "do not fear" (μὴ φοβοῦ). Following Matthew, John then omitted "righteous and salvific is he." From Matthew, John left out that the king was coming "to you" (σοι) and that he was "meek" (πραΰς). Finally, John looked to Matt. 21:7 and used a synonymous verb for sitting, and John used Matthew's two nouns to describe one young ass.

Matthew and John by no means present identical quotations, but there are significant agreements that have gone unappreciated in previous scholarship. Compared with Mark and Luke, Matthew and John specify that the animal was a donkey and give a quotation of Zech. 9:9 along with the claim that Jesus fulfills the prophecy. If Mark had in mind at all that Jesus was reenacting an Old Testament text, it might well have been Solomon's coronation (1 Kgs. 1:33, 38, 44), for the crowd not only greets Jesus as they would a king but also mentions "the kingdom of our father David" (Mark 11:8, 10). It is somewhat peculiar that Matthew and John even claim that Jesus fulfills Zechariah's prophecy. All Jesus does is sit on a donkey, whereas Zechariah's "salvific" (σώζων; נוֹשָׁע) king actually tramples his enemies.[100] So in

---

100. *Pace* Ruth Sheridan, *Retelling Scripture: 'The Jews' and the Scriptural Citations in John 1:19–12:15* (Biblical Interpretation Series 110; Leiden/Boston: Brill, 2012), 220–21; Sheridan says that in fulfilling Zech. 9:9, Jesus is not characterized by "triumphalism and war" (p. 220)—even though the rest of Zechariah 9 is full of bloody warfare.

their respective quotations of Zech. 9:9, John and Matthew omit this essential word; in fact, they omit the same two phrases totaling seven words. If John were quoting Zechariah from memory or making his own translation, then one would not expect John to abbreviate the verse in precisely the same ways as Matthew had done. In summary, John's makeshift quotation more closely resembles Matthew's quotation and surrounding narrative than any of the eight extant Hebrew and Greek versions of Zech. 9:9 down to the third century. Matthew's redacted gospel thus serves as the most likely source for John's use of Zech. 9:9 when describing Jesus' entry into Jerusalem.

**The Role of the Spirit: John's Supplement to Matthew**

Throughout the Gospels of Matthew and John, the narrators explain Jesus' actions as fulfilling Old Testament Scriptures. Out of the eleven fulfillment sayings in Matthew and the eight similar type of sayings in John,[101] the donkey prophecy from Zechariah is the only one that Matthew and John have in common. In this one instance, John corrects Matthew's presentation of Jesus riding on two donkeys simultaneously. In all the other cases, John supplements Matthew by showing additional Scriptures Jesus fulfilled. To the evangelists, these fulfillments prove that Jesus is the Messiah. Upon further reflection, the question arises as to why so few people believed in Jesus if he was enacting so many clear proofs from prophecy. To answer this question, John supplements Matthew in another way: John explains that it was impossible for anyone to comprehend the prophetic significance of Jesus' actions in the moment; such comprehension could only come by receiving the Holy Spirit, which did not happen until Jesus had risen from the dead.

The Spirit's mnemonic and interpretive role unfolds across John's gospel. At the first Passover, Jesus disrupts the commerce in the temple

---

101. Matthew's fulfillment citations are found in 1:22–23 (Isa. 7:14); 2:15 (Hos. 11:1), 17–18 (Jer. 31:15), 23 (?); 4:14–16 (Isa. 8:23–9:1); 8:17 (Isa. 53:4); 12:17–21 (Isa. 42:1–4); 13:14–15 (Isa. 6:9–10), 35 (Ps. 78:2); 21:4–5 (Zech. 9:9); 27:9–10 (Zech. 11:13; cf. Jer. 18:1–2; 32:6–15). John's fulfillment sayings are found in 2:17 (Ps. 69:9); 12:14–16 (Zech. 9:9), 38–39a (Isa. 53:1), 39b–40 (Isa. 6:10); 19:24 (Ps. 22:18), 28 (?), 36 (Ps. 34:20), 37 (Zech. 12:10).

(2:15–16). John says, "His disciples remembered that it is written, 'Zeal for your house consumes me'" (2:17; cf. Ps. 69:9a). Then in response to a request for a sign, Jesus says, "Destroy this temple and in three days I will raise it" (2:19). After explaining that Jesus was speaking figuratively about his body (2:21), John adds, "And so when he was raised from the dead, his disciples remembered that he said this, and they believed the Scripture and the word that Jesus said" (2:22).[102] Nearly a year and a half later at Sukkot, Jesus talks about living water bubbling up within those who believe in him (7:38). John explains, "But this he said concerning the Spirit, which the ones who believed in him were about to receive; for there was not yet a Spirit because Jesus was not yet glorified" (7:39). At Jesus' final Passover, he sits on a donkey to fulfill Zechariah's prophecy (12:14–15). John explains, "These things his disciples did not comprehend at first, but when Jesus was glorified, then they remembered that these things had been written concerning him and these things were done to him" (12:16). Finally, after the resurrection, Jesus gives the Holy Spirit to the disciples (20:22). Only thereafter could the disciples remember Jesus' deeds and interpret them as fulfillments of prophecies.

In conclusion, proofs from prophecy provide an important point of contact between Matthew and John. In general, these gospels similarly interpret many of Jesus' actions as literally fulfilling Old Testament prophecies. In particular, Matthew and John state explicitly that Jesus' entry into Jerusalem upon a donkey fulfills the prophecy from Zech. 9:9 about the coming of Israel's king. John's fulfillment citation nevertheless reveals insight into his estimation of Matthew's gospel. John finds it necessary to correct Matthew's overly literal depiction of Jesus riding upon two donkeys at once. Accordingly, John revises the narrative and the quotation so that Jesus sits upon only one donkey. At the same time, John shows no intention of replacing Matthew altogether, for without Matthew's gospel, the church would not know the ten other prophecies Jesus is said to fulfill. Finally, John explains

---

102. Jaime Clark-Soles (*Scripture Cannot Be Broken*, 294–97) is exactly right in saying that John's use of "memory" (μιμνήσκομαι) and "fulfillment" (πληρόω) shows that John's gospel counts as Scripture—on par with the Old Testament.

that disciples can only understand the prophetic significance of Jesus' actions in light of the resurrection and with the Holy Spirit operating as *aide-mémoire*. John's proofs from prophecy can be read on their own, but John's pneumatology can also reinterpret why Jesus is not widely accepted as the Messiah in Matthew's gospel—despite Matthew's insistence that Jesus had fulfilled so many messianic proofs from prophecy.

5

# Samaritan Inclusion or Exclusion?

In Matthew's gospel, Jesus avoids Samaria and tells the disciples not to evangelize there. So why in John's gospel does Jesus travel through Samaria and evangelize Samaritans? In this chapter, I advance a rather counterintuitive argument: With regard to the Samaritans, John differs so much from Matthew that John must be consciously disagreeing with Matthew. Surprisingly, these two gospels can be harmonized such that Jesus actually tells the disciples not to evangelize in Samaria while he himself was in the process of doing so. Jesus' Samaritan mission in John does not in fact contradict Jesus' prohibition of a Samaritan mission in Matthew.

In what follows, I will give an overview of Samaria and Samaritans in the Gospels, and then I will show how John's Samaritan mission and Matthew's prohibition of a Samaritan mission can be harmonized. The key is a metaphorical saying about the harvest, which refers to disciples' evangelism. Although the synoptic version of the saying is widely attested and was in all likelihood orally transmitted (Matt. 9:37b–38; Q/Luke 10:2; *Gos. Thom.* 73),[1] only Matthew's saying occurs in

---

1. Literary dependence and oral tradition need not be mutually exclusive; see Andrew F. Gregory, "What Is Literary Dependence?," in *New Studies in the Synoptic Problem: Oxford Conference, April 2008;*

close proximity to the question concerning evangelism to Samaritans (Matt. 10:5b). I find that John (4:35b) once again shows knowledge of a Matthean saying in its redacted context.

## Samaria and Samaritans in the Gospels

Mark never mentions the Samaritans explicitly, yet he does subtly depict Jesus avoiding Samaria en route to Jerusalem from Galilee. Setting out from Capernaum (Mark 9:33), Jesus went "into the regions of Judea and across the Jordan" (10:1).[2] Since Capernaum lies in Galilee to the north, Mark implies that Jesus traveled south to Judea via Perea, a narrow territory on the east side of the Jordan River; some copyists later made this route explicit.[3] Mark next locates Jesus and the disciples on the road to Jerusalem (10:32), and shortly thereafter they arrive at Jericho (10:46); by this point they have necessarily re-crossed the Jordan. Matthew follows Mark closely when reporting that Jesus leaves Capernaum in Galilee and crosses to the other side of the Jordan (Matt. 19:1), most likely via the Sea of Galilee. Jesus would then head south until past Samaria, at which point he could cross the Jordan into Judea, for in Matt. 20:17 Jesus and the Twelve are on the road to Jerusalem, and as of Matt. 10:29 they have entered and departed Jericho.

At least since the early nineteenth century, scholars have observed that Jesus' travels in Matthew and Mark avoid Samaria,[4] yet the two prevailing explanations prove inadequate. Some scholars suppose that Jews avoided Samaria because of purity concerns.[5] On the contrary, other rabbis do not question the piety of Rabbi Jonathan, who talked to a Samaritan near Mount Gerizim (Gen. Rab. 32.10).[6] Others such as

---

*Essays in Honour of Christopher M. Tuckett*, ed. Paul Foster et al. (BETL 239; Leuven: Peeters, 2011), 87–114.
2. εἰς τὰ ὅρια τῆς Ἰουδαίας καὶ πέραν τοῦ Ἰορδάνου (Mark 10:1); the absence of καί in the Western text most likely represents assimilation to Matt. 19:1.
3. E.g., by adding διά in Codex Alexandrinus and Byzantine MSS as well as ܒ in the Harklean, Jesus travels to Judea via the Transjordan.
4. E.g., Friedrich Schleiermacher, *The Life of Jesus*, ed. Jack C. Verheyden, trans. S. Maclean Gilmour (Lives of Jesus Series; Philadelphia: Fortress Press, 1975), 366; more recently, see R. T. France, *Matthew* (NICNT; Grand Rapids: Eerdmans, 2007), 709.
5. Andreas Köstenberger, *John* (BECNT; Grand Rapids: Baker, 2004), 146; Leon Morris, *The Gospel according to John* (rev. ed.; NICNT; Grand Rapids: Eerdmans, 1995), 226.

John Meier explain that bypassing Samaria was "a common route for Jewish pilgrims wishing to avoid the hostility of Samaritans."[7] This requires qualification, however. Such Samaritan hostility arose more than twenty years after Jesus' ministry ended. Josephus records an attack on Galilean pilgrims passing through Samaria in 52 CE, but he introduces the account as follows: "It was the custom among the Galileans coming to the festivals in the holy city to travel via the region of Samaria" (*Ant.* 20.6.1). Thus Samaritan hostility may very well explain Jesus' travel itinerary in Matthew and Mark, but the route would anachronistically reflect the time of the evangelists rather than Jesus' own day.

Compared with Matthew and Mark, Luke is ambiguous as to whether Jesus ever entered Samaria. At the outset of the travel narrative, Jesus sent messengers who entered a Samaritan village (κώμην Σαμαριτῶν; 9:52). Jesus himself did not enter that village because its inhabitants were unreceptive (9:53), so Jesus and his disciples proceeded into a different village (ἑτέραν κώμην; 9:56); Luke does not specify whether the second village was a Samaritan one. The next geographic marker comes when Jesus encounters ten men afflicted with leprosy, one of whom was a Samaritan (17:12, 16b). That encounter took place in a village along the border between Samaria and Galilee (διὰ μέσον Σαμαρείας καὶ Γαλιλαίας; 17:11–12), but Luke does not clarify which side of the border. Later still, Jesus shows up near Jericho (18:35) and subsequently in Jericho (19:1), but Luke takes over those references from Mark. Since Luke never reports Jesus traveling east of the Jordan, readers may reasonably infer that Jesus indeed traveled through Samaria. Yet Luke never specifies this, and so John remains the only gospel according to which Jesus explicitly does so.

Jesus' self-revelation to Samaritans in John appears particularly surprising considering Matthew's distinctive ethnic delineations and

---

6. Craig S. Keener, *The Gospel of John: A Commentary* (2 vols.; Peabody, Mass.: Hendrickson, 2003), 1:590 n. 46.
7. John P. Meier, *A Marginal Jew: Rethinking the Historical Jesus* (4 vols.; A[Y]BRL; New York: Doubleday; Hartford, CT: Yale University Press, 1991–2009), 3:546; similarly Urban C. von Wahlde, *The Gospels and Letters of John* (3 vols.; ECC; Grand Rapids: Eerdmans, 2010), 2:170.

prohibition of evangelism to Samaritans. In Matthew's mission discourse, Jesus commands the Twelve to proclaim that the kingdom of the heavens has come, and he authorizes them to perform miracles (10:7-8). The apostolic mission expressly excludes Samaritans, though: "Into a road of Gentiles you may not go, and into a city of Samaritans you may not enter. Go instead to the lost sheep of the house of Israel" (Matt. 10:5b-6).[8] From Matthew's standpoint, then, humanity divides into three groups, namely Gentiles, Samaritans, and the house of Israel.

Jesus reiterates that he was sent only "to the lost sheep of the house of Israel"—a uniquely Matthean phrase—when he speaks to the "Canaanite" woman (15:24). As in the Old Testament, Canaanites would be included among the Gentiles (גוים; ἔθνη). The question arises as to whether Samaritans could also count as Jews or Gentiles. On the one hand, 2 Kgs. 17:29 might include the Samaritans among the ἔθνη by referring to "the Samaritan ethnicity" (οἱ Σαμαρῖται ἔθνη).[9] On the other hand, the Samaritans could represent the Israelites of the former northern kingdom, who are more akin to the Judahites, Judeans, or Jews in the southern kingdom of Judah. In the Gospel of Matthew, only Jews constitute members of the house of Israel; for example, King of Israel (Matt. 27:42b) is synonymous with King of the Jews (Matt. 27:37), and Matthew never uses the term Israelite. At the same time, Matthew does not associate Samaritans with pagan beliefs and practices such as polytheism and idolatry.

According to Matthew, Samaritans constitute a distinct ethnicity, neither Jew nor Gentile.[10] At the end of the gospel, Matthew has the

---

8. Pragmatically Jesus issues commands in Matt. 10:5b, and so the verbs are usually translated as imperatives (e.g., NIV and NRSV); morphologically, though, the verbs are subjunctives, and so I prefer "may not." Regarding Matt. 10:5b, see Amy-Jill Levine, *The Social and Ethnic Dimensions of Matthean Salvation History* (Studies in the Bible and Early Christianity 14; Lewiston, NY: Mellen, 1988).
9. When used in the absolute, I prefer the rendering *Gentile* for ἔθνος. In 2 Kgs. 17:29, I use *people group* since ἔθνος appears juxtaposed with a specific gentilic; the term's etymological derivative *ethnicity* would also work in that instance, but I consider the common rendering *nation* anachronistic. In Matthew, I maintain the separation of Samaritans from Gentiles as stated in 10:5b.
10. Regarding Samaritans as neither Jews nor Gentiles according to Matthew, see Gary N. Knoppers, *Jews and Samaritans: The Origins and History of their Early Relations* (Oxford: Oxford University Press, 2013), 221; John P. Meier, "The Historical Jesus and the Historical Samaritans: What can be Said?" *Bib* 81, no. 2 (2000): 202-32, here 221; Reinhard Pummer, *The Samaritans in Flavius Josephus* (TSAJ 129; Tübingen: Mohr Siebeck, 2009), 37; Stefan Schapdick, *Auf dem Weg in den Konflikt*:

risen Jesus lift the ban on apostles' evangelizing Gentiles, for the Great Commission commands the Eleven to go and make disciples of "all the Gentiles" (πάντα τὰ ἔθνη; Matt. 28:19).[11] Based on the explicit distinction between Samaritans and Gentiles in Matt. 10:5b, the Samaritans would remain excluded from Matthew's evangelistic purview.

Read in light of Matt. 10:5b, John 4 constitutes the Fourth Gospel's concern for Samaritan inclusion. Johannine scholars have often pointed out the opposition between Jesus telling the Twelve not to enter any city of the Samaritans (Matt. 10:5b) and the disciples accompanying Jesus to the Samaritan city of Sychar (John 4).[12] However, considering John and Matthew independent, most scholars have not attempted to reconcile that opposition.[13] Those who do try to harmonize John 4 with Matt. 10:5 simply claim that Jesus' trip to Samaria occurred long before Matthew's mission discourse. For example, A. T. Robertson dated the events of John 4 approximately two years prior to the events of Matthew 10.[14] Thus for Robertson, John's account and Matthew's can both be historically accurate, even though a tension would remain between the two evangelists' perspectives toward Samaritans.

Previous scholarship has also misstated the Samaritan influence on, or audience of, the Fourth Gospel. It would be an overstatement to

---

*Exegetische Studien zum theologischen Profil der Erzählung vom Aufenthalt Jesu in Samarien (Joh 4,1-42) im Kontext des Johannesevangeliums* (BBB 126; Berlin: Philo, 2000), 131; pace Jürgen Zangenberg, *Frühes Christentum in Samarien: topographische und traditionsgeschichtliche Studien zu den Samarientexten im Johannesevangelium* (Texte und Arbeiten zum neutestamentlichen Zeitalter 27; Tübingen: Francke, 1998), 189.

11. Other scholars translating ἔθνη as "Gentiles" in the Great Commission include Douglas R. A. Hare and Daniel J. Harrington, "Make Disciples of all the Gentiles (Mt 28:19)," *CBQ* 37, no. 3 (1975): 359-69; Amy-Jill Levine, "'To All the Gentiles': A Jewish Perspective on the Great Commission," *RevExp* 103, no. 1 (2006): 139-58.

12. E.g., Raymond Brown, *The Gospel according to John* (2 vols.; AB 29-29A; Garden City, N.Y.: Doubleday, 1966-1970), 1:175; Oscar Cullmann, *The Early Church: Studies in Early Christian History and Theology,* ed. A. J. B. Higgins (Philadelphia: Westminster, 1956), 189; Rudolf Schnackenburg, *The Gospel according to St. John,* trans. Kevin Smyth et al. (3 vols.; HTKNT 4; New York: Herder & Herder; Seabury; Crossroad, 1968-1982; repr. New York: Crossroad, 1990), 1:458-9.

13. E.g., based in part on Matt. 10:5, Barnabas Lindars (*The Gospel of John* [NCB; London: Oliphants, 1972; repr. Grand Rapids: Eerdmans, 1982], 175) finds Jesus' Samaritan mission unlikely historically, but Lindars does not consider John 4 a direct response to Matt. 10:5.

14. A. T. Robertson, *A Harmony of the Gospels for Students of the Life of Christ: Based on the Broadus Harmony in the Revised Version* (New York: George H. Doran, 1922). John 4:5-42 constitutes ch. 35, which Robertson dates to 27 CE; Matt. 9:35-11:1 appears in ch. 70, which Robertson dates to 29 CE.

conclude that John's gospel must have originated within the Samaritan church or that the Samaritans were John's primary audience.[15] Conversely, it would be an understatement to deny John's knowledge of Samaritan beliefs or to exclude any Samaritans from John's intended audience.[16] I prefer the mediating position that John wanted both Jews and Samaritans (as well as Gentiles) to believe in Jesus.[17] In my estimation, John 4 is—at least in part—intended to show unequivocally that Samaritans were welcome in the church because Jesus had revealed himself to them.

### Harmonizing John's and Matthew's Mission Discourses

I propose a new reading whereby the Matthean mission discourse and the Johannine Samaritan mission are supposed to occur simultaneously. The link is that, in both Matthew and John, Jesus talks about sending the disciples out into the harvest, which is a metaphor for evangelism. I readily acknowledge that Matthew's version of the harvest saying circulated widely, for it appears nearly verbatim in Q/Luke 10:2 and in *Gos. Thom.* 73. Nevertheless, Q does not mention Samaritans at all, and the *Gospel of Thomas* (60) includes only one reference to a Samaritan—a saying about ritual slaughter. Accordingly, these other attested harvest sayings or a free-floating orally transmitted one would not evoke any question about whether to preach to Samaritans. Matthew's harvest saying lies in close proximity to the prohibition of a Samaritan mission, and so I consider the Samarian setting of John's harvest saying more than mere coincidence. In this section, I argue that John composed his discourse so that readers

---

15. *Pace* George Wesley Buchanan, "The Samaritan Origin of the Gospel of John," in *Religions in Antiquity: Essays in Memory of Erwin Ramsdell Goodenough*, ed. Jacob Neusner (Leiden: Brill, 1968), 149–75, here 175; John Bowman, *The Samaritan Problem: Studies in the Relationships of Samaritanism, Judaism, and Early Christianity*, trans. Alfred M. Johnson, Jr. (PTMS 4; Pittsburgh: Pickwick, 1975), 89.
16. *Pace* Margaret Pamment, "Is There Convincing Evidence of Samaritan Influence on the Fourth Gospel?," ZNW 73, no. 4 (1982): 221–30, here 225; Keener, *Gospel of John*, 1:169–70: "Few would argue … that the Samaritans are John's primary audience, and it is tenuous to assert that their presence in the Gospel makes them part of its original audience at all."
17. Edwin D. Freed, "Did John Write His Gospel Partly to Win Samaritan Converts?," *NovT* 12, no. 3 (1970): 241–56, here 256; Andrew T. Lincoln, *The Gospel according to Saint John* (BNTC; Peabody, Mass.: Hendrickson, 2005), 181–82.

of both Matthew and John could link the two sayings. John reinterprets Matthew such that Jesus was in Samaria evangelizing Samaritans when he instructed the disciples to go and evangelize elsewhere.

Matthew has Jesus use a harvest saying as the rationale for the mission discourse (chapter 10). There is too much work for one person, and so Jesus commissions the Twelve to share the responsibility:

> And Jesus was going around all the cities and the villages teaching in their synagogues and preaching the gospel of the kingdom and healing every disease and every sickness. And seeing the crowds, he had compassion on them because they were troubled and tossed about like sheep without a shepherd. Then he says to his disciples, "The harvest is a lot, but the workers few. So ask of the Lord of the harvest that he send out workers into his harvest." (Matt. 9:35-38)

At that point Jesus summons the Twelve and gives them authority over unclean spirits (Matt. 10:1), but he tells them to avoid Samaritan cities when working miracles and preaching the gospel (10:5b, 7-8). Despite Jesus' extensive instructions to the Twelve (10:5-11:1), Matthew never reports that they actually went out to preach and heal (cf. Mark 6:7-13; Luke 9:1-6; 10:1-17).[18]

The harvest metaphor conveys two basic meanings in the Gospel of Matthew, namely proclamation and judgment. Because Jesus refers to the disciples as preachers and healers, in Matt. 9:37b-38 the harvest symbolizes evangelistic work; similarly the Parable of the Sower (Matt. 13:3b-9 par. Mark 4:3-9; Luke 8:5-8) allegorizes planting seed as preaching the gospel. Elsewhere in Matthew the harvest serves as a vehicle for eschatological judgment. For example, in the Parable of the Wheat and Tares (13:24-30) the person sows (13:24) but has others harvest (13:30), and there the harvest signifies the "consummation of the age" (συντέλεια αἰῶνος; 13:39) when angels will throw evildoers into the fiery furnace (13:40-42; cf. Rev. 14:15, 16). Jesus later tells the disciples that they too will play a role in eschatological judgment

---

18. Matthew 11:1 has Jesus preach in the disciples' cities, perhaps implying that he was alone while they carried out his instructions, but Matthew does not say so explicitly.

(Matt. 19:28b), but in the context of the mission discourse the harvest represents proclamation rather than judgment.[19]

In the Gospel of John, harvest language (θερισμός/θερίζω) appears only in the abbreviated mission discourse Jesus has with his disciples in Samaria (4:35–38). When Jesus travels through Samaria, he grows tired and sits by Jacob's Well outside the city of Sychar (John 4:4–6). While his disciples enter the city to buy food (4:8), Jesus speaks with an unnamed Samaritan woman (4:7, 9–26).[20] Just after the disciples return (4:27a), the woman leaves and enters the city (4:28). Then Jesus says to the disciples:

> Do you not say, "There are four months still, and the harvest comes"? I say to you, lift up your eyes and look at the fields because they are white for harvest. Already the harvester receives pay and gathers fruit for eternal life, so that the sower may rejoice even with the harvester. For in this way, the word is true: "One is the sower and another the harvester." I sent you to harvest that for which you did not labor. Others have labored, and you have entered into their labor. (John 4:35–38)

Meanwhile the woman testifies about Jesus, and many Samaritans believe in him (4:39). Jesus then stays with the city-people for two days (4:40), and many more come to believe that he is "the Savior of the world" (4:41–42). At the same time, Jesus' talk about sending the disciples to labor in the harvest never materializes. In other words, John never reports them as doing any agricultural or evangelistic work, and the Samaritans believe in Jesus based on the woman's testimony and Jesus' own testimony (4:39, 41).

John explains the harvest as a metaphor for eternal life (4:36). Throughout the gospel, eternal life results from belief in Jesus and/

---

19. Matthew's only other uses of θερισμός/θερίζω are when Jesus says that birds neither sow nor harvest (6:26) and when the lead character in the Parable of the Talents harvests what he does not sow (25:24, 26).
20. Rabbis would sometimes name otherwise unnamed biblical characters; e.g., R. Abba bar Kahanan names Noah's wife Naʿamah because she was "pleasing" (Gen. Rab. 23.3). Similarly, feminist critics have named female characters; e.g., Mieke Bal ("Dealing/With/Women: Daughters in the Book of Judges," in *Women in the Hebrew Bible*, ed. Alice Bach [New York: Routledge, 1998], 317–33, here 319) names Jephthah's daughter Bath, the Hebrew word for "daughter." I would call the woman at the well "Sami" because it is not only an abbreviated form of "Samaritan" but also the nickname of Samantha "Sami" Brady (from the NBC daytime drama *Days of Our Lives*), who likewise has had five husbands, viz. Austin, Brandon, Lucas, E.J., and Rafe.

or in the one who sent him, and eternal life protects believers from judgment or condemnation (for example, 3:16, 18a; 5:24); conversely those who do not believe are condemned (3:18b). Individuals' eternal salvation and condemnation are thus present realities for John, and the immediate readiness of a harvest still four months away fits with John's notion of realized eschatology.[21] For John, then, proclamation and judgment are one and the same, and nobody has to wait until the end of the world to sort out the saved and the damned.

Even though Matthew's and John's harvest sayings are not identical, they are widely acknowledged as close parallels.[22] Matthew's reads, "The harvest is a lot, but the workers few. So ask of the Lord of the harvest that he send out workers into his harvest" (9:37b–38), as compared with John's, "I say to you, lift up your eyes and look at the fields because they are white for harvest. . . . I sent you to harvest that for which you did not labor" (4:35b, 38a). Both sayings refer to a ready harvest and to the disciples being sent out to work in it. Yet the two gospels use different words for "send out" and "work": Matthew uses ἐκβάλλω and ἐργάτης as compared with the synonymous terms ἀποστέλλω and κοπιάω/κόπος in John.[23] Although in both gospels Jesus intimates the disciples' evangelistic work, neither gospel records that the disciples did any such work at that time. Furthermore, Matthew's harvest saying occurs just prior to Jesus' prohibiting the disciples from entering any Samaritan city, whereas John's harvest saying occurs on the outskirts of a Samaritan city that the disciples have just entered.

The Samarian location of John's discourse can accord with Matthew's narrative, for in Matt. 9:35 Jesus traveled throughout "all the cities and the villages teaching in the synagogues and preaching the gospel of the kingdom." Even though Matthew intended to exclude

---

21. D. Moody Smith, *John* (ANTC; Nashville: Abingdon, 1999), 120; similarly Rudolf Bultmann (*The Gospel of John: A Commentary*, trans. G. R. Beasley-Murray [Philadelphia: Westminster, 1971], 197–8) pointed out the paradoxical simultaneity of sowing and harvesting, and C. H. Dodd (*Historical Tradition in the Fourth Gospel* [Cambridge: Cambridge University Press, 1963], 400–401) noted the tension between future expectation and present reality of the harvest.
22. See, e.g., Brown, *Gospel according to John*, 1:18; James M. Robinson, Paul Hoffmann, and John S. Kloppenborg, eds., *The Critical Edition of Q* (Hermeneia; Minneapolis: Fortress Press, 2000), 160–61.
23. John's term for labor parallels his description of Jesus' weariness (κοπιάω) at the beginning of the episode (John 4:6).

the Samaritans from the church, John could exploit Matthew's phrase "all the cities" to include the Samaritan city of Sychar, thereby subverting Matthew's Samaritan exclusion. Readers of John could then reinterpret the Matthean Jesus' instruction that the disciples preach to the house of Israel and not to the Samaritans (10:5b). That is, readers of John could recall that Jesus was preaching in a Samaritan city when he told the disciples not to go preach in Samaritan cities. In other words, there was no need for the disciples to go and do what Jesus had already gone and done; their preaching was needed elsewhere.

Since John's harvest sayings evince parallels with several synoptic harvest sayings but do not agree verbatim with any one, scholars such as C. H. Dodd have concluded that John 4:35–38 arose independently via oral tradition.[24] As I see it, though, John's knowledge of the redacted Matthean saying accounts for two crucial details that Dodd remains at a loss to explain. One is the oddity that John refers to unfulfilled missionary work on the part of the disciples.[25] In this regard, I point out that John and Matthew align against Mark and Luke. Mark (6:7-13) and Luke (9:1-6; 10:1-20) record not only that Jesus instructed the disciples to go and preach but also that the disciples did so. If Matthew served as John's source for the harvest sayings, though, John would simply be following Matthew; both fail to mention that the disciples leave to evangelize and subsequently return to report their success. Arguments for oral tradition also fail to explain why the harvest sayings appear at all in John 4,[26] since verses 35–38 do not clearly relate to the rest of the chapter.[27] According to my interpretation, the setting of Samaria is essential for recasting the Matthean prohibition of a Samaritan mission. The seeming non sequitur of harvest sayings in John 4 is in fact the key to harmonizing with the Matthean mission discourse, and Matthew's Samaritan prohibition is the *raison d'être* for the Johannine Samaritan mission.

I would add a supporting argument that Matthew's and John's

---

24. Dodd, *Historical Tradition in the Fourth Gospel*, 392–93, 400, 404–5; see also Smith, *John*, 120.
25. Ibid., 405.
26. Ibid., 400.
27. Ibid., 391.

chronologies further allow the two harvest sayings to coincide, since these mission discourses occur prior to the feeding of the five thousand (see Table 5.1 below). All three Synoptics use the report of John the Baptist's death to transition to the feeding of the five thousand, which Augustine identified as a "meeting-point" of all four gospels (*Cons.* 2.94). According to Matthew (4:12), John the Baptist was in prison and still alive during Jesus' mission discourse (chapter 10). Immediately thereafter the Baptist sent disciples to Jesus (Matt. 11:2), and Herod Antipas had John the Baptist executed sometime before the feeding of the five thousand (chapter 14). According to the Fourth Gospel, John the Baptist was still baptizing (3:23) and not yet in prison (3:24) when Jesus and the disciples enter Samaria (4:4–5). The Gospel of John never again reports whether the Baptist was free or imprisoned or alive or dead. However, based on the unanimity of the Synoptics, any gospel harmonizer would infer the Baptist's death upon reading about the feeding of the five thousand.

While the overall chronology of the Fourth Gospel by no means aligns with that of the Synoptics, John's account of the feeding of the five thousand (6:1–13) indeed occurs after the Samaritan mission, just as Matthew's mission discourse precedes this feeding miracle. Even if John 6 originally preceded chapter 5,[28] John would still fit Jesus' two days in Sychar into the only possible position that could align with Matthew's chronology. I do not intend to overemphasize this point. I simply have in mind to correct Hans Windisch's overstatement that "nowhere are there gaps in which one can insert the synoptic narratives John skipped over. Every attempt at harmonization and combination pits the fourth evangelist in the greatest opposition."[29] In at least this one case, Matthew's mission discourse can plausibly be inserted into John's Samaritan mission.[30]

---

28. Jesus leaves Judea for the Galilee via Samaria (John 4:3–4) and later heals the royal official's son at Cana in the Galilee (4:46). As has long been observed, it may make more sense for chapter 6 to come next, since Jesus would have been in Galilee and in position to cross the sea (6:1). If chapter 5 then followed, Jesus would go to Jerusalem for a feast (5:1), and after the Sabbath-healing controversy he would return to Galilee "because the Jews were seeking to kill him" (7:1).

29. Hans Windisch, *Johannes und die Synoptiker: wollte der vierte Evangelist die Älteren Evangelien ergänzen oder ersetzen?* (UNT 12; Leipzig: J.C. Hinrichs, 1926), 88.

30. I do not attempt to reconstruct compositional stages of the Fourth Gospel, but those who have

Table 5.1: The Sequence of Mission Discourses and Notices about John the Baptist

| John | Matthew | Luke | Mark |
|---|---|---|---|
| John is baptizing (3:23). | John is baptizing (3:15). | John is baptizing (3:16). | John is baptizing (1:9). |
| John is *not yet* in prison (3:24). | John is in prison (4:12). | John is in prison (3:20). | John is in prison (1:14). |
| Jesus delivers a mission discourse including harvest sayings (4:35–38). | Jesus delivers a mission discourse including harvest sayings (9:37b–38). | | Jesus delivers a mission discourse *without* a harvest saying (6:7–11). |
| | | | Mission accomplished (6:12–13). |
| | John is still in prison (11:2). | John is still in prison (7:19). | |
| | | Jesus delivers a mission discourse *without* a harvest saying (9:1–5). | |
| | | Mission accomplished (9:6). | |
| | John is beheaded (14:2, 10). | John is beheaded (9:7, 9). | John is beheaded (6:14, 16). |
| Jesus feeds the 5000 (6:1–15). | Jesus feeds the 5000 (14:13–21). | Jesus feeds the 5000 (9:10–17). | Jesus feeds the 5000 (6:32–34). |
| | | Jesus delivers a mission discourse including a harvest saying (10:2). | |
| | | Mission accomplished (10:17). | |

done so could allow for John's use of Matthew as I have argued here. E.g., M.-É. Boismard et al. placed a visit to Sychar in Document C; II-A later added John 4:40, the two-day stay with the Samaritans; vv. 35–36 come from II-B; vv. 37-38 enter at stage III. Although he considers John II-B to have been influenced by Matthew, Boismard (*Synopse des quatre Évangiles en français: avec parallèles des apocryphes et des pères* [3 vols.; Paris: Cerf, 1965–1977] 3:140–144) never refers to Matt. 10:5b as a cross-reference or an impetus for the story in John 4. Also, von Wahlde (*Gospel and Letters of John*, 2:190, 193–4) attributes John 4:35–38 either to the second or third (i.e., the final) stage, for which Matthew served as a source; von Wahlde does not posit John's use of Matthew here, though.

## Conclusions

In arguing for John's use of Matthew, I could not ignore the seeming contradiction regarding Samaritan inclusion within the church: According to Matthew (10:5b), Jesus prohibits the disciples from traveling to Samarian cities and preaching to Samaritans; according to John (chapter 4), Jesus spends two days in a Samarian city preaching to Samaritans. Upon closer examination, John's narrative can harmonize with Matthew's mission discourse. Matthew's discourse begins with Jesus' saying that a plentiful harvest requires more workers (9:37-38). The point is that the disciples must help Jesus by preaching to the troubled masses. John's abbreviated mission discourse has Jesus say that the harvest is ready and that the disciples have been sent to labor in the harvest (4:35-38). Jesus told this to the disciples after he had revealed himself as the Messiah to the Samaritan woman (4:25-26); he then spent two days in the Samarian city of Sychar, and many Samaritans believed in Jesus as "the savior of the world" (4:42). I have proposed that John intended his harvest saying to harmonize with Matthew's. This harmonization effectively recontextualized Matthew's Samaritan exclusion. Jesus only told the disciples not to preach to the Samaritans because he was already doing so himself.

I consider it less probable historically that Jesus actually preached to Samaritans as recorded in John 4.[31] In my opinion, John composed the entire story in response to Matt. 10:5b, and John used a similarly worded harvest saying to link his mission discourse to Matthew's. Thus there is multiple independent attestation for neither a mission discourse by Jesus nor a mission by the disciples.[32] In terms of social memory theory, I would suggest that John is implanting a memory rather than remembering an event that actually happened.

Historically, it is highly probable that some Samaritans would have

---

31. *Pace* Susan Miller, "The Woman at the Well: John's Portrayal of the Samaritan Mission," in *John, Jesus, and History, Volume 2: Aspects of Historicity in the Fourth Gospel,* ed. Paul N. Anderson, Felix Just, and Tom Thatcher (SBLECL 2; Atlanta: Society of Biblical Literature, 2009), 73-81.

32. Scholars claiming the authenticity of the harvest saying based on multiple attestation include Dodd (*Historical Tradition in the Fourth Gospel*, 405) and Peter W. Ensor ("The Authenticity of John 4.35," *Evangelical Quarterly* 72, no. 1 [2000]: 3-21).

joined the church at a relatively early date; otherwise there would be no need for the New Testament to explain the origins of Samaritan believers.[33] Since Matthew intended his gospel for an expanding audience,[34] sooner or later Samaritan believers would have read or heard Matthew's gospel, thereby taking offense at its anti-Samaritan prejudice. John carefully constructed Jesus' Samaritan mission as a corrective. To employ Windisch's terms, John 4 both supplements and critically reinterprets Matt. 10:5b; in my estimation, John could not reasonably have expected to supplant Matthew's gospel altogether. Instead John wrote a self-standing narrative about Jesus' conversation with a Samaritan woman by Jacob's well. Of course, readers can understand John's Samaritan inclusion on its own terms, without knowing that the Matthean Jesus had forbidden the disciples to preach to Samaritans. John's story would, however, mitigate the offensiveness of Samaritan exclusion among readers who did know Matthew's gospel.

---

33. In addition to John 4, see also Acts 8.
34. Daniel W. Ulrich, "The Missional Audience of the Gospel of Matthew," *CBQ* 69, no. 1 (2007): 64–83.

# 6

## Conclusion

Chapter 1 traced the history of research concerning John's relation to the Synoptics. Fundamental questions arose during the patristic era. Should the four gospels be combined into a single harmony or be read separately? If the Gospels are read separately, must they be interpreted as harmonious, or can their discord be admitted? And if the Gospels are admittedly discordant, does that render them false and uninspired? In the fourth century, the opinion emerged that John had written with all three Synoptics in view, and for centuries thereafter the church predominantly read the Gospels separately while interpreting them harmoniously. In the modern era, scholars called into question John's knowledge and use of the Synoptics, and in the twentieth century Percival Gardner-Smith initiated the paradigm shift to Johannine independence.[1] That is, John relied on orally transmitted Synoptic tradition rather than the written Synoptic Gospels. For the last two hundred years, the Gospel of Matthew has generally been considered the least likely written source for the Gospel of John.

Chapter 2 detailed my methodology and hermeneutic for

---

1. Percival Gardner-Smith, *Saint John and the Synoptic Gospels* (Cambridge: Cambridge University Press, 1938; repr. 2011).

establishing John's use of Matthew. The fundamental question is how to decide between oral tradition and literary dependence. I have followed Helmut Koester's criterion that a subsequent gospel must reveal knowledge of a source text's redactional work.[2] Previous scholarship has uncovered two good examples of this. M.-É. Boismard observed that John most likely knows Matthew's redactional placement of Jesus' remote healing of a centurion's boy; both gospels call attention to the precise hour when the healing occurred, and John's notice that "the fever left him" comes from Matthew's immediately ensuing story where Jesus heals Peter's mother-in-law such that "the fever left her."[3] Frans Neirynck demonstrated that Jesus' appearance to Mary Magdalene in John reflects knowledge of Matthew's christophany, specifically that Matthew changes Mark's "disciples" to "brothers;" also, Jesus tells Mary Magdalene to let go of him, thereby interlocking with Matthew's report that Mary had taken hold of Jesus.[4]

If John is indeed dependent on Matthew, then Hans Windisch's question must be answered, namely whether John intended to be read alongside or instead of Matthew.[5] Except for three separate episodes involving a deaf man, a blind man, and a naked man, Matthew took over Mark's gospel almost entirely. It stands to reason, then, that Matthew might have intended his gospel as Mark's replacement. By contrast, John took over relatively few synoptic stories, and so the majority of the Fourth Gospel supplements the Synoptics. At the same time, John's gospel would have gained credibility by repeating and reworking well known stories such as Jesus' feeding the five thousand, his anointing, and his passion. The (eventually) extracanonical gospels employ the same strategy of "grounding" new material in stories found in gospels that were already accepted as authoritative.[6] John definitely

---

2. Helmut Koester, "Written Gospel or Oral Tradition?," *JBL* 113, no. 2 (1994): 293–97.
3. M.-É. Boismard et al., *Synopse des quatre Évangiles en français: avec parallèles des apocryphes et des pères* (3 vols.; Paris: Cerf, 1965–77), 3:149.
4. Frans Neirynck, "Les Femmes au Tombeau: Étude de la rédaction Matthéenne," *NTS* 15, no. 2 (1968–69): 168–90.
5. Hans Windisch, *Johannes und die Synoptiker: wollte der vierte Evangelist die Älteren Evangelien ergänzen oder ersetzen?* (UNT 12; Leipzig: J.C. Hinrichs, 1926).
6. The term *grounding* comes from Vernon K. Robbins's (*Who Do People Say I Am? Rewriting Gospel*

disagreed with Matthew in some places, but—as Benedict Viviano has shown—Windisch poses a false dichotomy between supplementation and replacement.[7]

Chapter 3 focused on Matthew's saying about binding and loosing and John's saying about forgiving and retaining sins. Readers have noticed this parallel since the patristic era, and over the last fifty years these sayings have generated two important arguments for oral tradition. John Emerton posited that a single Aramaic saying about opening and shutting (based on Isa. 22:22) could have morphed into the Matthean and Johannine logia. The main weakness of this argument is the dearth of evidence that the Aramaic term for *open* (פתח) could also mean both *loose* (λύω) and *forgive* (ἀφίημι) anytime near the first century. The other argument for oral tradition rightly observes that in Aramaic (שרי) and in Greek (λύω) the same word can mean both *loosen* and *forgive*. This argument nevertheless errs by supposing binding and loosing to be synonymous with retaining and forgiving sins. Matthew's binding and loosing refer to the rabbinic authority to prohibit and permit beliefs and practices, and rabbis do not forgive people for doing something that is permitted. If the sayings are at all related and if John actually understood what Matthew's saying meant, then these Matthean and Johannine logia must be explained in some other way.

I have argued that binding and loosing transformed into forgiving and retaining sins because John knew Matthew's redactional transition (in chapter 18) from Jesus' binding and loosing saying to Peter's question about the limits of forgiveness. Jesus answered with a parable extolling exceeding forgiveness of others so as to secure one's own forgiveness from God. Matthew tightly arranges the entire discourse, and John's knowledge of if its redacted form sufficiently explains how John maintained the structure of the binding and loosing saying while

---

in *Emerging Christianity* [Grand Rapids: Eerdmans, 2013], 185–86) discussion of the *Infancy Gospel of Thomas*. D. Moody Smith ("The Problem of John and the Synoptics in Light of the Relation between Apocryphal and Canonical Gospels," in *John and the Synoptics*, ed. Adelbert Denaux [BETL 101; Leuven: Leuven University Press, 1992], 147–62) also considered John the first apocryphal gospel, in a sense, and I join Ulrich Wilckens (*Das Evangelium nach Johannes* [NTD 4; Göttingen: Vandenhoeck & Ruprecht, 2000]) in applying this hermeneutic in a systematic way.

7. Benedict T. Viviano, "John's Use of Matthew: Beyond Tweaking," *RB* 111, no. 2 (2004): 209–37.

interchanging forgiveness and non-forgiveness terminology from the ensuing passages. John's change in wording reveals a deliberate correction to Matthew's theology: whereas Matthew insists on granting practically limitless forgiveness (on the condition of repentance), John qualifies that disciples have the authority and responsibility to withhold forgiveness in some instances. John's corrective in no way implied outright rejection of Matthew's gospel, and the first Johannine epistle shows that the same circle who produced the Gospel of John continued reading the Gospel of Matthew alongside it.

Chapter 4 scrutinized the proof from prophecy associated with Jesus' entry into Jerusalem. Matthew and John quote Zechariah's oracle about Israel's king coming on a donkey, and both gospels specify that Jesus rode a donkey; Mark and Luke lack these elements. Although John's quotation does not match Zechariah's or Matthew's exactly, John aligns more closely with Matthew than with any other attested version of Zech. 9:9, and there is no evidence that this prophecy stood in a *testimonium* as of the first or second centuries. In the first half of the verse, John and Matthew omit the same two phrases from Zechariah. In the second half of the verse, John's wording derives from Matthew's surrounding narrative. By depicting Jesus riding two donkeys at once, Matthew seemingly misunderstands Zechariah's synonymous parallelism, and so John included only one donkey in his quotation. Despite this clear corrective, John was not attempting to replace Matthew's gospel altogether. There are ten other fulfillments in Matthew that John leaves alone while adding seven of his own proofs from prophecy. John further supplements Matthew by explaining that no one, including the disciples, was able to understand the prophetic significance of Jesus' actions in the moment. Only after the risen Jesus had bestowed the Spirit on the disciples could they remember and reinterpret all that Jesus had done.

Chapter 5 took up the question of Samaritan inclusion in the early church. According to Matthew, Jesus prohibits the disciples from entering Samaria and evangelizing Samaritans. According to John,

Jesus spends two days in Samaria, and Samaritans believe in Jesus as the Savior of the world. Although these Matthean and Johannine pericopes appear contradictory, each contains a metaphorical saying about Jesus sending his disciples into a ready harvest. This saying undeniably circulated via oral tradition, but I have argued that John knows Matthew's saying in its redacted context, in which Jesus appears to exclude Samaritans from the church. The harvest sayings thus facilitate a surprising harmonization: Jesus could have delivered the Matthean mission discourse while he was in Samaria. In other words, Jesus spent two days there evangelizing Samaritans while he sent the disciples elsewhere to evangelize Jews. Here the Fourth Gospel supplements Matthew insofar as it tells something that Matthew did not. John also critically reinterprets Matthew by engendering a complete reversal from Samaritan exclusion to inclusion. Nevertheless, by allowing for this subtle harmonization, John would not have tried to replace, but instead invited comparison with, Matthew's gospel.

John the Baptist, Jesus' feeding the five thousand, a woman anointing Jesus with oil, and the passion narrative are the main characters and events common to all four gospels. In all of these episodes, there are minor details where Matthew and John align against Mark and Luke. *Pace* Mark (1:4) and Luke (3:3), John the Baptist's baptism is not said to forgive sins, and only in Matthew (3:7) and John (1:24) do Pharisees inquire of John the Baptist. In John's story of the feeding of the five thousand, Jesus goes up a mountain and sits down (6:3), which has a parallel elsewhere in Matthew (15:29).[8] When a woman anoints Jesus, someone complains that the expensive ointment could have been sold to benefit the poor, and Jesus responds that the poor will always be there but that he himself will not be; except for slightly different word order, this saying is nearly verbatim in Matthew (26:11) and John (12:8), and they both omit Mark's phrase "and when you want, you are able to do good to (the poor)" (14:7).[9]

---

8. Burnett Hillman Streeter, *The Four Gospels: A Study of Origins: Treating of the Manuscript Tradition, Sources, Authorship, & Dates* (London: Macmillan, 1925), 412–15.

9. πάντοτε γὰρ τοὺς πτωχοὺς ἔχετε μεθ' ἑαυτῶν, ἐμὲ δὲ οὐ πάντοτε ἔχετε (Matt. 26:11); πάντοτε γὰρ τοὺς

Finally, there is a long list of agreements in the passion narrative, to which I would add that Matthew and John have the chief priests conspire with the Pharisees in Jerusalem (John 7:45; 11:47, 57; 18:3; Matt. 21:45; 27:62). Table 6.1 lists these and other prominent John-Matthew parallels, twenty in all.

At least two additional minor agreements emerge when studying ecclesial authority and proofs from prophecy. Regarding ecclesial authority, Mark and Luke depict Jesus alone as shepherd,[10] but Matthew and John delegate Jesus' pastoral role to the disciples. Matthew's Parable of the Lost Sheep figures the disciples as shepherds who should regain church members who fall into sin (18:10–14), and John's gospel ends with Peter becoming the pastor of Jesus' flock (21:15–17). Regarding proofs from prophecy, John narrates a crowd debating whether Jesus could be the Messiah, since Jesus comes from Galilee and yet the Scriptures say that the Messiah comes from Bethlehem (7:40–43). Rather than assuming John's ignorance of Matthew's nativity story,[11] I would suggest that John is interlocking with Matthew's fulfillment citations. According to Matthew, Jesus' birth in Bethlehem fulfills Micah's prophecy (5:2; cf. Matt. 2:4–6), and Jesus' residence in Galilee fulfills a prophecy from Isaiah (8:23; Eng. 9:1; cf. Matt. 4:12–16). In other words, John's debate about the location of the Messiah collects puzzle pieces, which readers of Matthew could connect.

---

πτωχοὺς ἔχετε μεθ' ἑαυτῶν καὶ ὅταν θέλητε δύναθε αὐτοῖς εὖ ποιῆσαι, ἐμὲ δὲ οὐ πάντοτε ἔχετε (Mark 14:7); τοὺς πτωχοὺς γὰρ πάντοτε ἔχετε μεθ' ἑαυτῶν, ἐμὲ δὲ οὐ πάντοτε ἔχετε (John 12:8). In Codex Bezae, John 12:8 is a Western non-interpolation.

10. Mark describes Jesus as the shepherd of a crowd (6:34) and the disciples (14:27), and Luke's Parable of the Lost Sheep compares Jesus to the shepherd who brings the "lost" to repentance (15:1–7).
11. Edwin R. Goodenough, "John: A Primitive Gospel," *JBL* 64, no. 2 (1945): 145–82, here 171.

| Table 6.1 John–Matthew Parallels | John | Matthew |
|---|---|---|
| 1 | John the Baptist's baptism is *not* said to forgive sins. | 1:24-28 | 3:1-6 |
| 2 | Pharisees inquire of John the Baptist. | 1:24 | 3:7 |
| 3 | Jesus calls Simon Peter the son of John/Jonah. | 1:42 | 16:17 |
| 4 | Jesus heals the son/boy of an imperial official/centurion "at that hour," and "the fever left him." | 4:52, 53 | 8:13, 15 |
| 5 | Jesus says either I am or you are the light of the world. | 8:12 | 5:14 |
| 6 | Chief priests conspire with Pharisees in Jerusalem. | 11:47 | 21:45 |
| 7 | Zechariah 9:9 is quoted when Jesus enters Jerusalem. | 12:15 | 21:5 |
| 8 | Jesus says that slaves are not greater than their masters. | 13:16 | 10:24 |
| 9 | Jesus commands a disciple to put away his sword. | 18:11 | 26:52 |
| 10 | Caiaphas is specified as the high priest. | 18:13, 24 | 26:3, 57 |
| 11 | Releasing a prisoner at Passover is customary. | 18:39 | 27:15 |
| 12 | Soldiers put a crown of thorns on Jesus' head. | 19:2 | 27:29 |
| 13 | Pilate sits on the judgment seat ($\beta\tilde{\eta}\mu\alpha$). | 19:13 | 27:19 |
| 14 | Jesus' name is inscribed on the *titulus*. | 19:19 | 27:37 |
| 15 | Joseph of Arimathea is called a disciple. | 19:38 | 27:57 |
| 16 | Jesus is buried in a new tomb. | 19:41 | 27:60 |
| 17 | Mary Magdalene is *not* going to anoint Jesus' corpse. | 20:1 | 28:1 |
| 18 | An angel or two appear(s) to Mary Magdalene. | 20:12 | 28:2-3, 5 |
| 19 | The risen Jesus sends Mary Magdalene to his "brothers." | 20:17 | 28:10 |
| 20 | John's forgiving and retaining sins logion parallels Matthew's binding and loosing saying. | 20:23 | 18:18; cf. 16:19 |

I readily acknowledge that John's use of Matthew appears far less obvious than Matthew's use of Mark. Even so, several instances of Matthean redaction in John meet Koester's strict criterion for claiming literary dependence rather than defaulting to oral tradition. At the very least, I hope that my findings correct Rudolf Schnackenburg's mischaracterization of John–Matthew parallels as "rare and unimportant."[12] I agree with Windisch that John used Matthew and

---

12. Rudolf Schnackenburg, *The Gospel according to St. John*, trans. Kevin Smyth, et al. (3 vols.; HTKNT 4; New York: Herder & Herder; Seabury; Crossroad, 1968-82; repr. New York: Crossroad, 1990), 1:30.

that John constructed a self-standing narrative. Yet I disagree with Windisch that John intended to replace Matthew. The vast majority of John's gospel consists of special material that supplements the Synoptics, and John's instances of harmonization and interlocking indicate John's intention that his gospel be read alongside, not instead of, Matthew's.

At least since the 1800s, the Gospel of Mark had been the most widely accepted written source for the Fourth Gospel. Gardner-Smith's *Saint John and the Synoptic Gospels* challenged those assumptions and propelled a wave of studies on John and the Synoptics. For the last two hundred years, the Gospel of Matthew has remained the least accepted written Johannine source. I hope that my source-critical arguments for John's use of Matthew will add energy to the new wave of studies on the perennial question of John and the Synoptics.

# Bibliography

Abbott, H. Porter. "Secondary Orality." Pages 521–22 in *Routledge Encyclopedia of Narrative Theory*. Edited by David Herman, Manfred Jahn, and Marie-Laure Ryan. New York: Routledge, 2005.

Aland, Kurt. *Synopsis Quattuor Evangeliorum*. 15th ed. Stuttgart: Deutsche Bibelgesellschaft, 1996.

Albl, Martin. *"And Scripture Cannot Be Broken": The Form and Function of the Early Christian Testimonia Collections*. Supplements to Novum Testamentum 96. Boston: Brill: 1999.

Albrecht, Felix. "Das Zwölfprophetenbuch und seine Rezeption im frühen Christentum am Beispiel Justins des Märtyrers." Pages 349–57 in *Textual History and the Reception of Scripture in Early Christianity*. Edited by Johannes de Vries and Martin Karrer. Septuagint and Cognate Studies 60. Atlanta: Society of Biblical Literature, 2013.

Allert, Craig D. *Revelation, Truth, Canon and Interpretation: Studies in Justin Martyr's Dialogue with Trypho*. Supplements to Vigiliae Christianae 64. Boston: Brill, 2002.

Anderson, Gary A. *Sin: A History*. New Haven: Yale University Press, 2009.

Anderson, Paul N. *The Christology of the Fourth Gospel: Its Unity and Disunity in the Light of John 6*. Wissenschaftliche Untersuchungen zum Neuen Testament 78. Tübingen: Mohr Siebeck, 1996. Repr. with a new introduction, outlines, and epilogue. Eugene, OR: Cascade, 2010.

———. *The Fourth Gospel and the Quest for Jesus: Modern Foundations Reconsidered*. London: T&T Clark, 2006.

———. "'You have the words of eternal life!' Is Peter Presented as *Returning* the

Keys of the Kingdom to Jesus in John 6:68?" *Neotestamentica* 41, no. 1 (2007): 6–41.

Annet, Peter. *The Resurrection of Jesus Considered: In Answer to the Trial of the Witnesses*. London: 1744.

Attridge, Harold W. "'Don't Be Touching Me': Recent Feminist Scholarship on Mary Magdalene." Volume 2, Pages 140–66 in *A Feminist Companion to John*. Edited by Amy-Jill Levine with Marianne Blickenstaff. 2 vols. Sheffield: Sheffield Academic Press, 2003.

Aquinas, Thomas. *Commentary on the Gospel of John*. Translated by Fabian Larcher and James A. Weisheipl. 3 vols. Thomas Aquinas in Translation. Washington, DC: Catholic University of America Press, 2010.

Bachmann, E. Theodore, ed. *Luther's Works, Vol. 35: Word and Sacrament I*. Philadelphia: Muhlenberg, 1960.

Bacon, Benjamin W. *The Fourth Gospel in Research and Debate: A Series of Essays on Problems concerning the Origin and Value of the Anonymous Writings attributed to the Apostle John*. New York: Moffat, Yard and Company, 1910).

_____. *An Introduction to the New Testament*. New York: Macmillan, 1900.

Baird, William. *History of New Testament Research, Vol. 1: From Deism to Tübingen*. Minneapolis: Augsburg Fortress, 1992.

Bal, Mieke. "Dealing/With/Women: Daughters in the Book of Judges." Pages 317–33 in *Women in the Hebrew Bible*. Edited by Alice Bach. New York: Routledge, 1998.

Barchiesi, Alessandro. *Homeric Effects in Vergil's Narrative*. Translated by Ilaria Marchesi and Matt Fox. Princeton: Princeton University Press, 2015.

Bardenhewer, Otto. *Geschichte der altkirchlichen Litteratur, bd. 1*. 2d ed. Freiburg: Herder, 1913.

Barker, James W. "Ancient Compositional Practices and the Gospels: A Reassessment." *Journal of Biblical Literature*, forthcoming.

_____. "The Reconstruction of *Kaige/Quinta* Zechariah 9,9." *Zeitschrift für die alttestamentliche Wissenschaft* 126, no. 4 (2014): 584–88.

_____. Review of Frank Schleritt, *Der vorjohanneische Passionsbericht*. *Catholic Biblical Quarterly* 74, no. 2 (2012): 397–98.

_____. "Written Gospel or Oral Tradition? Patristic Parallels to John 3:3, 5." *Early Christianity*, forthcoming.

Barrett, C. K. *The Gospel according to St. John: An Introduction with Commentary and Notes on the Greek Text*. 2d ed. Philadelphia: Westminster, 1978.

Barthélemy, Dominique. *Les Devanciers d'Aquila: première publication intégrale du texte des fragments du Dodécaprophéton trouvés dans le désert de Juda*. Leiden: Brill, 1963.

———. "Redécouverte d'un chaînon manquant de l'histoire de la Septante." *Revue biblique* 60 (1953): 18–29.

Basser, Herbert W. "Derrett's 'Binding' Reopened." *Journal of Biblical Literature* 104, no. 2 (1985): 297–300.

Bauckham, Richard. *Jesus and the Eyewitnesses: The Gospels as Eyewitness Testimony*. Grand Rapids: Eerdmans, 2006.

———. "John for Readers of Mark." Pages 147–71 in *The Gospels for All Christians: Rethinking the Gospel Audiences*. Edited by Richard Bauckham. Grand Rapids: Eerdmans, 1998.

Bauer, Walter. *Das Johannesevangelium*. 3d ed. Handbuch zum Neuen Testament 6. Tübingen: Mohr Siebeck, 1933.

———. "The 'Colt' of Palm Sunday (Der Palmesel)." *Journal of Biblical Literature* 72, no. 4 (1953): 220–29.

Baum-Bodenbender, Rosel. *Hoheit in Niedrigkeit: Johanneische Christologie im Prozeß Jesu vor Pilatus (Joh 18, 28-19,16a)*. Forschung zur Bibel 49. Würzburg: Echter Verlag, 1984.

Baur, Ferdinand Christian. *Kritische Untersuchungen über die kanonischen Evangelien: ihr Verhältniß zu einander, ihren Charakter und Ursprung*. Tübingen, 1847.

Beasley-Murray, George R. *John*. Word Biblical Commentary 36. Waco: Word Books, 1987.

Bellinzoni, Arthur J. "The Gospel of Luke in the Apostolic Fathers: An Overview." Pages 45–68 in *Trajectories through the New Testament and the Apostolic Fathers*. Edited by Andrew Gregory and Christopher Tuckett. Oxford: Oxford University Press, 2005.

———. *The Sayings of Jesus in the Writings of Justin Martyr*. Supplements to Novum Testamentum 17. Leiden: Brill, 1967.

Berkowitz, Luci, and Karl A. Squitier. *Thesaurus Linguae Graecae: Canon of Greek Authors and Works*. 3d ed. New York: Oxford University Press, 1990.

Bernard, J. H. *A Critical and Exegetical Commentary on the Gospel according to St. John*. 2 vols. International Critical Commentary 29. Edinburgh: T&T Clark, 1928.

Bird, Michael F. *The Gospel of the Lord: How the Early Church Wrote the Story of Jesus*. Grand Rapids: Eerdmans, 2014.

Blanton IV, Thomas R. "Saved by Obedience: Matthew 1:21 in Light of Jesus' Teaching on the Torah." *Journal of Biblical Literature* 132, no. 2 (2013): 393–413.

Blenkinsopp, J. "The Oracle of Judah and the Messianic Entry." *Journal of Biblical Literature* 80, no. 1 (1961): 55–64.

Bock, Darrell. *Luke*. 2 vols. Baker Exegetical Commentary on the New Testament. Grand Rapids: Baker, 1994–96.

Boismard, M.-É. et al. *Synopse des quatre Évangiles en français: avec parallèles des apocryphes et des pères*. 3 vols. Paris: Cerf, 1965–77.

Borgen, Peder. "John and the Synoptics in the Passion Narrative." *New Testament Studies* 5, no. 4 (1958–59): 246–59.

Boring, M. Eugene. *Mark: A Commentary*. New Testament Library. Louisville: Westminster John Knox, 2006.

Bowman, John. *The Samaritan Problem: Studies in the Relationships of Samaritanism, Judaism, and Early Christianity*. Translated by Alfred M. Johnson Jr. Pittsburgh Theological Monograph Series 4. Pittsburgh: Pickwick, 1975.

Brodie, Thomas L. *The Birthing of the New Testament: The Intertextual Development of the New Testament Writings*. New Testament Monographs 1. Sheffield: Sheffield Phoenix Press, 2004.

———. *The Quest for the Origin of John's Gospel: A Source-Oriented Approach*. New York: Oxford University Press, 1993.

Brown, Raymond. *The Epistles of John*. Anchor Bible 30. New York: Doubleday, 1982.

———. *The Gospel according to John*. 2 vols. Anchor Bible 29–29A. Garden City: Doubleday, 1966–70.

———. *An Introduction to the Gospel of John*. Edited by Francis J. Moloney. Anchor Bible Reference Library. New York: Doubleday, 2003.

———. Review of M.-É. Boismard and A. Lamouille, *L'Évangile de Jean* (Synopse des quatre Évangiles en français 3). *Catholic Biblical Quarterly* 40, no. 4 (1978): 624–28.

Bruce, F. F. *The Gospel of John: Introduction, Exposition, and Notes.* Grand Rapids: Eerdmans, 1983.

Buchanan, George Wesley. "The Samaritan Origin of the Gospel of John." Pages 149–75 in *Religions in Antiquity: Essays in Memory of Erwin Ramsdell Goodenough.* Edited by Jacob Neusner. Leiden: Brill, 1968.

Büchsel, Friedrich. "δέω (λύω)." Volume 2, Pages 60–61 in *Theological Dictionary of the New Testament.* Edited by Gerhard Kittel and Gerhard Friedrich. Translated by Geoffrey W. Bromiley. 10 vols. Grand Rapids: Eerdmans, 1964–76.

Bultmann, Rudolf. *The Gospel of John: A Commentary.* Translated by G. R. Beasley-Murray. Philadelphia: Westminster, 1971.

———. *The Johannine Epistles.* Translated by R. Philip O'Hara with Lane C. McGaughy and Robert W. Funk. Hermeneia. Philadelphia: Fortress Press, 1973.

Burkitt, F. Crawford. *Evangelion da-Mepharreshe: The Curetonian Version of the Four Gospels, with the readings of the Sinai Palimpsest and the early Syriac Patristic evidence.* 2 vols. Cambridge: Cambridge University Press, 1904.

Byrskog, Samuel. Review of Rudolf Bultmann, *The History of the Synoptic Tradition. Journal of Biblical Literature* 122, no. 3 (2003): 549–55.

———. *Story as History—History as Story: The Gospel Tradition in the Context of Ancient Oral History.* Wissenschaftliche Untersuchungen zum Neuen Testament 123. Tübingen: Mohr Siebeck, 2000.

———. "The Transmission of the Jesus Tradition: Old and New Insights." *Early Christianity* 1, no. 3 (2010): 441–68.

Cadbury, Henry J. "The Meaning of John 20:23, Matthew 16:19, and Matthew 18:18." *Journal of Biblical Literature* 58, no. 3 (1939): 251–54.

von Campenhausen, Hans. *Ecclesiastical Authority and Spiritual Power in the Church of the First Three Centuries.* Translated by J. A. Baker. Stanford: Stanford University Press, 1969.

Carey, Greg. "Moving Things Ahead: A Lukan Redactional Technique and Its Implications for Gospel Origins." *Biblical Interpretation* 21, no. 3 (2013): 302–19.

Carson, D. A. *The Gospel according to John*. Pillar New Testament Commentary. Grand Rapids: Eerdmans, 1991.

Catchpole, David R. "The 'triumphal' entry." Pages 319–34 in *Jesus and the Politics of His Day*. Edited by Ernst Bammel and C. F. D. Moule. Cambridge: Cambridge University Press, 1984.

Ceriani, Antonio Maria, ed. *Codex Syro-Hexaplaris Ambrosianus*. London: Williams & Norgate. 1874.

Clark-Soles, Jaime. *Scripture Cannot Be Broken: The Social Function of the Use of Scripture in the Fourth Gospel*. Boston: Brill, 2003.

Collins, Adela Yarbro. *Mark: A Commentary*. Hermeneia. Minneapolis: Fortress Press, 2007.

———. "Redaction Criticism in Theory and Practice." Pages 59–77 in *Method and Meaning: Essays on New Testament Interpretation in Honor of Harold W. Attridge*. Edited by Andrew B. McGowan and Kent Harold Richards. Resources for Biblical Study 67. Atlanta: Society of Biblical Literature, 2011.

*Comprehensive Aramaic Lexicon Project*. url:cal1.cn.huc.edu.

Conte, Gian Biagio. *The Rhetoric of Imitation: Genre and Poetic Memory in Virgil and Other Latin Poets*. Translated by Charles Segal. Cornell Studies in Classical Philology 44. Ithaca: Cornell University Press, 1986.

Cribbs, F. Lamar. "The Agreements that Exist between Luke and John." Volume 1, Pages 215–61 in *SBL Seminar Papers, 1979*. 2 vols. Missoula, MT: Society of Biblical Literature, 1979.

———. "A Study of the Contacts that Exist between St. Luke and St. John." Volume 1, Pages 1–93 in *SBL Seminar Papers, 1973*. 2 vols. Cambridge, MA: Society of Biblical Literature, 1973.

Crook, Zeba. "Collective Memory Distortion and the Quest for the Historical Jesus." *Journal for the Study of the Historical Jesus* 11, no. 1 (2013): 53–76.

Cullmann, Oscar. *The Early Church: Studies in Early Christian History and Theology*. Edited by A. J. B. Higgins. Philadelphia: Westminster, 1956.

Culpepper, R. Alan. *Luke*. New Interpreter's Bible 9. Nashville: Abingdon, 1994.

———. "The Relationship between the Gospel of John and 1 John." Pages 95–119 in *Communities in Dispute: Current Scholarship on the Johannine Epistles*. Edited by R. Alan Culpepper and Paul N. Anderson. Society of Biblical Literature Early Christianity and Its Literature 13. Atlanta: SBL Press, 2014.

Dahl, Nils A. "Die Passionsgeschichte bei Matthäus." *New Testament Studies* 2, no. 1 (1955–56): 17–32.

Dalman, Gustaf. *The Words of Jesus: Considered in the Light of Post-Biblical Jewish Writings and the Aramaic Language.* Translated by D. M. Kay. Edinburgh: T&T Clark, 1902. Repr., Eugene, OR: Wipf & Stock, 1997.

Damm, Alex. *Ancient Rhetoric and the Synoptic Problem: Clarifying Markan Priority.* Bibliotheca Ephemeridum Theologicarum Lovaniensium 252. Leuven: Peeters, 2013.

Danker, Frederick W., Walter Bauer, William F. Arndt, and F. Wilbur Gingrich. *A Greek-English Lexicon of the New Testament and Other Early Christian Literature.* 3d ed. Chicago: University of Chicago Press, 2000.

Dauer, Anton. *Die Passionsgeschichte im Johannesevangelium: Eine traditionsgeschichtliche und theologische Untersuchung zu Joh 18,1–19,30.* Studien zum Alten und Neuen Testaments 30. Munich: Kösel-Verlag, 1972.

Davies, W. D. and Dale C. Allison. *A Critical and Exegetical Commentary on the Gospel according to Saint Matthew.* 3 vols. International Critical Commentary. Edinburgh: T&T Clark, 1988–97.

Davis, Stephen J. *Christ Child: Cultural Memories of a Young Jesus.* Synkrisis. New Haven: Yale University Press, 2014.

DeConick, April D. *Voices of the Mystics: Early Christian Discourse in the Gospels of John and Thomas and Other Ancient Christian Literature.* Journal for the Study of the New Testament Supplement Series 157. Sheffield: Sheffield Academic Press, 2001.

Denaux, Adelbert, ed. *John and the Synoptics.* Bibliotheca Ephemeridum Theologicarum Lovaniensium 101. Leuven: Leuven University Press, 1992.

Derrenbacker Jr., R. A. *Ancient Compositional Practices and the Synoptic Problem.* Bibliotheca Ephemeridum Theologicarum Lovaniensium 186. Leuven: Peeters, 2005.

Derrett, J. Duncan M. "Binding and Loosing (Matt. 16:19; 18:18; John 29:23 [sic: 20:23])." *Journal of Biblical Literature* 102, no. 1 (1983): 112–17.

———. "Law in the New Testament: The Palm Sunday Colt." *Novum Testamentum* 13, no. 4 (1971): 241–58.

Desreumaux, Alain. *Codex sinaiticus Zosimi rescriptus: Description codicologique des feuillets araméens melkites des manuscrits Schøyen 35, 36 et 37 (Londres-Oslo) comprenant l'édition de nouveaux passages des Évangiles et des Catéchèses de Cyrille*. Histoire du texte biblique 3. Lausanne: Éditions du Zèbre, 1997.

Dodd, C. H. *According to the Scriptures: The Sub-structure of New Testament Theology*. London: James Nisbet & Co., 1952.

———. *Historical Tradition in the Fourth Gospel*. Cambridge: Cambridge University Press, 1963.

Donahue, John R., and Daniel J. Harrington. *The Gospel of Mark*. Sacra Pagina 2. Collegeville, Minn.: Liturgical Press, 2002.

Downing, F. Gerald. "Compositional Conventions and the Synoptic Problem." *Journal of Biblical Literature* 107, no. 1 (1988): 69–85.

Dunderberg, Ismo. *The Beloved Disciple in Conflict? Revisiting the Gospels of John and Thomas*. Oxford: Oxford University Press, 2006.

———. *Johannes und die Synoptiker: Studien zu Joh 1-9*. AASF Dissertationes Humanarum Litterarum 69. Helsinki: Suomalainen Tiedeakatemia, 1994.

Dungan, David Laird. *A History of the Synoptic Problem: The Canon, the Text, the Composition, and the Interpretation of the Gospels*. Anchor Bible Reference Library. New York: Doubleday, 1999.

Dunn, James D. G. "John's Gospel and the Oral Gospel Tradition." Pages 157–85 in *The Fourth Gospel in First-Century Media Culture*. Edited by Anthony Le Donne and Tom Thatcher. Library of New Testament Studies 426. London: T&T Clark, 2011.

Elliger, Karl, and Wilhelm Rudolph, eds. *Biblia Hebraica Stuttgartensia*. 4th ed. Stuttgart: Deutsche Bibelgesellschaft, 1990.

Emerton, John A. "Binding and Loosing—Forgiving and Retaining." *Journal of Theological Studies* 13, no. 2 (1962): 325–31.

Ensor, Peter W. "The Authenticity of John 4.35." *Evangelical Quarterly* 72, no. 1 (2000): 3–21.

Esler, Philip F. and Ronald A. Piper. *Lazarus, Mary and Martha: Social-Scientific Approaches to the Gospel of John*. Minneapolis: Fortress Press, 2006.

Evans, Craig A. *Matthew*. New Cambridge Bible Commentary. New York: Cambridge University Press, 2012.

———. "Zechariah in the Markan Passion Narrative." Pages 64–80 in *Biblical Interpretation in Early Christian Gospels, Vol. 1*. Edited by Thomas Hatina. Library of New Testament Studies 304. London: T&T Clark, 2006.

Eve, Eric. *Behind the Gospels: Understanding the Oral Tradition*. Minneapolis: Fortress Press, 2014.

Faller, Otto, and Michaels Zelzer, eds. *Ambrosii Opera: Epistulae et acta*. 4 vols. Corpus Scriptorum Ecclesiasticorum Latinorum 82. Vienna: F. Tempsky, 1968–96.

Farrell, Joseph. *Vergil's Georgics and the Traditions of Ancient Epic: The Art of Allusion in Literary History*. New York: Oxford University Press, 1991.

Fernández Marcos, Natalio. *The Septuagint in Context: Introduction to the Greek Versions of the Bible*. Translated by Wilfred G. E. Watson. Leiden: Brill, 2000.

Fortna, Robert Tomson. *The Fourth Gospel and Its Predecessor: From Narrative Source to Present Gospel*. Philadelphia: Fortress Press, 1988.

Foster, Paul. "The Epistles of Ignatius of Antioch and the Writings that Later Formed the New Testament." Pages 160–86 in *The Reception of the New Testament in the Apostolic Fathers*. Edited by Andrew F. Gregory and Christopher M. Tuckett. New York: Oxford University Press, 2005.

―――. "Memory, Orality, and the Fourth Gospel: Three Dead-Ends in Historical Jesus Research." *Journal for the Study of the Historical Jesus* 10, no. 3 (2012): 191–227.

France, R. T. *The Gospel of Mark*. New International Greek Testament Commentary. Grand Rapids: Eerdmans, 2002.

―――. *Matthew*. New International Commentary on the New Testament. Grand Rapids: Eerdmans, 2007.

Freed, Edwin D. "Did John Write His Gospel Partly to Win Samaritan Converts?" *Novum Testamentum* 12, no. 3 (1970): 241–56.

―――. "The Entry into Jerusalem in the Gospel of John." *Journal of Biblical Literature* 80, no. 4 (1961): 329–38.

Frey, Jörg. "Das Vierte Evangelium auf dem Hintergrund der älteren Evangelientradition: Zum Problem: Johannes und die Synoptiker," Pages 60–118 in *Johannesevangelium—Mitte oder Rand des Kanons? Neue Standortbestimmungen*. Edited by Thomas Söding et al. Quaestiones Disputatae 203. Freiburg: Herder, 2003.

Gamble, Harry Y. *Books and Readers in the Early Church*. New Haven: Yale University Press, 1995.

Gardner-Smith, Percival. *Saint John and the Synoptic Gospels*. Cambridge: Cambridge University Press, 1938. Repr., 2011.

Gnilka, Joachim. *Das Matthäusevangelium*. Herders Theologischer Kommentar zum Neuen Testament 1. 2 vols. Freiburg: Herder, 1986.

Goodacre, Mark. *Thomas and the Gospels: The Case for Thomas's Familiarity with the Synoptics*. Grand Rapids: Eerdmans, 2012.

Goodenough, Edwin R. "John: A Primitive Gospel." *Journal of Biblical Literature* 64, no. 2 (1945): 145–82.

Green, Joel. *The Gospel of Luke*. New International Commentary on the New Testament. Grand Rapids: Eerdmans, 1997.

Greenspahn, Frederick E. Review of Raphael Weiss, *The Aramaic Targum of Job*. *Journal of the American Oriental Society* 101, no. 4 (1981): 452–53.

Greenspoon, Leonard. "The *Kaige* Recension: The Life, Death, and Postmortem Existence of a Modern—and Ancient—Phenomenon." Pages 1–16 in *XII Congress of the International Organization for Septuagint and Cognate Studies: Leiden, 2004*. Edited by Melvin K. H. Peters. Septuagint and Cognate Studies 54. Atlanta: Society of Biblical Literature, 2006.

Gregory, Andrew F. and Christopher M. Tuckett. "Reflections on Method: What Constitutes Use of the Writings that later formed the New Testament in the Apostolic Fathers?" Pages 61–82 in *The Reception of the New Testament in the Apostolic Fathers*. Edited by Andrew F. Gregory and Christopher M. Tuckett. New York: Oxford University Press, 2005.

Gregory, Andrew F. "What is Literary Dependence?" Pages 87–114 in *New Studies in the Synoptic Problem: Oxford Conference, April 2008: Essays in Honour of Christopher M. Tuckett*. Edited by Paul Foster et al. Bibliotheca Ephemeridum Theologicarum Lovaniensium 239. Leuven: Peeters, 2011.

Gundry, Robert H. *Mark: A Commentary on His Apology for the Cross*. Grand Rapids: Eerdmans, 1993.

———. *Matthew: A Commentary on His Literary and Theological Art*. Grand Rapids: Eerdmans, 1982.

Hägerland, Tobias. *Jesus and the Forgiveness of Sins: An Aspect of His Prophetic Mission*. Society for New Testament Studies Monograph Series 150. Cambridge: Cambridge University Press, 2012.

Hagner, Donald A. *Matthew*. 2 vols. Word Biblical Commentary 33A–33B. Dallas: Word Books, 1993–95.

Hare, Douglas R. A. and Daniel J. Harrington. "Make Disciples of all the Gentiles (Mt 28:19)." *Catholic Biblical Quarterly* 37, no. 3 (1975): 359–69.

Harrington, Daniel J. *The Gospel of Matthew*. Sacra Pagina 1. Collegeville, Minn.: Liturgical Press, 1991.

Harris, Rendel. *Testimonies*. 2 vols. Cambridge: Cambridge University Press, 1916–20.

Hays, Richard B. *Echoes of Scripture in the Letters of Paul*. New Haven: Yale University Press, 1989.

⎯⎯⎯. *Reading Backwards: Figural Christology and the Fourfold Gospel Witness*. Waco: Baylor University Press, 2014.

Heider, George C. "The Gospel according to John: The New Testament's Deutero-Deutronomy?" *Biblica* 93, no. 1 (2012): 68–85.

Hillmer, Melvyn R. "The Gospel of John in the Second Century." Th.D. diss., Harvard Divinity School, 1966.

Hock, Ronald F. *The Infancy Gospels of James and Thomas*. The Scholars Bible 2. Santa Rosa, CA: Polebridge, 1995.

⎯⎯⎯. *The Life of Mary and the Birth of Jesus: The Ancient Infancy Gospel of James*. Berkeley, CA: Ulysses Press, 1997.

Holmes, Michael W. *The Apostolic Fathers: Greek Texts and English Translations*. 3d ed. Grand Rapids: Baker Academic, 2007.

Horner, George. *The Coptic Version of the New Testament in the Northern Dialect, otherwise called Memphitic and Bohairic*. 4 vols. Oxford: Clarendon, 1898–1905.

van der Horst, Pieter W. "Macarius Magnes and the Unnamed Anti-Christian Polemicist: A Review Article." Pages 181–89 in *Jews and Christians in Their Graeco-Roman Context: Selected Essays on Early Judaism, Samaritanism, Hellenism, and Christianity*. Wissenschaftliche Untersuchungen zum Neuen Testament 196. Tübingen: Mohr Siebeck, 2006.

Hunt, Steven A. *Rewriting the Feeding of the Five Thousand: John 6.1–15 as a Test Case for Johannine Dependence on the Synoptic Gospels*. Studies in Biblical Literature 125. New York: Peter Lang, 2011.

Irenaeus of Lyons. *On the Apostolic Preaching*. Translated by John Behr. Popular Patristics Series. Crestwood, N.Y.: St. Vladimir's Seminary Press, 1997.

———. *Proof of the Apostolic Preaching*. Translated by Joseph P. Smith. Ancient Christian Writers 16. New York: Paulist, 1978.

Jastrow, M. *A Dictionary of the Targumim, the Talmud Babli and Yerushalmi, and the Mishnaic Literature*. 2d ed. New York, 1903.

Jennings, Mark. "The Fourth Gospel's Reversal of Mark in John 13,31–14,3." *Biblica* 94, no. 2 (2013): 210–36.

*Josephus*. Translated by Henry St. J. Thackeray et al. 10 vols. Loeb Classical Library. Cambridge: Harvard University Press, 1926–65.

Kautzsch, E., ed. *Genesius' Hebrew Grammar*. Translated by A. E. Cowley. 2d. ed. Oxford: Clarendon, 1910.

Kazen, Thomas. "Sectarian Gospels for Some Christians? Intention and Mirror Reading in the Light of Extra-Canonical Texts." *New Testament Studies* 51, no. 4 (2005): 561–78.

Keener, Craig. *A Commentary on the Gospel of Matthew*. Grand Rapids: Eerdmans, 1999.

———. *The Gospel of John: A Commentary*. 2 vols. Peabody, Mass.: Hendrickson, 2003.

Keith, Chris. *Jesus' Literacy: Scribal Culture and the Teacher from Galilee*. Library of New Testament Studies 413. New York: Bloomsbury T&T Clark, 2011.

———. "Memory and Authenticity: Jesus Tradition and What Really Happened." *Zeitschrift für die neutestamentliche Wissenschaft* 102, no. 2 (2011): 155–77.

———. "Social Memory Theory and the Gospels: The First Decade." *Early Christianity* 6 (2015), forthcoming.

Kinman, Brent. *Jesus' Entry into Jerusalem: In the Context of Lukan Theology and the Politics of His Day*. Arbeiten zur Geschichte des antiken Judentums und des Urchristentums 28. Leiden: Brill, 1995.

Kiraz, George Anton, ed. *Comparative Edition of the Syriac Gospels: Aligning the Sinaiticus, Curetonianus, Peshitta and Harklean Versions*. 4 vols. New Testament Tools and Studies 21–24. Leiden: Brill, 1996.

Kline, Leslie L. *The Sayings of Jesus in the Pseudo-Clementine Homilies*. Society of Biblical Literature Dissertation Series 14. Missoula, MT: Society of Biblical Literature, 1975.

Klostermann, Erich, ed. *Origenes Werke, vol. 10: Matthäuserklärung, vol. 1*. Die griechischen christlichen Schriftsteller der ersten drei Jahrhunderte 40. Leipzig: J.C. Hinrichs, 1935.

Knauer, Georg Nicolaus. *Die Aeneis und Homer: Studien zur poetischen Technik Vergils mit Listen der Homerzitate in der Aeneis.* Hypomnemata 7. Göttingen: Vandenhoeck & Ruprecht, 1964.

Knoppers, Gary N. *Jews and Samaritans: The Origins and History of their Early Relations.* Oxford: Oxford University Press, 2013.

Köhler, Wolf-Dietrich. *Die Rezeption des Matthäusevangeliums in der Zeit vor Irenäus.* Wissenschaftliche Untersuchungen zum Neuen Testament 24. Tübingen: Mohr Siebeck, 1987.

Köstenberger, Andreas. *John.* Baker Exegetical Commentary on the New Testament. Grand Rapids: Baker, 2004.

Koester, Helmut. *Ancient Christian Gospels: Their History and Development.* Philadelphia: Trinity Press International; London: SCM, 1990.

———. "Septuaginta und Synoptischer Erzählungsstoff im Schriftbeweis Justins des Märtyrers." *Habilitationsschrift*, Heidelberg, 1956.

———. *Synoptische Überlieferung bei den Apostolischen Vätern.* Texte und Untersuchungen 65. Berlin 1957.

———. "Written Gospel or Oral Tradition?" *Journal of Biblical Literature* 113, no. 2 (1994): 293–97.

Konradt, Matthias. *Israel, Church, and the Gentiles in the Gospel of Matthew.* Translated by Kathleen Ess. Baylor-Mohr Siebeck Studies in Early Christianity. Waco: Baylor University Press, 2014.

Künzle, Beda O. *Das Altarmenische Evangelium.* 2 vols. Europäische Hochschulschriften, Reihe XXI, Linguistik und Indogermanistik, bd. 33. New York: Peter Lang, 1984.

Kuhn, Heinz W. "Das Reittier Jesu in der Einzugsgeschichte des Markusevangeliums." *Zeitschrift für die neutestamentliche Wissenschaft* 50, no. 1 (1959): 82–91.

Kvalbein, Hans. "The Authorization of Peter in Matthew 16:17-19: A Reconsideration of the Power to Bind and Loose." Pages 145–74 in *The Formation of the Early Church.* Edited by Jostein Ådna. Wissenschaftliche Untersuchungen zum Neuen Testament 183. Tübingen: Mohr Siebeck, 2005.

Kysar, Robert. Review of M.-É. Boismard and A. Lamouille, with the collaboration of G. Rochais, *Synopse des quatre Évangiles en français*, Tome III. *Journal of Biblical Literature* 98, no. 4 (1979): 605–7.

Labahn, Michael. *Jesus als Lebensspender: Untersuchungen zu einer Geschichte der johanneischen Tradition anhand ihrer Wundergeschichten*. Beihefte zur Zeitschrift für die neutestamentliche Wissenschaft 98. Berlin: Walter de Gruyter, 1999.

LaBianca, Øystein Sakala, et al. *Faunal Remains: Taphonomical and Zooarchaeological Studies of the Animal Remains from Tell Hesban and Vicinity*. Hesban 13. Berrien Springs, Mich.: Andrews University Press, 1995.

Lagrange, P. M.-J. *Évangile selon Saint Marc. Etudes biblique*. Paris: J. Gabalda, 1947.

Le Donne, Anthony and Tom Thatcher, eds. *The Fourth Gospel in First-Century Media Culture*. Library of New Testament Studies 426. London: T&T Clark, 2011.

Le Donne, Anthony. *The Historiographical Jesus: Memory, Typology, and the Son of David*. Waco: Baylor University Press, 2009.

Leloir, Louis. "Le Diatessaron de Tatien." *L'orient syrien* 1 (1956): 208–31, 313–34.

Levine, Amy-Jill. *The Social and Ethnic Dimensions of Matthean Salvation History*. Studies in the Bible and Early Christianity 14. Lewiston, N.Y.: Mellen, 1988.

\_\_\_\_\_. "'To All the Gentiles': A Jewish Perspective on the Great Commission," *Review and Expositor* 103, no. 1 (2006): 139–58.

Lewis, Agnes Smith and Margaret Dunlop Gibson, eds. *The Palestinian Syriac Lectionary of the Gospels: Re-edited from two Sinai MSS. and from P. de Lagarde's edition of the "Evangeliarium Hierosolymitanum."* London: Kegan Paul, Trench, Trübner & co., 1899.

Liddell, Henry George, Robert Scott, and Henry Stuart Jones. *A Greek-English Lexicon*. 9th ed. with revised supplement. Oxford: Clarendon, 1996.

Lieu, Judith. *I, II, & III John: A Commentary*. New Testament Library. Louisville: Westminster John Knox, 2008.

\_\_\_\_\_. "Justin Martyr and the Transformation of Psalm 22." Pages 195–211 in *Biblical Traditions in Transmission: Essays in Honour of Michael A. Knibb*. Edited by Charlotte Hempel and Judith M. Lieu. Supplements to the Journal for the Study of Judaism 3. Boston: Brill, 2006.

Lincoln, Andrew T. *The Gospel according to Saint John*. Black's New Testament

Commentaries. London: Continuum, 2005. Repr., Peabody, Mass.: Hendrickson, 2006.

Lindars, Barnabas. *The Gospel of John*. New Century Bible Commentary. London: Marshall, Morgan & Scott, 1972. Repr., Grand Rapids: Eerdmans, 1982.

———. *New Testament Apologetic: The Doctrinal Significance of the Old Testament Quotations*. London: SCM, 1961.

Lust, Johan, Erik Eynikel, and Katrin Hauspie, eds. *Greek-English Lexicon of the Septuagint*. Rev. ed. Stuttgart: Deutsche Bibelgesellschaft, 2003.

Luz, Ulrich. *Matthew*. Translated by James E. Crouch. 3 vols. Hermeneia. Minneapolis: Fortress Press, 2001–7.

Macarios de Magnésie. *Le Monogénès: Introduction générale, édition critique, traduction française et commentaire*. Edited by Richard Goulet. 2 vols. Textes et Traditions 7. Paris: Librairie Philosophique J. Vrin, 2003.

MacDonald, Dennis R. *The Gospels and Homer: Imitations of Greek Epic in Mark and Luke-Acts*. Lanham, Md.: Rowman & Littlefield, 2015.

———. *The Homeric Epics and the Gospel of Mark*. New Haven: Yale University Press, 2000.

———. *Luke and Vergil: Imitations of Classical Greek Literature*. Lanham, Md.: Rowman & Littlefield, 2015.

März, Claus-Peter. *"Siehe, dein König kommt zu dir..."*: *eine traditionsgeschichtliche Untersuchung zur Einzugsperikope*. Erfurter theologische Studien 43. Leipzig: St. Benno, 1980.

Manor, T. Scott. "Papias, Origen, and Eusebius: The Criticisms and Defense of the Gospel of John." *Vigiliae Christianae* 67, no. 1 (2013): 1–21.

Mantey, Julius. "Distorted Translations in John 20:23; Matthew 16:18-19 and 18:18." *Review and Expositor* 78, no. 3 (1981): 409–16.

———. "Evidence That the Perfect Tense in John 20:23 and Matthew 16:19 Is Mistranslated." *Journal of the Evangelical Theological Society* 16, no. 3 (1973): 129–38.

———. "The Mistranslation of the Perfect Tense in John 20:23, Mt 16:19, and Mt 18:18." *Journal of Biblical Literature* 58, no. 3 (1939): 243–49.

Mara, M. G., ed. *Évangile de Pierre: Introduction, Texte Critique, Traduction, Commentaire et Index*. Sources Chrétiennes 201. Paris: Cerf, 1973.

Marcovich, Miroslav, ed. *Iustini Martyris Dialogus cum Tryphone*. Patristische Texte und Studien 47. Berlin: de Gruyter, 1997.

Marcus, Joel. *Mark*. 2 vols. AB 27–27A. New York: Doubleday; New Haven: Yale University Press, 2000–2009.

Marinack, Makayla. "Searching for Baptism in the Gospel of John." Paper presented at the Annual Meeting of the Upper Midwest Region of the SBL. Saint Paul, Minn., 18 April 2015.

Massaux, Édouard. *The Influence of the Gospel of Saint Matthew on Christian Literature before Saint Irenaeus*. Translated by Norman J. Belval and Suzanne Hecht. 3 vols. New Gospel Studies 5. Macon, Ga.: Mercer University Press, 1990–93.

Matson, Mark A. *In Dialogue with Another Gospel? The Influence of the Fourth Gospel on the Passion Narrative of the Gospel of Luke*. Society of Biblical Literature Dissertation Series 178. Atlanta: Society of Biblical Literature, 2001.

Mayo, Maria. *The Limits of Forgiveness: Case Studies in the Distortion of a Biblical Ideal*. Minneapolis: Fortress Press, 2015.

McLay, Tim. "*Kaige* and Septuagint Research." *Textus* 19 (1998): 127–39.

*Mechon Mamre*. url: mechon-mamre.org (INTR 1998-08-16).

Meier, John P. "The Historical Jesus and the Historical Samaritans: What can be Said?" *Biblica* 81, no. 2 (2000): 202–32.

———. *A Marginal Jew: Rethinking the Historical Jesus*. 4 vols. Anchor [Yale] Bible Reference Library. New York: Doubleday; Hartford, CT: Yale University Press, 1991–2009.

Mekerttschian, Karapet Ter, and S. G. Wilson, eds. "The Proof of the Apostolic Preaching." Pages 653–731 in Patrologia Orientalis 12. Paris, 1919.

Menken, M.J.J. *Matthew's Bible: The Old Testament Text of the Evangelist*. Bibliotheca Ephemeridum Theologicarum Lovaniensium 173. Leuven: Leuven University Press, 2004.

———. *Old Testament Quotations in the Fourth Gospel: Studies in Textual Form*. Contributions to Biblical Exegesis and Theology 15. Leuven: Peeters, 1996.

———. "The Quotations from Zech. 9,9 in Mt 21,5 and in Jn 12,15." Pages 571–78 in *John and the Synoptics*. Edited by A. Denaux. Bibliotheca Ephemeridum Theologicarum Lovaniensium 101. Leuven: Leuven University Press, 1992.

Micaelli, Claudio, and Charles Munier. *La pudicité*. 2 vols. Sources Chrétiennes 394–95. Paris: Cerf, 1993.

Michel, Otto. "Eine philologische Frage zur Einzugsgeschichte." *New Testament Studies* 6, no. 1 (1959): 81–82.

Miller, Susan. "The Woman at the Well: John's Portrayal of the Samaritan Mission." Pages 73–81 in *John, Jesus, and History, Volume 2: Aspects of Historicity in the Fourth Gospel*. Edited by Paul N. Anderson, Felix Just, and Tom Thatcher. Society of Biblical Literature Early Christianity and Its Literature 2. Atlanta: Society of Biblical Literature, 2009.

Moloney, Francis. *The Gospel of John*. Sacra Pagina 4. Collegeville, Minn.: Liturgical Press, 1998.

―――. *The Gospel of Mark: A Commentary*. Peabody, Mass.: Hendrickson, 2002.

Morris, Leon. *The Gospel according to John*. Rev. ed. New International Commentary on the New Testament. Grand Rapids: Eerdmans, 1995.

―――. *Studies in the Fourth Gospel*. Grand Rapids: Eerdmans, 1969.

Moss, Charlene McAfee. *The Zechariah Tradition and the Gospel of Matthew*. Beihefte zur Zeitschrift für die neutestamentliche Wissenschaft 156. Berlin: Walter de Gruyter, 2008.

Moulton, James H., and George Milligan. *The Vocabulary of the Greek New Testament*. London, 1930. Repr., Peabody, Mass.: Hendrickson, 1997.

Müller-Kessler, Christa. "Christian Palestinian Aramaic and Its Significance to the Western Aramaic Dialect Group." *Journal of the American Oriental Society* 119, no. 4 (1999): 631–36.

Munier, Charles, ed. *Justin Martyr: Apologie pour les Chrétiens*. Sources Chrétiennes 507. Paris: Cerf, 2006.

Muraoka, Takamitsu, ed. *A Greek-English Lexicon of the Septuagint*. Leuven: Peeters, 2009.

Nairn, J. Arbuthnot, ed. *De Sacerdotio of John Chrysostom*. Cambridge Patristic Texts. Cambridge: Cambridge University Press, 1906.

Nauck, Wolfgang. *Die Tradition und Charakter des ersten Johannesbriefes*. Wissenschaftliche Untersuchungen zum Neuen Testament 3. Tübingen: Mohr Siebeck, 1957.

Neirynck, Frans et al. *Jean et les Synoptiques: Examen critique de l'exégèse de M.-*

É. Boismard. Bibliotheca Ephemeridum Theologicarum Lovaniensium 49. Leuven: Leuven University Press, 1979.

Neirynck, Frans. "Les Femmes au Tombeau: Étude de la rédaction Matthéenne." *New Testament Studies* 15, no. 2 (1968–69): 168–90.

———. "John and the Synoptics." Pages 73–106 in *L'Évangile de Jean: Sources, Rédaction, Théologie*. Edited by M. de Jonge et al. Bibliotheca Ephemeridum Theologicarum Lovaniensium 44. Leuven: Leuven University Press, 1977.

———. "John and the Synoptics: 1975–1990." Pages 3–62 in *John and the Synoptics*. Edited by Adelbert Denaux. Bibliotheca Ephemeridum Theologicarum Lovaniensium 101. Leuven: Leuven University Press, 1992.

———. "John and the Synoptics: The Empty Tomb Stories." *New Testament Studies* 30, no. 2 (1984): 161–87.

———. "Note on Mt 28, 9-10." *Ephemerides Theologicae Lovanienses* 71, no. 1 (1995): 161–65.

Nestle, Eberhard et al., eds. *Novum Testamentum Graece*. 27th ed. Stuttgart: Deutsche Bibelgesellschaft, 1993.

Nieuviarts, Jacques. *L'Entrée de Jésus à Jérusalem (Mt 21,1-17)*. Lectio Divina 176. Paris: Cerf, 1999.

Nineham, D. E. *Saint Mark*. Pelican. London: SCM, 1963.

Nolland, John. *The Gospel of Matthew: A Commentary on the Greek Text*. New International Greek Testament Commentary. Grand Rapids: Eerdmans, 2005.

Obermann, Andreas. *Die christologische Erfüllung der Schrift im Johannesevangelium: Eine Untersuchung zur johanneischen Hermeneutik anhand der Schriftzitate*. Wissenschaftliche Untersuchungen zum Neuen Testament 2/83. Tübingen: Mohr Siebeck, 1996.

O'Brien, Kelli S. *The Use of Scripture in the Markan Passion Narrative*. Library of New Testament Studies 384. New York: T&T Clark, 2010.

O'Leary, Anne M. *Matthew's Judaization of Mark: Examined in the Context of the Use of Sources in Graeco-Roman Antiquity*. Library of New Testament Studies 323. New York: T&T Clark, 2006.

Owen, Henry. *Observations on the Four Gospels: Tending Chiefly To Ascertain the Times of Their Publication and To Illustrate the Form and Manner of Their Composition*. London: T. Payne, 1764.

Pamment, Margaret. "Is There Convincing Evidence of Samaritan Influence on the Fourth Gospel?" *Zeitschrift für die neutestamentliche Wissenschaft* 73, no. 4 (1982): 221-30.

Perrin, Norman. *What is Redaction Criticism?* Guides to Biblical Scholarship. Philadelphia: Fortress Press, 1969.

Petersen, William L. *Tatian's Diatessaron: Its Creation Dissemination, Significance, and History in Scholarship.* Supplements to Vigiliae Christianae 25. Leiden: Brill, 1994.

*Philo.* Translated by F. H. Colson et al. 12 vols. Loeb Classical Library. Cambridge: Harvard University Press, 1929-53.

Pichler, Josef. "Setzt die Johannespassion Matthäus voraus? " Pages 495-505 in *The Death of Jesus in the Fourth Gospel*. Edited by G. van Belle. Bibliotheca Ephemeridum Theologicarum Lovaniensium 200. Leuven: Leuven University Press, 2007.

*Plutarch's Lives.* Translated by Bernadotte Perrin. 11 vols. Loeb Classical Library. Cambridge: Harvard University Press, 1914-26.

Pummer, Reinhard. *The Samaritans in Flavius Josephus.* Texte und Studien zum antiken Judentum 129. Tübingen: Mohr Siebeck, 2009.

Qimron, Elisha, and James H. Charlesworth, eds. "Rule of the Community (1QS; cf. 4QS MSS A-J, 5Q11)." Pages 1-51 in *The Dead Sea Scrolls: Hebrew, Aramaic, and Greek Texts with English Translations, Volume 1: Rule of the Community and Related Documents*. Edited by James H. Charlesworth. Tübingen: Mohr Siebeck; Louisville: Westminster John Knox, 1994.

Rahlfs, Alfred. *Septuaginta.* Stuttgart: Deutsche Bibelgesellschaft, 1979.

Reim, Günter. *Studien zum alttestamentlichen Hintergrund des Johannesevangeliums.* Society for New Testament Studies Monograph Series 22. Cambridge: Cambridge University Press, 1974.

Robbins, Vernon K. *Who Do People Say I Am? Rewriting Gospel in Emerging Christianity.* Grand Rapids: Eerdmans, 2013.

Robertson, A. T. *A Harmony of the Gospels for Students of the Life of Christ: Based on the Broadus Harmony in the Revised Version.* New York: George H. Doran, 1922.

Robinson, James M., Paul Hoffmann, and John S. Kloppenborg, eds. *The Critical Edition of Q.* Hermeneia. Minneapolis: Fortress Press, 2000.

Rodriguez, Rafael. *Structuring Early Christian Memory: Jesus in Tradition,*

*Performance, and Text*. Library of New Testament Studies 407. New York: T&T Clark, 2010.

Rostowzew, M. "Angariae." *Klio* 6 (1906): 249–58.

Rothfuchs, Wilhelm. *Die Erfüllungszitate des Matthäus-Evangeliums: Eine biblisch-theologische Untersuchung*. Beiträge zur Wissenschaft vom Alten und Neuen Testament 88. Stuttgart: W. Kohlhammer, 1969.

Rousseau, Adelin, et al., eds. *Irénée de Lyon: Contre les hérésies*. 11 vols. Sources Chrétiennes. Paris: Cerf, 1952–82.

Sabbe, Maurits. "John and the Synoptists: Neirynck vs. Boismard," *Ephemerides Theologicae Lovanienses* 56, no. 1 (1980): 125–31.

Sandmel, Samuel. "Parallelomania." *Journal of Biblical Literature* 81, no. 1 (1962): 1–13.

Schapdick, Stefan. *Auf dem Weg in den Konflikt: Exegetische Studien zum theologischen Profil der Erzählung vom Aufenthalt Jesu in Samarien (Joh 4,1-42) im Kontext des Johannesevangeliums*. Bonner biblische Beiträge 126. Berlin: Philo, 2000.

Schleiermacher, Friedrich. *The Life of Jesus*. Edited by Jack C. Verheyden. Translated by S. Maclean Gilmour. Lives of Jesus Series. Philadelphia: Fortress Press, 1975.

Schleritt, Frank. *Der vorjohanneische Passionsbericht: Eine historisch-kritische und theologische Untersuchung zu Joh 2,13-22; 11,47-14,31 und 18,1-20,29*. Beihefte zur Zeitschrift für die neutestamentliche Wissenschaft 154. Berlin: de Gruyter, 2007.

Schnackenburg, Rudolf. *The Gospel according to St. John*. Translated by Kevin Smyth et al. 3 vols. Herders Theologischer Kommentar zum Neuen Testament 4. New York: Herder & Herder; Seabury; Crossroad, 1968–82. Repr. New York: Crossroad, 1990.

―――. *The Gospel of Matthew*. Translated by Robert R. Barr. Grand Rapids: Eerdmans, 2002.

―――. *The Johannine Epistles: A Commentary*. Translated by Reginald and Ilse Fuller. New York: Crossroad, 1992.

Schnelle, Udo. *Das Evangelium nach Johannes*. 2d ed. Theologischer Handkommentar zum Neuen Testament 4. Leipzig: Evangelische Verlagsanstalt, 2000.

_____. *The History and Theology of the New Testament Writings*. Translated by M. Eugene Boring. Minneapolis: Fortress Press, 1998.

Schröter, Jens. "The Gospels as Eyewitness Testimony? A Critical Examination of Richard Bauckham's *Jesus and the Eyewitnesses*." *Journal for the Study of the New Testament* 31, no. 2 (2008): 195–209.

Schuchard, Bruce G. *Scripture within Scripture: The Interrelationship of Form and Function in the Explicit Old Testament Citations in the Gospel of John*. Society of Biblical Literature Dissertation Series 133. Atlanta: Scholars Press, 1992.

Schulthess, Friedrich. *Lexicon Syropalestinum*. Berlin: Georgii Reimer, 1903. Repr., Amsterdam: APA, 1979.

Schwartz, Eduard and Theodor Mommsen. *Eusebius Werke, vol. 2: Die Kirchengeschichte*. 3 vols. Berlin: Akademie Verlag, 1999.

Schweizer, Eduard. *The Good News according to Mark*. Translated by Donald H. Madvig. Atlanta: John Knox, 1970.

Segal, M. H. *A Grammar of Mishnaic Hebrew*. Oxford: Clarendon, 1927. Repr., Eugene, OR: Wipf & Stock, 2001.

Shellard, Barbara. "The Relationship of Luke and John: A Fresh Look at an Old Problem." *Journal of Theological Studies* 46, no. 1 (1995): 71–98.

Sheridan, Ruth. *Retelling Scripture: 'The Jews' and the Scriptural Citations in John 1:19–12:15*. Biblical Interpretation Series 110. Leiden/Boston: Brill, 2012.

Sim, David C. "Matthew's Use of Mark: Did Matthew Intend to Supplement or to Replace His Primary Source?" *New Testament Studies* 57, no. 2 (2011): 176–92.

Skinner, Christopher W. *John and Thomas—Gospels in Conflict? Johannine Characterization and the Thomas Question*. Princeton Theological Monograph Series 115. Eugene, OR: Pickwick, 2009.

Smith, D. Moody. *The Composition and Order of the Fourth Gospel: Bultmann's Literary Theory*. New Haven: Yale University Press, 1965.

_____. *John*. Abingdon New Testament Commentaries. Nashville: Abingdon, 1999.

_____. "John 12:12ff. and the Question of John's Use of the Synoptics." *Journal of Biblical Literature* 82, no. 1 (1963): 58–64.

_____. *John among the Gospels*. 2d ed. Columbia: University of South Carolina Press, 2001.

_____. "The Problem of John and the Synoptics in Light of the Relation between

Apocryphal and Canonical Gospels." Pages 147–62 in *John and the Synoptics*. Edited by Adelbert Denaux. Bibliotheca Ephemeridum Theologicarum Lovaniensium 101. Leuven: Leuven University Press, 1992.

Soares-Prabhu, George M. *The Formula Quotations in the Infancy Narrative of Matthew: An Enquiry into the Tradition History of Mt 1-2*. Analecta Biblica 63. Rome: Biblical Institute Press, 1976.

de Solages, Bruno. *Jean et les Synoptiques*. Leiden: Brill, 1979.

Stanton, Graham N. *A Gospel for a New People: Studies in Matthew*. Edinburgh: T&T Clark, 1992.

———. "Revisiting Matthew's Communities." Pages 9–23 in *SBL Seminar Papers, 1994*. Society of Biblical Literature Seminar Papers 33. Atlanta: Scholars Press, 1994.

Stec, David M. *The Targum of Psalms*. The Aramaic Bible 16. Collegeville, Minn.: Liturgical Press, 2004.

Stendahl, Krister. *The School of St. Matthew and Its Use of the Old Testament*. Philadelphia: Fortress Press, 1968.

Strack, H. L., and P. Billerbeck. *Kommentar zum Neuen Testament aus Talmud und Midrasch*. 6 vols. Munich, 1922–61.

Streeter, Burnett Hillman. *The Four Gospels: A Study of Origins: Treating of the Manuscript Tradition, Sources, Authorship, & Dates*. London: Macmillan, 1925.

Thatcher, Tom. *Why John Wrote a Gospel: Jesus—Memory—History*. Louisville: Westminster John Knox, 2006.

Theobald, Michael. *Herrenworte im Johannesevangeliums*. Herder's Biblical Studies 34. Freiburg: Herder, 2002.

Thomson, Robert W. *An Introduction to Classical Armenian*. Delmar, N.Y.: Caravan Books, 1975.

Thyen, Hartwig. *Das Johannesevangelium*. Handbuch zum Neuen Testament 6. Tübingen: Mohr Siebeck, 2005.

von Tischendorf, Constantin. *Evangelia Apocrypha*. Leipzig: Hermann Mendelssohn, 1876.

Tov, Emanuel. *The Greek Minor Prophets Scroll from Naḥal Ḥever (8ḤevXIIgr)*. Discoveries in the Judaean Desert 8. Oxford: Clarendon, 1990.

Ulrich, Daniel W. "The Missional Audience of the Gospel of Matthew." *Catholic Biblical Quarterly* 69, no. 1 (2007): 64–83.

Uro, Risto. "'Secondary Orality' in the Gospel of Thomas? Logion 14 as a Test Case." *Forum* 9, no. 3/4 (1993): 305–29.

Van Belle, Gilbert and David R. M. Godecharle. "C. H. Dodd on John 13:16 (and 15:20): St John's Knowledge of Matthew Revisited." Pages 86–106 in *Engaging with C. H. Dodd on the Gospel of John: Sixty Years of Tradition and Interpretation*. Edited by Tom Thatcher and Catrin H. Williams. Cambridge: Cambridge University Press, 2013.

Verheyden, Jos. "P. Gardner-Smith and 'The Turn of the Tide.'" Pages 423–52 in *John and the Synoptics*. Edited by Adelbert Denaux. Bibliotheca Ephemeridum Theologicarum Lovaniensium 101. Leuven: Leuven University Press, 1992.

Viviano, Benedict T. "John's Use of Matthew: Beyond Tweaking." *Revue biblique* 111, no. 2 (2004): 209–37.

von Wahlde, Urban C. *The Gospel and Letters of John*. 3 vols. Eerdmans Critical Commentary. Grand Rapids: Eerdmans, 2010.

Watson, Francis. *Gospel Writing: A Canonical Perspective*. Grand Rapids: Eerdmans, 2013.

──────. "A Response to Richard Bauckham and Heike Omerzu." *Journal for the Study of the New Testament* 37, no. 2 (2014): 210–18.

Way, Kenneth C. "Donkey Domain: Zechariah 9:9 and Lexical Semantics." *Journal of Biblical Literature* 129, no. 1 (2010): 105–14.

Weihrich, Francisci, ed. *Augustini Opera: De consensu Evangelistarum*. Corpus Scriptorum Ecclesiasticorum Latinorum 43. Leipzig: G. Freytag, 1904.

Weren, W.J.C. "Jesus' Entry into Jerusalem." Pages 117–41 in *The Scriptures in the Gospels*. Edited by C. M. Tuckett. Bibliotheca Ephemeridum Theologicarum Lovaniensium 131. Leuven: Leuven University Press, 1997.

Wilckens, Ulrich. *Das Evangelium nach Johannes*. Das Neue Testament Deutsch 4. Göttingen: Vandenhoeck & Ruprecht, 2000.

Willems, Radbod. *Augustini Opera: In Iohannis Evangelium Tractatus CXXIV*. Corpus Christianorum Series Latina 36. Turnhout: Brepols, 1954.

Wilson, E. Jan, ed. *The Old Syriac Gospels: Studies and Comparative Translations*. 2 vols. Eastern Christian Studies 1–2. Piscataway, NJ: Gorgias Press, 2002

Windisch, Hans. *Johannes und die Synoptiker: wollte der vierte Evangelist die älteren Evangelien ergänzen oder ersetzen?* Untersuchungen zum Neuen Testament 12. Leipzig: J.C. Hinrichs, 1926.

Witherington III, Ben. *John's Wisdom: A Commentary on the Fourth Gospel.* Louisville: Westminster John Knox, 1995.

Wright, Jacob L. *David, King of Israel, and Caleb in Biblical Memory.* New York: Cambridge University Press, 2014.

Zahn, Theodor. *Introduction to the New Testament.* 3 vols. Translated by M. W. Jacobus et al. Edinburgh: T&T Clark, 1909.

Zangenberg, Jürgen. *Frühes Christentum in Samarien: topographische und traditionsgeschichtliche Studien zu den Samarientexten im Johannesevangelium.* Texte und Arbeiten zum neutestamentlichen Zeitalter 27. Tübingen: Francke, 1998.

Zumstein, Jean. *Kreative Errinerung: Relecture und Auslegung im Johannesevangelium.* 2d ed. Abhandlungen zur Theologie des Alten und Neuen Testaments 84. Zürich: Theologischer Verlag, 2004.

# Index of Ancient Sources

Old Testament

Genesis
32:16......65, 69
49:11......65, 68–69, 88

Exodus
20:13–15......85

Deuteronomy
5:17–19......85

Judges
10:4......65, 69
12:14......65, 69

1 Kings
1:33......76, 89
1:38, 44......76, 88–89

2 Kings
17:29......96
24:16......43

Job
42:9......44, 46
42:10......44–45

Psalm
22:18......90
34:20......90
69:9......90
78:2......90

Proverbs
5:19......65, 69

Isaiah
6:9–10......90
6:10......90
7:14......90
8:23; 9:1......90, 112
19:1......88
22:22......39–40, 43, 109
30:24......69
40:9......88
42:1–4......90
44:2......88

53:1......90
53:4......90
62:11......77–78, 82, 86

Jeremiah
18:1–2......90
32:6–15......90
31:15......90

Hosea
11:1......90

Micah
4:1–7......80

Zephaniah
3:14......77–79, 87
3:16......87–88

Zechariah
9:2......80
9:9......63–65, 69, 74, 76–81, 84–91, 110
11:13......90
12:10......90

New Testament

Matthew
1:21......58
1:22–23......90
2:4–6......112
2:15......90
2:16......31
2:17–18......90
2:23......90
3:1–6......113
3:6......58
3:7......111, 113
3:14......58
3:15......18, 104
4:12......103, 104
4:12–16......112
4:14–16......90
5:2......112
5:14......14, 113
5:17–20......58
6:4, 6, 18, 23......82
6:12......53
6:14–15......53
6:26......100
8:5–13......23
8:6......23
8:13......113
8:15......23, 25, 113
9:1–8......53
9:6......53
9:8......53
9:35–38......99, 101
9:37–38......93, 99, 104–5
10......97, 99, 103
10:1......99
10:5–11:1......99
10:5......94, 96–97, 99, 102, 105–6
10:5–6......96
10:7–8......96, 99
10:24......14, 113
10:29......94

10:39......20–22, 25
11:1......99
11:2......103–4
11:14......34
12:5......34
12:17–21......90
12:47......82
13:3–9......99
13:14–15......90
13:24–30......99
13:35......90
13:39, 40–42......99
14......103
14:2, 10......104
14:13–21......104
15:24......96
15:28......82
15:29......111
16......49–50
16:13, 15–18......50
16:17–19......47
16:17......14, 113
16:19......14, 37–40, 43–47, 49–51, 53–54, 60, 113
16:20......50
16:25......20–21, 25
18......48–51, 53–56, 59, 109
18:1–14......50
18:10–14......112
18:15–35......38, 59
18:15–17......50, 52, 56
18:15......48, 51, 53, 59
18:16......51
18:17......48, 51

18:18......12, 14, 37–38, 40, 43–51, 53–54, 56–57, 60–61, 113
18:19–20......50–51
18:21......38, 50–51, 53, 57
18:22......50–51
18:23–35......50–51, 56
18:26–27......52
18:28......52
18:29–30......52
18:31–34......52
18:32......52
18:34–35......56
18:35......52
19:1......94
19:16–30......84
19:18......85
19:28......55, 100
20:17......94
21:1–9......63
21:2......88–89
21:4–5......90
21:5......14, 77–79, 82–83, 86, 89, 113
21:6......88
21:7......34, 80, 88–89
21:45......112, 113
24:14......16
25:24, 26......100
26:3......14
26:7......9
26:11......9, 111
26:13......16
26:28......58
26:52......14, 113
26:57......14, 113

26:61......33
27:5......56
27:9–10......90
27:15......14, 113
27:19......14, 113
27:29......14, 87, 113
27:37, 42......96
27:37......14, 113
27:46......4
27:57......14, 113
27:60......14, 113
27:62......112
28:1......14, 113
28:2–3, 5......14, 113
28:9–10......24
28:9......24, 33
28:10......14, 24–25, 113
28:19......97
28:19–20......16

Mark
1:4......58, 111
1:9......104
1:12......5
1:14......104
1:31......23
1:39......31
2:1–12......53
2:10......53
3:4......34
4:3–9......99
6:7–13......99, 102, 104
6:14, 16......104
6:32–34......104

6:34......112
8:27–30......47
8:35......20–21, 25
9:33......94
10:1......94
10:17–31......84
10:19......85
10:32......94
10:46......94
11:1–10......63
11:2, 4, 5, 7......65, 68
11:8......89
11:10......76, 89
14:3......9
14:5......9
14:7......9, 111–12
14:24......58
14:27......112
14:58......33
15:34......4
15:47......6
16:1......6
16:6–7......24–25

Luke
2:7......32
2:21......32
2:41–52......32
2:42......32
3:3......58, 111
3:16, 20......104
4:38–39......24
5:17–26......53
5:24......53

7:1–10......23
7:2......23
7:19......104
7:37......9
8:5–8......99
9:1–17 ......104
9:1–6......99, 102
9:24......20–21, 25
9:52, 53, 56......95
10:1–17......99
10:1–20......102
10:2......93, 98, 104
10:17......104
15:1–7......112
17:11–12, 16......95
17:33......25
18:18–30......84
18:20......85
18:35......95
19:1......95
19:29–38......63
19:30, 33, 35......68
19:32......75
22:30......55
23:34......2
23:46......4
23:55......6
24:1......6

John
1:21......34
1:24......111, 113
1:24–28......113
1:29......58

1:29, 35–36......5
1:42......14, 113
1:43......5
2......2
2:1......5
2:15–17......90
2:17......90
2:19......33, 91
2:21–22......91
3:3, 5......57
3:16, 18......101
3:23, 24......103–4
4......2, 97–98, 102, 105–6
4:2......57–58
4:3–4......103
4:4–28......100
4:4–5......103
4:6......101
4:14......21
4:25–26......105
4:35–38......100–102, 104–5
4:35......94
4:39–42......100
4:40......104
4:42......105
4:46......103
4:46–54......23
4:52......23, 25, 113
4:53......113
5......2, 103
5:1......103
5:17......34
5:24......101
6......2, 103

6:1–15......104
6:1–13......103
6:1......103
6:3......111
7......2
7:1......103
7:38–39......91
7:40–43......112
7:45......112
8:12......14, 113
11:47, 57......112, 113
12:3......14
12:5......9
12:8......9, 111–12
12:12–19......63
12:14–16......90
12:14......34, 88, 91
12:15......14, 77–83, 86, 88–89, 91, 113
12:16......91
12:25......20–22, 25
12:38–39......90
12:39–40......90
13:16......14, 113
14:29......42
16:7–8......59
17:12......56
18......61
18:3......112
18:11......14, 113
18:13, 24......14, 113
18:31–19:40......42
18:39......14, 41–42, 113
19:2......14, 87, 113
19:13......14, 113

19:19......14, 113
19:24......90
19:26......2
19:28......90
19:30......4
19:36......90
19:37......90
19:38......14, 113
19:39......7
19:41......14, 113
20:1......14, 113
20:11–18......24
20:12......14, 113
20:17......14, 24–25, 33, 113
20:19......54
20:20......54
20:21–23......54, 56
20:22......91
20:22–23......59
20:23......12, 14, 37–38, 40, 43–44, 46–47, 49, 53–56, 58–61, 113
20:24......56
21:15–17......112

Acts
8......106
15......51

Romans
6:1–2......58

1 John
1:7, 9......58
2:2, 12......58

2:20, 27......57
3:5......58
4:10......58
5:6......57
5:16......59–60
5:16–17......59

3 John
9–10......47

Revelation
1:5......42
14:15, 16......99

## Early Christian Texts

Ambrose
*ep.* 74.9......83

Augustine
*Cons.*......5–6, 103
*Tract. Ev. Jo.* ......24

Eusebius of Caesarea
*Hist. eccl.* 3.24......4–5
*Hist. eccl.* 6.14......3

*Gospel of Thomas*
60......98
73......93, 98

Hippolytus
*Trad. ap.* 3.4......57

Ignatius of Antioch
*Smyrn.* 1.1......18

Irenaeus of Lyons
*Epid.* 65......77–78, 81–83
*Haer.* 3.11......2–3

John Chrysostom
*Sac.* 3.5......54

Justin Martyr
*1 Apol.* 32.1–6......69
*1 Apol.* 35.10......83
*1 Apol.* 35.11......77–79
*1 Apol.* 54.7......69, 71
*Dial.* 53.3......77–81
*Dial.* 109.2–3......80

Macarius Magnes
*apocr.* 2.12......4

Origen of Alexandria
*Comm. Jo.* 10.3......3
*Comm. Matt.* 13.31......52
*Comm. Matt.* 16.16......77–78

*Protevangelium of James*
22......31

Tertullian
*Pud.* 1.6......60
*Pud.* 2.13–14......60
*Pud.* 19.24, 25, 28......60
*Pud.* 21.9–10......57, 60

*Pud.* 21......51

## Greco-Roman Literature

### Papyri
*BGU* 1.15......73
Egerton Papyrus 2......29
*P.Oxy.* 1222.1......66, 68

### Aelian
*Nat. an.* 8.17.20......66–67

### Homer
*Od.* 11.204–209......35

### Pausanias
*Descr.* 5.8–9......67
*Descr.* 10.7......67

### Plutarch
*Alex.* 6......75

### Vergil
*Aen.* 2.790–794......35
*Aen.* 6.700–701......35

### Xenophon
*Eq. mag.* 2.1......66

## Early Jewish Texts

### Dead Sea Scrolls
1QS 8.20–9.2......45

### Josephus
*Ant.* 20.6.1......95
*B.J.* 1.111......46, 51

### Philo
*Spec. Laws* 3.47......68, 71

### Mishnah

Kil.
8:4–5......72

Šabb.
24:2–4......70

Yebam.
1:4......45, 50

B. Meṣiʿa
5:4......75
6:3......73

### Babylonian Talmud

Šabb.
155a–b......70

Moʾed Qat.
16a......45

Giṭ.
88a......43

Sanh.

38a......43

99a......44

Targums

Tg. N. Gen. 4:7......40

Tg. J. Isa. 22:22......40

Tg. J. Zech. 9:9......83

Tg. Ps. 105:20......41

Tg. Ps. 108:11......41

Tg. Job 12:14......41

Midrash

Genesis Rabbah

23.3......100

32.10......94

Sipre Deuteronomy

32:25......43

Tanḥuma Noah

3......43

# Index of Subjects and Modern Authors

Anderson, Gary A., 46, 53
Anderson, Paul N., ix, 11, 46–48, 55, 57, 61, 105

Bauckham, Richard, 11, 15, 26, 30–31
Bauer, Walter, 40, 65–69, 71, 75
Boismard, M.-É., 10, 22–23, 25, 33, 104, 108
Bultmann, Rudolf, 10, 18, 26, 33, 44, 57, 86, 101

*Diatessaron*, 2, 28
Dodd, C. H., 9–10, 13, 44, 53, 84, 86, 101–2, 105

Emerton, John A., 39–43, 109

Freed, Edwin D., xviii, 64, 86, 88, 98

Gardner-Smith, Percival, xvi–xvii, 9–10, 12, 107, 114

Hays, Richard B., 16–17, 37, 74

Hesban, 72–73

*Infancy Gospel of Thomas*, 31–32

*kaige*, 80–81
Koester, Helmut, xvii, 16–20, 23, 25, 30, 76, 108, 113
Kuhn, H.-W., 65, 68–69, 71

literary dependence, xvi–xvii, 7–13, 16–19, 22, 25, 37, 84, 93, 108, 113

Menken, M.J.J., 78, 84, 86–88
Michel, Otto, 65, 69–71

Naḥal Ḥever, 80
Neirynck, Frans, 10, 22, 24, 25, 33, 87, 108

*oppositio in imitando*, 15, 27, 35
oral tradition, xvi–xvii, 7, 9, 10, 12–13, 16–23, 26, 38–39, 47, 49, 53, 56, 60, 93, 102, 108–9, 111, 113

*Protevangelium of James*, xv, 30–32

Quinta. See kaige

redaction, xvii, 11, 15–16, 18–19, 23–27, 33, 36, 38, 47, 49, 53, 55–56, 61, 108–9, 113
Robbins, Vernon K., 32, 108

Schnackenburg, Rudolf, 10, 13, 44, 57, 74, 84, 86, 97, 113
Smith, D. Moody, xv–xvi, 2, 8, 10, 15, 22, 28–29, 32, 86, 88, 101–2, 109
Stendahl, Krister, 78, 84, 87

Streeter, Burnett Hillman, 8, 13, 63, 111

*testimonium*, xviii, 64, 76–77, 80–86, 110

Viviano, Benedict T., 33–34, 64, 86, 109
von Wahlde, Urban C., 11–12, 20–22, 25, 33, 44, 57, 95, 104

Watson, Francis, 15, 30, 36
Wilckens, Ulrich, 12–13, 29–30, 109
Windisch, Hans, xvi–xvii, 8–9, 12–13, 27–32, 34, 103, 106, 108–9, 113–14

www.ingramcontent.com/pod-product-compliance
Lightning Source LLC
Chambersburg PA
CBHW072138160426
43197CB00012B/2157